Do You Need a Guru?

understanding the student-teacher relationship in an era of false prophets

Mariana Caplan

Thorsons

The Way of Failure: Winning Through Losing (Hohm Press, 2001)

Halfway Up the Mountain: the Error of Premature Claims to Enlightenment
(Hohm Press, 1999)

To Touch is to Live: the Need for Genuine Affection in an Impersonal World
(Hohm Press, 2002)

When Holidays are Hell ...! A Guide to Surviving Family Gatherings
(Hohm Press, 1997)

When Sons and Daughters Choose Alternative Lifestyles (Hohm Press, 1996)

If you do not have the being of a disciple, how can you hope to find a guru?

ARNAUD DESJARDINS

Thorsons
An Imprint of HarperCollins*Publishers*
77–85 Fulham Palace Road,
Hammersmith, London W6 8JB

The Thorsons website address is:
www.thorsons.com

and *Thorsons* are trademarks of
HarperCollins*Publishers* Ltd

Published by Thorsons 2002

10 9 8 7 6 5 4 3 2 1

A catalogue record of this book
is available from the British Library

ISBN 0 00 711865 1

Printed and bound in Great Britain by
Creative Print and Design, Wales (Ebbw Vale)

Dedication

This book is dedicated to my spiritual lineage – Lee Lozowick, Yogi Ramsuratkumar, Swami Papa Ramdas – and to the glory of the relationships of Love and Truth that exist between them. I would particularly like to honor Yogi Ramsuratkumar (December 1, 1918 – February 20, 2001), who lived as an expression of the highest possibility of humanity, and who mercifully blessed me with His profound benediction and compassionate regard. I also dedicate this book to my personal lineage – my mother, Mollie Caplan (August 10, 1936 – March 17, 2001), who, before I could even spell, had written in her own journal that I would one day become a writer, and my father, Herbert Caplan, who taught me to pray.

Mariana Caplan and
Lee Lozowick

Yogi Ramsuratkumar
and Lee Lozowick

Yogi Ramsuratkumar
and Mariana Caplan

"Mariana Caplan's book is the most comprehensive, lucid, well-argued, utterly straightforward and honest work on the whole guru question that there is. She unapologetically tackles the most difficult, controversial, nitty-gritty issues without hedging, flinching, or smoothing over any of the rough edges. This book is must-reading for any serious spiritual seeker, as well as for anyone who wants to understand what the relation to a spiritual master is all about."

John Welwood, author of *Toward a Psychology of Awakening*

"An honest, well-researched and informative guide to this much misunderstood and yet important spiritual topic ... A clear, insightful, and humorous look at the drama of the student–teacher relationship."

Llewellyn Vaughan-Lee, Sufi teacher and author,
Sufism: The Transformation of the Heart and *The Face Before I Was Born*

"Mariana Caplan's *Do You Need a Guru?* answers this question better than any book I've read. If you are curious about the subtle gifts and traps of the student–teacher relationship, or if you are interested in authenticating mature heart-devotion rather than following your unresolved childhood hope for love down the wrong spiritual road, then read this book."

David Deida, author of *Naked Buddhism* and *Finding God Through Sex*

"The rising of spiritual aspirations in the West, where the values of 'having' have smothered those of 'being', is a source of hope for the future of mankind. However, the interest in traditional teachings transmitted by masters to their disciples is developing in a context of confusion, misunderstanding, if not of scandals. And what was a promise of peace becomes a source of suffering. Many spiritual seekers think it is their right to meet a guru, and even an outstanding guru, without ever asking themselves: 'Who am I as a disciple to have such a claim?' Mariana Caplan explores the essential matter through her own experience and throws precious light on this theme. It pays homage to the truth, the truth being always greater than any illusions."

Arnaud Desjardins, author of *Jump into Life* and *Toward the Fullness of Life*

'Essential reading for those on the spiritual path, and for those who want to see effective spiritual paths developed in our culture."

Charles Tart, author of *Altered States of Consciousness* and *Waking Up*

Acknowledgements

Often when I give talks and seminars on my books, people credit me for the knowledge contained within them or for the help they receive from them. Much as my ever-hungry ego would like to take credit for either, and as indebted as I feel for the privilege of being able to convey this timeless body of teachings, I am fully aware that when I came to the master, my soul was an unwatered seed. The transmission of the master is the divine water that awakens the soul-seed and initiates the sprouting of Self-remembering. The wisdom that arises is a bursting forth of the same Knowledge of Everything that is the birthright of all human beings, a Knowledge that is kept alive through a living transmission from individual to individual. Thus, everything of value I have to offer has come directly from my teacher and through our lineage.

To say this is neither a form of psychological self-deprecation nor a sentimental adulation of the master, but a recognition of and appreciation for the extraordinary process of transmission of living wisdom – a process in which an individual takes full responsibility for everything that passes through him or her, yet assumes no credit for it, nor falsely basks in a glory that does not rightfully belong to them. My teacher attributes everything to his own teacher, and his own teacher insists that "All is Father, Father Alone." Thus I offer my respectful obeisances to my master, Lee Lozowick, and to his master, Yogi Ramsuratkumar.

Many of the teachers, scholars, and senior practitioners I most respect in the field of contemporary spirituality supported me with my research by granting me extensive personal interviews: Lama Palden Drolma, Father Bruno Barnhart, Ma Jaya Sati Bhagavati, Arnaud Desjardins, Gilles Farcet, Georg Feuerstein, Robert Frager, the Kanyas of the Sakuri Ashram, Sam Keen, Krishna Dass, George Leonard, Daniel Moran, Ram Dass, Swami Satchitananda of Anandashram, Charles Tart, Vimala Thakar, Jai Uttal, Llewellyn Vaughan-Lee, and John Welwood. I am grateful to each of them for their generosity and commitment to this project.

I would like to extend further appreciation to my editor at Thorsons, Carole Tonkinson, who is willing to stand behind a controversial topic with steadfast integrity; to Nancy Lewis for generously reviewing the manuscript; to Regina Sara Ryan, editor of Hohm Press, who ever assists me in editing the cycles of my spiritual journey; to Sandra Hurlong and my doctoral committee at Union Institute for supporting my research; to Jorge Ferrer, for his steadfast support and zest in work and friendship; to Nicole Bureau and Rabia Trudeau for transcribing and proofreading; as well as to my dear friends, study group members, and *sangha*-mates who weather my "stormy search for Self" as I attempt to engage ruthlessly my own relationship to the principles and practices of conscious discipleship.

Lastly, my gratitude, love, and awe to Sita for her exemplary modeling of discipleship.

Contents

Introduction

The Call to Conscious Discipleship

I am in danger. I am in danger of being taken advantage of by a male, hierarchical, patriarchal authority figure. Yes, I have a GURU – that hairy term that has come to be so feared in the Western world. And worse than that, my guru is not even a Divine Mother. He is a *man*. A Jew from New Jersey, at that. He wears hot-pink knitted sweatpants and 12-year-old Teva sandals held together by string. He does not adorn himself with flowing white garments. His name is not 'Shanti'-anything. He does not stare into my eyes and tell me I am Divine. He does not walk on air. He does not materialize gold bracelets for his disciples. He does not expound in hushed tones about the divine consciousness of all animate and inanimate matter. Nor does he tell his disciples that they are already enlightened and that there is nowhere to go and nothing to do.

Instead, my teacher makes demands. He is fond of telling jokes, often erring on the edge of vulgarity. He appreciates beautiful women. On occasion he reprimands me harshly. It is not his voice that is so harsh, but what the correction is aimed at: those squirmy secret spots buried within me that are so unsettling I usually do not dare admit them even to myself. My teacher works within a hierarchical framework: He is the head of it. I am but a nun – in the most unconventional sense of the word. All of those hair-raising dangers of power and corruption broadcast by the media and scorned by the New Age are present in my life. I am in danger of surrendering and submitting my helpless, feeble psyche to fraudulent and unsafe spiritual authority.

Yes, I participate in a traditional, committed guru – disciple relationship with a spiritual master who I am fully convinced can, *with* my conscious, mature, and complete participation, personally guide me to the expression of my highest potential in this lifetime. I am in it for the long haul. In eight years of life with my teacher and his teacher, I have seen and experienced feats of extraordinariness that few people would believe possible, and that even fewer have known. The miracles of matter and spirit are fascinating, but what has grabbed my heart and reorganized my mind are the miracles of love – experiences that have permanently expanded limiting beliefs about the possibility for a human being to participate in a technology that produces love without limitation and service free of all selfish motivation: the literal cellular and alchemical transformation of the heart and the body. The price for this possibility, I am told, is one's life.

Thus the danger I am faced with comes from both sides. In addition to the threat of being manipulated, taken advantage of, having my power taken from me, I am also in grave danger of profound abandonment into love; of dying to all false perception, selfishness, vanity, cruelty and prideful aspects of myself. I am in danger of melting into the hot lava of the Divine, of burning to a crisp in the fire of love, and of dissolving into deep surrender, unshakable clarity, and ceaseless service to humanity. Indeed, I am in danger. My life is not safe.

Maybe it was safer when I lived only according to my own whim. When I lived in the jungles of Costa Rica, the villages of Mexico, the beaches of Belize ... imitating a brand of freedom, convincing myself that I was unafraid of life, and attempting to free myself from the shackles of cultural conditioning. Or when I roamed the cities of San Salvador, Bogotá, Jerusalem, Rome, Delhi, Managua, Katmandu, Johannesburg ... scanning the depths of human wretchedness and splendor in search of hints of truth. But as we all know in our heart of hearts, life – and especially death – is not about playing it safe.

We find ourselves in precarious times – so shaky that even those of us most prone to blanket denial acknowledge the all-too-real danger, if not likelihood, of nuclear or biological warfare. We face as well unprecedented shifts in global and atmospheric conditions. This frightening intensification is all but forcing a surge of interest in spiritual matters. The reality of what G. I. Gurdjieff called "the horror of the situation" is manifesting without as well as within: a sense of desperation is compelling, even in the most fearful and cynical, to hunger for a type of nourishment that can only be found through the wisdom and depth the inner life offers.

As a representative of a younger generation of writers in the field of contemporary spirituality, I was born into a circumstance in which global crisis was in full swing. Whereas the GenXers fall just shy of my ripening age, I know all too well what it feels like to experience existential planetary crises inside my bones. I know the restless panic of finding myself born into a world that is pulling me into its dry cynicism and hopelessness while simultaneously propelling me into an urgency to act on behalf of all humanity. People of my generation who are serious about spiritual life cannot afford to be irresponsible hippies preaching the gospel of love and light, but are commanded from within to learn to be functional, efficient, and precise in order to work within such a complex system. Given the radical nature of the present crises, I cannot believe other than that we are in dire need of reliable resources for spiritual guidance and wisdom – those who can not only inspire us but facilitate authentic and enduring transformation.

I am aware that in a culture built upon values of independence and autonomy, a culture in which most of our authorities have not only failed to live up to their stature but in many cases have acted in a hypocritical if not reprehensible manner, the idea of the teacher is unpopular. Within the current climate of interest in spirituality, the teacher or guru is still not favored and the student–teacher relationship is poorly understood. Even those who give it lip service, talking about "gurus" and "spiritual teachers" as easily as they chat about their pets, understandably have well-considered concerns and confusion regarding the question of the spiritual teacher. And they should, given the complexity of the issue.

My response to the challenge of spiritual authority is the principle and practice of *conscious discipleship*, consisting of a fully empowered, intelligent, discriminating studenthood. Conscious discipleship – the topic I intend to consider in depth in this book – will be the connecting thread in the unfolding study of the great labyrinth of the student–teacher relationship in Western culture that I set before you. The contents of this study come from masters and disciples of numerous traditions, spiritual academicians, scriptures, and over 15 years of my own contact and personal involvement with just about every kind of guru, shmuru, tulku, sensei, sheik, shaman, rabbi, therapist, sage, mentor, "no teacher"-teacher, healer, psychic, and divine mother you can imagine and not imagine.

In the initial years, my involvement with such authorities was from the perspective of a seeker desperately looking for anything or anyone that would help me find sanity, truth, and wholeness in a world that seemed utterly mad and heading for its own demise. In the years following the meeting with my teacher and a formal commitment to my particular tradition, my relationship with these individuals turned from that of a seeker to one of a researcher, not only in an academic context, but in the most personal sense of the term. The purpose of my ongoing study is twofold: one, to augment my understanding of my own transformational process; and two, to fulfill an internal commitment to do my small part in helping spiritual seekers in the West gain a spiritual education such that their path may unfold with as much understanding, clarity, and efficiency as possible.

Here in the Western world we have not learned *how to learn* when it comes to knowledge of the soul. We are taught to use our minds in such a way that many of us can process large amounts of complex data in many fields, achieving unprecedented advances in the material world and even in the arts. Yet we receive no instruction on how to educate the higher heart, higher emotions, higher mind – to refine the subtle systems necessary to perceive those qualities that lie at a deeper dimension of our experience.

My commitment to assist in the creation of a body of literature that would help seekers learn how to approach the spiritual path effectively first materialized with the publication of my fourth book, *Halfway Up the Mountain: The Error of Premature Claims to Enlightenment* (Hohm Press, 1999), in which I detailed the numerous pitfalls, obstacles, and forms of self-deception that Western seekers and teachers are likely to encounter on the spiritual path. From the perspective of ego, the book was full of bad news, and I expected to be highly criticized. I was wonderfully surprised to discover the tremendous willingness that readers had to having the whistle blown on the New Age party, and delighted by the receptivity seekers had to hearing really *bad news* about their own egoic investment in their spiritual path. For as much as the reality check stings initially (and the reader will soon learn how often and sharply my ego has been stung with the potent venom of reality), there is great satisfaction in hearing and acknowledging what is true about our lives as they are. It is the singular starting point for any authentic transformation to occur. My readers' response led me to believe that people had begun to tire of promises of transcendence, eternal bliss, and instant enlightenment, when the reality of their lives revealed that in spite of countless experiences of rapture and cosmic unity, the immediate challenge of spiritual expression still had more to do with the struggle to become deeply human, and to express that humanness in the domains of intimacy, sex, childraising, career, and serving a greater planetary and evolutionary need.

This book not only asks the question, "Do you need a guru?", but takes the consideration much further by delving into a consideration of what to do with a guru, mentor, or spiritual teacher once you have one – how to cope with the paradoxes, confusions, rough edges, and disillusionments that will inevitably arise in relationship to the spiritual teacher, even in the best of circumstances. What has not yet been widely available in contemporary spiritual literature on the subject is a consideration of what it takes *to make the student–teacher relationship work* given the internal circumstance of Western culture. Far too often the discussion remains at the level of the integrity and qualifications of the teacher, by implication relegating the function of the disciple to one of passivity, with the accompanying psychological dynamic being that of a disempowered and unconscious victimization. *Conscious discipleship* places the power and responsibility back into the hands and heart of the disciple as he or she learns to engage in studenthood from a perspective of increasing maturity, awareness, and authenticity.

A further intention of the book is to provide a map to spiritual aspirants, academicians and even curiosity-seekers regarding the vast terrain of the student–teacher relationship. For this land is often undervalued and experienced as alien, much as one might feel when first coming to the desert after living at the coast or in the mountains. At times I feel like a resident of the interior of the Grand Canyon looking up at the millions of visitors who come each year to the rim of the canyon, spend a few minutes looking down, snap a few photos, and move along on their travels, telling themselves they have been there without having *been* there. They see only the surface, which is but a shell of the vast interior.

"Come on down and have a look!" I call from within. "The pathways are steep and it will require effort, but you might find a beauty that will bring you to tears, and a wilderness you had not even dared to imagine."

That which the teacher represents is vaster, more complex, more challenging than even the Grand Canyon. For, intimidating as it is to consider backpacking into such geological vastness with only what you can carry on your back, such a journey is an afternoon stroll compared with the one into the interior of the human and universal soul and psyche. This is the domain we are approaching when standing at the rim of the student–teacher relationship, and when the journey is done, you are not the same person as the one who began it.

Speaking of rims of the universe, my initial research for this book began in the Indian subcontinent, interviewing a selected handful of the surviving disciples of the great Eastern masters of our era, spiritual giants like J. Krishnamurti, Swami Papa Ramdas, Swami Nityananda, Neem Karoli Baba, Mother Mayee of Kanyakumari, and Upasani Maharaj. And I *worked* for the data I collected. In one case I voyaged 42 hours on a variety of trains, planes and automobiles from Katmandu to Dalhousie in order to interview the Advaita master Vimala Thakar for two one-hour meetings; in another instance I bused through potholes and around minor landslides in my sweat-drenched Indian sari with my scarf over my face to keep from inhaling strange bacteria and toxic exhaust in order to interview several women at the Sakuri ashram – the only ashram run exclusively by and for women in patriarchal-driven India; and still another time I was chased out of an Indian village by a pseudo-spiritual mafia who perceived my interviewing the one remaining disciple of a great saint to be an economic threat to a local journalist working on a largely unrelated article about the same individual for a local Indian newspaper. Of course, there were the inevitable three days of the dreaded and unavoidable "Delhi belly" in which even soda water ran through me like an 18-wheeler truck, and countless other encounters with rare insects, rare diseases, rare people, and inconveniences common to anyone mad enough to conduct low-budget research in India on a Western corporate schedule.

Yet, having traveled 6,000 miles in order to collect data for my readers, it became evermore and undeniably evident that we as Westerners are in a distinctly different situation in relationship to the spiritual teacher. Whereas the nature of the ego is the same across all cultures, the elements of the psyche form a totally different constellation in the West than they do in the East. In a country like India, a context for spiritual understanding is woven into the culture, and spiritual principles and problems are discussed in and through daily life. In the West, that matrix remains to be developed. If the center of spiritual activity is moving from East to West, as the sages prophesized, one of many tasks will be to educate ourselves on how to interpret, integrate, and make use of these imported teachings. We must be extremely careful not to adopt Eastern forms superficially and presume that the language of the Eastern psyche immediately translates to the language of the Western psyche.

With notable exceptions, this text deals more with the student–teacher relationship as practiced in the Eastern traditions than it does with Judeo-Christian models. I am not a Judeo-Christian scholar, thus my knowledge is too scant to assume authority on these issues. I was most grateful when a Christian group created a study course based on *Halfway Up the Mountain*, suggesting how the principles set forth applied to a Christian-based spiritual path. I encourage readers of this book to do the same, and assure you that my negligence of that material is not an oversight, but rather a desire to refrain from presumptuously claiming authority in an area outside the domain of my personal expertise.

The book is divided into five sections. Section 1, "The Dilemma", considers the unavoidable challenge we are faced with in championing spiritual authority in Western culture. Included in this section are the major arguments *against* the student–teacher relationship, which I offer in order to give the reader a clear view of the intelligent rationale that lies behind this argument.

Section 2, "A Working Model of Relationship: Three Necessary Qualities for Student *and* Teacher" looks at three major challenges for students and teachers in Western culture – psychological balance, appropriate relationship to power dynamics, and trust – and suggests a means for accessing greater consciousness in these arenas so the aspiring student might avoid the traps that commonly arise in association with them.

Section 3, "Finding Your Teacher: The Fine Art of Discrimination", focuses on criteria useful in evaluating spiritual teachers as well as on the dangers and limitations of trying to "democratize" and institutionalize the wild card of spiritual mastery.

Section 4, "Hot Issues", considers controversial aspects of the student–teacher relationship commonly highlighted by the media, including: obedience; imperfections in the teacher; sex, money, drugs and alcohol.

Finally, Section 5, "For the Glory of Love", delves into the domain of objective power that arises within oneself through the process of conscious discipleship, and considers the glory of divinized human love that is shared among those who travel the path of the personal Beloved in their quest for self-realization.

Each chapter of the book begins with a personal narrative of my own antics, disillusionments, and adventures as I traveled the often muddy path that leads to the spiritual teacher, and continues even after one finds and is found by the teacher. Because I was as naïve, ambitious, and crazy as I was, the stories may seem exaggerated, but they are always true. Their outlandishness serves to highlight important points that are played out in most seekers' psyches and spiritual journeys, but not always in such a dramatic fashion. Next, I present a theoretical overview of the principles of conscious discipleship as they pertain to the topics covered in that section. Each chapter concludes with an interview I personally conducted with a contemporary authority in the field. In my research for this project I consulted over a dozen of the most renowned scholars and teachers in the world of Eastern and Western mysticism, and I present the spiritual "nuggets" of each of these encounters in order to provide the reader with additional perspectives on the issues under consideration.

I have been burned many times over in my quest for truth, and I have learned to use my mistakes to my advantage. I feel that any individual in serious pursuit of truth and God should have the same right: both to be deeply disillusioned by the unconscious playing out of their weaknesses, and to find a source of strength, power, and self-knowledge amid the inevitable pain and failings of trying to express living divinity through the human form. Unfortunately, many people never go beyond the disillusionment in order to discover the illumination, as the pain feels too overwhelming to confront. Yet from the perspective of *conscious discipleship*, we can see that the model does not need to be discarded; but rather that our own misunderstanding and lack of cultural preparation needs to be tended to and augmented. In the words of Winston Churchill, "Success is going from one failure to the next without a loss of enthusiasm."

Whereas this book is ultimately optimistic in the sense that it proposes a working model of the student–teacher relationship in Western culture, the truth of the matter is that I would not seriously consider undertaking a long-term spiritual apprenticeship with approximately 95 per cent of the individuals who profess themselves to be spiritual teachers, either because I do not feel they are strong or clear enough to guide me to the fulfillment of my highest possibility, or because their style or personality does not personally attract me. Yet, in spite of the overwhelming odds against the spiritual seeker finding a productive and harmonious discipleship with an authentic spiritual teacher, I hold an unwavering conviction that the value of this possibility makes it a worthwhile pursuit. I also believe that if we educate and train ourselves well in the art of conscious discipleship, there is an exponential increase in the possibility that we will find ourselves in a working and fruitful relationship to spiritual authority, in spite of cultural trends. The power is in our hands; we simply need to learn how to use it. But we will get to that later ...

My story begins well over a decade ago, in a remote desert village in the heart of Mexico. I am not yet 20, but imagine myself to be a blossoming goddess of significant maturity. I am the specially chosen apprentice of Hozi – a renowned Aztec shaman, mystic, and artist. I have come to Mexico as his invited guest in order to fulfill the first segment of the shared destiny he has informed me that we have together, as fated by the gods.

I am feigning sleep on a makeshift cot that passes for a bed in a one-room cottage/art studio that has been donated to Hozi by one of the mothers (who were also "specially chosen" apprentices) of his various children, so he can afford to paint and teach. I am lying on my stomach with a blanket covering my arm, which is tucked under my pillow, my fingers firmly gripping a large, stainless steel kitchen knife I sneaked from the kitchen moments before on a trip to the outhouse.

My personal shaman is stoned and drunk in the loft, creating erotic life-sized paintings of forests, gods, daemons, cosmic vaginas, ethereal dimensions, sacred objects, sublime interior landscapes. I am all too aware that there are only two telephones in the whole town, and that I do not know where either of them is. I make a mental note to locate them the following day – if I make it through the night. I contemplate various escape plans, but am internally tormented by my thirst for the wisdom I will not receive if I flee. For a moment I rationalize just sleeping with him for the sake of the higher knowledge I wish to obtain, but my stomach curdles at the thought of his whisky breath and his smoke-saturated, bristly gray moustache.

I hear him breathing. Following each smoke-filled in-breath, the out-breath echoes with carnal lust for the naïve, young wannabe shamaness in the bed just feet beneath him. I listen to the rhythm of his breathing, praying to whatever Aztec gods exist that he will pass out from intoxication before his shamanic balls take over. Instead, the breath deepens into a combination of lust mixed with aggression, frustration, vengefulness. My hand held firmly on the knife and my resolve firmly upon doing what is required to save my remaining innocence, I prepare to be attacked.

And so the story begins ...

MARIANA CAPLAN

FAIRFAX, CALIFORNIA

JANUARY 2002

Section One

The Dilemma

Spiritual responsibility means that we take responsibility for all of our spiritual choices, including the choice to place ourselves in the hands of charlatans who then disappoint us, and including the freedom that results from the courage to accept true help in the face of ego's stormy resistance.

We are faced with a great dilemma when it comes to the question of spiritual discipleship. Individuals who wholly dedicate their lives to the fulfillment of the great goal of humankind quickly discover that many self-proclaimed teachers cannot provide them with what they want and may even gravely disappoint them; but, at the same time, such individuals recognize unequivocally that they need guidance. This section explores the dilemma of the conscious spiritual aspirant as he or she wades into the turbulent waters of spiritual mastery. Launching the lifeboat of inquiry, it considers questions such as: What is a spiritual teacher? Are there different gradations of teachers? What is at the root of the great spiritual scandals so commonly spoken of? Why do we need a teacher?

CHAPTER I

You Get What You Ask For (But You Need to Know What You Want)

If frequently enough, the question of the guru is not properly considered, it is because the question of the disciple is not properly considered.

ARNAUD DESJARDINS

I didn't arrive at the shaman's battlefield as my first destination on the spiritual sojourn. It began long before that. It began in a family with a father whose own father did not know how to love him, because his father did not know how to love him, and who thus could not help but to bring some of that same fate to his own children. But upon his youngest daughter the wound also sprinkled the graceful waters of discontentment with a sleeping world that was being increasingly drained of the living mystical possibilities of compassion, inner harmony, selflessness. It began with an imported and patriarchal distortion of the Jewish religion that damaged the mind by instilling God-fear and damnation while simultaneously fertilizing the heart with its prayers and chants written in an objective language that engraved their perennial truth in the same heart and mind that they confused. It began with a car accident that almost took my life, but through grace left me instead with an acute awareness of the preciousness of an existence that could not be wasted and must be continually devoted to the fulfillment of its highest possibility.

By the time I hit 20, I was an overachieving hippy: a feminist activist who ran campus organizations I told myself would save the world, at least in part. I had managed to travel half of that world in my search for cultures that evidenced greater humanness than my own; I had undertaken a serious study of anthropology to justify my search on academic grounds; and I had already learned the necessary lesson that no culture, love affair, beach paradise, or adventure translated into the inner freedom that I already knew was the only thing worth living for.

So when Luna, a self-proclaimed Wiccan priestess and the elder sister of one of my college roommates, waltzed into the living room of our 1930s Victorian household in Ann Arbor, Michigan, and led us through meditations and guided visualizations about the inner self and our life's "true purpose" – the first time I had ever heard those terms I was eventually to come to loathe in their New Age context – I was ripe and ready. Luna hosted the Grand Opening of my psyche, and for the next seven years I was like the ugly duckling going up to every yoga teacher, Tai Chi master, massage therapist, philosophy professor, guru, Hassidic rabbi, and Native American wannabe shaman asking, "Are you my mother?", "Are you my father?"

"How do you find your way through the desert when there is no road?" ask the Sufis. I was new to the path in a culture that did not provide an instruction manual for spiritual seekers. What do you do in middle America when circumstance conspires such that the rigid walls of the psyche crack open wide enough to hear the soul's cry for truth? At that point, I joined with billions of other human beings – past, present and future – in the shared questions: Where do I begin? A book? A teacher? A friend? A place? A martial art? An LSD trip? A pilgrimage to India? How do I know where and how to look? Am I really crazy like everyone from my past believes, or could this intuition of something far beyond my perceived limited perceptions possibly exist ... please?!

Start simple, I thought: Study. I discovered Ann Arbor's single New Age bookstore, went in, and was confronted with thousands of titles ranging from *Discovering the Child Within* and *Everyday Buddhism* to *The Way of the Shaman* and *Celestial Messages*. It only confused me more. I need recommendations, I thought, but whom to ask? Who was spiritual? The people who worked at the bookstore? The long-haired hippies on campus? The women's studies professor who wore the Ghanaian fertility goddess necklace? Did I even know anybody wise? I asked them all for recommendations, and looked for repeats among their lists.

It also struck me as obvious that I would need some guidance but, once again, where to begin? What was a guru? Was that the same as a lama? How did that compare with a shaman? And what on earth did it mean when somebody professed to be a Divine Mother? Could *avatars* – human incarnations of God – really exist among us? Is everyone who calls themselves a spiritual teacher a teacher? Is there a Board of Certification somewhere? Or is it true that every rock, child, lover and tree is my teacher and that I should avoid "intermediaries", as the more cosmic literature suggested? But if that was so, how could I truly trust that I was hearing the rock itself, and not my hoped-for interpretation of its message? Would a ladybug *really* tell me if I was going astray? Little as I knew, I knew enough about the nature of mind to want something more than a blade of grass as my master, and thus I loosely began my search for something called a spiritual teacher ...

Types of Authority

In beginning a book like this, it is important to define what is meant by spiritual teacher, master, guru, guide and so forth. The problem is that it is impossible to do so. Objective distinctions cannot be made, and there will always be gray areas and exceptions. The best I can do is to give an overview of the issues involved, suggest how I will be using the terms in this book, and allow the reader to make further distinctions and refinements as his or her own understanding unfolds.

RELATIVE AND ABSOLUTE AUTHORITY

In his book *Toward a Psychology of Awakening*,[1] John Welwood makes a distinction between relative and absolute authority. *Relative authorities* include those who, human like the rest of us but perhaps one or many steps ahead on the path, function as mentors or guides; *absolute authorities* include the gurus and masters – whatever we call them – who are seen either as incarnations of the divine, or as powerful (if not flawless) vehicles of transmission for divine direction.

Yet even within the model of relative versus absolute authorities, the function any given teacher serves in our lives will depend largely upon how we relate to them. There are spiritual leaders whom some people relate to as inspirations and guides, whereas others relate to that same person as master, or even an incarnation of God. His Holiness the Dalai Lama, for example, is an inspiration or teacher, in a loose sense of the word, to tens of thousands of people, but to his closest disciples he is master, a representative of God Itself, the ultimate authority to be obeyed and worshipped. Even in many contemporary Buddhist traditions, in which the teacher is not formally related to from a devotional stance and may refuse many of the outward expressions of adulation commonly bestowed upon a formal spiritual authority, his or her inner circle of students will often confer uncompromising reverence, obedience, discipleship. Similarly, there are great gurus who, though they have the capacity to serve in the formal function of master, are related to by various aspirants as "guide" or "friend" according to given students' needs at particular times in their spiritual development.

In my own case, there were several months in my life when I practiced rigorously in the company of the disciples of a very famous guru. From the beginning I had the unshakable sense that she wasn't *my* guru, much as I would have liked her to be, as at that time I was actively looking for a master. I was serious about my spiritual studies, too. Serious enough to get up at 5 a.m., walk a mile across town in sub-zero temperatures in the dark Ann Arbor winter, sit in a room lit only by candles, and chant an hour-and-a-half-long Sanskrit prayer I didn't understand, much less was able to pronounce. The students of the master thought that I was a disciple who just "didn't know it yet". But I knew I was not. I was in training for something and someone else whom I had not yet met. Therefore, the distance and lack of devotion with which I related to that guru was rightful for me given my circumstance at that time.

In the course of spiritual life we are also likely to encounter various relative spiritual authorities. We may find ourselves attending meditation sessions or retreats with a particular teacher whom we respect and admire, but do not wish to take as a main teacher. Or we may practice under the guidance of a senior practitioner of a particular teacher as we investigate that specific path. Relative spiritual authorities could include someone who functions in the role of spiritual friend, or an Aikido teacher, or conceivably even a wise therapist (but beware – many therapists who subtly assume this function do not live up to it!).

To learn from these relative authorities, we must offer them a certain amount of respect and trust – in order to receive what they have to offer us. It is no different than going into a yoga class or even a calculus class for the first time. If we go in to profess our knowledge and do what we want and what we think is best, not only will we irritate all the other students, but we will be too busy being full of ourselves to receive anything.

The majority of traditional Judeo-Christian spiritual authorities such as rabbis, ministers and priests tend to fall into the category of relative spiritual authorities, with some notable exceptions. The nature of the religions they represent in no way suggests that such individuals are, or should be, fully realized beings, much less divine incarnations, but rather that they have undergone a set course of study that certifies them to represent the spiritual teachings and ethical laws of their respective traditions.

Many such relative authorities, although they know the rules of their religion and may have a deep regard for others, do not express through their lives an understanding that elicits a natural response of reverence and trust, in their congregants. We may grant them respect and deference, but we do not feel genuine confidence in their wisdom. All too frequently, many of us unconsciously and automatically form a belief structure about all spiritual authorities based on this traditional model, a model that is not always suitable to deep spiritual development.

One way to consider this issue of relative versus absolute authority is according to Ken Wilber's model of spiritual translation versus spiritual transformation. *Translation* refers to a horizontal process in which the contents of ego or personality are progressively uncovered, understood, and worked with in order to create a greater sense of well-being within the individual, and hopefully a greater workability within their lives. *Transformation* is a vertical process in which the nature of ego itself is understood and undermined, and the individual shifts from an egoic identity to a universal identity. In his book *One Taste*, Wilber writes:

> *With typical* translation, *the self (or subject) is given a new way to think about the world (or objects); but with radical* transformation, *the self itself is inquired into, looked into, grabbed by its throat, and literally throttled to death ... [Transformative spirituality] does not legitimate the world, it breaks the world; it does not console the world, it shatters it. And it does not render the self content, it renders it undone.*[2]

A relative spiritual authority is more likely to effect a translational process, whereas absolute authority is more prone to engender transformational possibilities. It is my opinion that the most optimal relationship between teacher and student will include both translational and transformational elements, but translation without transformation will always fall short of the highest human possibility.

NON-TEACHER TEACHERS

An increasing number of teachers say they are not teachers. There are many reasons for taking this position. In certain adaptations of Advaita-Vedanta non-dual traditions, the label of teacher is considered a devaluation of the ultimate realization of the path as well as an obstacle to the realization of oneness. The reality of the situation, however, is that when two people are functioning in the respective roles of teacher and student, the power dynamics that commonly arise in student–teacher relationships generally take place in spite of what they do or do not call themselves, the difference being the language they use to describe (and often avoid) those dynamics. I call this type of teacher a "non-teacher teacher".

In contemporary times, perhaps the foremost non-teacher teacher was the late J. Krishnamurti, an authority of tremendous power and capacity who introduced hundreds of thousands of Westerners to the Eastern non-dual teachings. Declared a prophet and world savior in his youth, a label which he felt was a grave impediment in his authentic quest for liberation,

Krishnamurti worked hard to extract himself from the projection of holiness by his early followers. As Vimala Thakar, a revolutionary Advaita teacher and "non-successor" of Krishnamurti, said:

> *Krishnamurti lived his life, and thousands came to be helped through his communication and the presence of his person. Krishnamurti communicated his own understanding. He shared it because that was his role. It helped many, but he did not help.*[3]

THE INNER GURU

A further type of authority is the "inner guru", a subject I dealt with extensively in my book, *Halfway Up the Mountain.*[4] Since the guru is ultimately a function or aspect of the true Self, the reality of the inner guru is undeniable. However, for most people, the inner guru is not an adequate substitute for relationship with the outer guru – the manifest, individuated expression of the inner guru. Similarly, rarely does the master who is not in the body and whom the disciple has never met, serve as an alternative to a flesh-and-blood teacher. As I will discuss in a later chapter, the external teacher serves several very specific functions of instruction and transmission which the inner guru, as understood by most people, does not and cannot serve until a much later stage of discipleship. The ongoing presence of the external guru awakens and supervises the training of the inner guru as it passes through the necessary and often arduous stages of metaphorical kindergarten, grade school, high school, college, graduate school and so forth.

LIFE AS GURU

There are also those who proclaim that everything – rocks, trees, animals, children, and situations – are their teachers and gurus. Who could deny the validity of such a claim, in the sense that if we are wise and lucky we stand to learn from everything we encounter? Yet to use the term "teacher", or especially "guru", in these circumstances necessitates the widest definition and interpretation of the word – resulting in confusion and even a diminution of the term itself. Why not just say that we have a rich relationship with life, instead of padding our spiritual resumé by proclaiming we have a teacher when it is more simply true that our preferred approach is to learn from whatever circumstance life gives us?

ORGANIC AUTHORITY VS PRESUMED AUTHORITY

I suggest a further distinction in types of authority – that between those whose authority is an organic expression of inner wisdom, and those who presume authority from a place of their own (usually unconscious) egoic ambition. According to Welwood, "True masters have access to an absolute, unconditional source of authority – awakened being ... The genuine teacher is one who has realized the essential nature of human consciousness, usually through practicing a self-knowledge discipline such as meditation for many years."[5]

To function from an organic and authentic expression of inner authority suggests that egoic motivations are no longer the source of one's actions; the authority of the Absolute is then able to flow freely through that individual. When we recognize true authority we cannot help but feel a sense of reverence in relationship to It. For it is *It* – God, Truth, Clarity – that we find ourselves in awe of, not the personality of its carrier, which may or may not be pleasing to us. And yet the natural and appropriate response is to respect the human being who is the vehicle of this extraordinary authority. Such an individual is worthy of acknowledgement and, in most cases, over time and with little or no efforts toward self-promotion, their authority will be recognized. Would-be students will commonly approach them in some manner and ask for guidance because they are drawn to, not coerced or tantalized into doing so.

My teacher's master, the late Indian saint Yogi Ramsuratkumar, is an excellent example of organic authority. Throughout his life and until his death, he expressed no desire to be a spiritual master of any sort, and shunned the role whenever possible. On the contrary, he lived as a beggar on the streets, sleeping under a tree at the bus station or in vacated buildings filled with scorpions and snakes, allowing people to believe he was a madman. Slowly people began to recognize his mastery and would travel far and wide to sit with him at the bus stand, or to help him carry the bags of trash and newspapers he collected, or to follow him around the temples and hills of Tiruvannamalai, South India, where he liked to roam. Over the course of 50 years, they persuaded him first to live in a scant room in the marketplace, then a house, and, in his final year, on an ashram that they had spent two decades beseeching him to preside over. One impeccable "disciple", a Finnish woman, asked him to be her guru once a year for 25 years. Although he offered her ongoing guidance, Yogi Ramsuratkumar insisted that he was not a guru.

We can contrast this example of organic authority with one of presumed authority which I encountered last year. An author of a book on non-duality asked to meet me for lunch to "compare notes" on our various experiences in the field of contemporary spirituality. "I'm frustrated," he told me, "because I have become a teacher but nobody seems to recognize it and I don't know how to get them to. Do you have any suggestions?"

"Tell me more," I said, fascinated by the manifestation of ego that sat before me, housed within a very sincere human being.

"Well," he continued, "I recently had an experience in which one of my closest friends cut off contact with me over this. He said he couldn't deal with me in my new function of spiritual teacher."

"What did you make of that?" I asked.

"It made me realize that once you become enlightened you will probably have to lose a lot of friends because who you are is too threatening to them. If they are not strong enough to perceive who you are, their ego will instead react with criticism. I wish I could help him to see more."

I told this man that no matter how many books I wrote or experiences I had, I would never consider assuming a teaching function unless it was explicitly asked of me from *without*, and not from *within*.

This story is real, and common. Recently a middle-aged woman who had just divorced an abusive Presbyterian minister came to a seminar I was giving with the intention to learn how to become a spiritual teacher. She thought herself wise, and wanted to learn how to go about collecting students. Her intention was sincere enough, but her appreciation of her own wisdom was highly inflated, and distorted besides. She was a woman heavily laden with aggression, unconscious motivations for power, and a deeply repressed sexuality. I didn't have the heart to tell her directly that she was not in a place of spiritual maturity which was likely to attract even one good student, and instead told her that if she focused on her own spiritual maturation, if her destiny was indeed to become a teacher, the students would come naturally.

As the reader may have glimpsed, the spectrum of spiritual authority is vast, with hazy edges on every level. The ambiguity is not due to an inability to make definitions and distinctions, but rather to the fact that most individuals do not fall into any given concrete category but span a range of developmental capacities. As Ken Wilber suggests, different developmental lines (spiritual, cognitive, emotional, sexual, and so forth) can unfold independently from one another, so that a person can be highly evolved in some areas but not in others.[6] For example, a teacher may be highly developed in the capacity to view life from an impersonal perspective, and thus may be able to articulate the teachings with qualities of objective clarity and transcendent awareness, but still have tremendous difficulties in the area of interpersonal intimacy due to disruptions in the bonding process that occurred in infancy.

More important than the developmental level of the teacher, however, is the purity of intention of the disciple and the relational quality between them. An infinite number of potential qualities of relationship exist between teacher and student. As we know from intimate relationships, even a good student and a good teacher will not necessarily yield a powerful outcome without correct chemistry. The whole domain of spiritual authority and discipleship is not only subjective, but intersubjective. It is fully relational.

When I lay in bed clutching a knife in Hozi's studio, I was not a victim of a sleazy shaman's sexual advances, I was naïve and driven by still-unconscious psychological forces. As a Spanish—English translator for the Piscataway tribe with whom I kept an idealized company in the initial years of my spiritual quest before Native American spirituality became trendy, I had had the opportunity to become acquainted with an Aztec shaman they had flown in from Mexico to conduct a ceremony to invoke the spirit of a young native woman who had died unexpectedly and without proper time for closure in her life. Hozi looked the part, straight out of the script. He was 100 per cent Aztec (as opposed to the many white shamans wandering about claiming to be one-eighth or one-sixteenth Hopi on their step-grandmother's side), with thick charcoal hair that fell to his waist, adorned with clay beads, eagle feathers, arrowheads, and all the other garb you would expect from a superstar shaman. I felt a certain unease with him energetically, but I couldn't put my finger on it and interpreted my critique of his slightly shady and unattractive physical characteristics – browned teeth and glazy eyes – to be the result of my vanity instead of an indication of something more authentically intuitive.

Admittedly, my family was skeptical. For example, when Hozi came to my house one evening to celebrate my birthday when my parents were out of town, I did not know he would saturate the newly upholstered living room by burning quantities of the purifying herb sage, which to the untrained nose smells exactly like marijuana. Imagine trying to explain *that* to your elder teenage brothers who, with their girlfriends, were suppressing giggles in the next room where they sat watching *Monty Python* videos. Upon hearing sounds of howling wolves and screams of primal release as Hozi called upon the ancestors to bestow their blessings on me for my birthday, the neighbors called to check that everything was OK. I politely told them I had taken up an interest in theater and was practicing for an audition. What does one do in such a circumstance: ask the Aztec shaman to tone down his calling in of the ancestors? I rationalized that the ancestors must live so far away that one had to call that loudly in order to attract their attention.

When my eldest brother took revenge for ruining his sleep by pounding on his toy Indian drum outside my bedroom door at 20-minute intervals beginning at 5 a.m., I had to laugh. And when I tried to explain to my parents that their 19-year-old daughter had been invited to Mexico as the personal apprentice to a famous Aztec artist-shaman, instead of being impressed – as all my "spiritually evolved" friends were – they wanted to know what he could possibly want with me. But my conservative family was skeptical of everything I did, and I felt insulted. At the time I couldn't see in myself what I now recognize as a highly undeveloped capacity for discernment.

I remember sitting on the airplane from Washington D.C. to Mexico City shaking and sweating. Was I crazy or were they – "they" being the 99-plus per cent of the population who wouldn't be doing what I was doing for any price? I will never forget intensely scribbling in my journal that, although it would probably be difficult, if I worked *really hard* – far more intensely than most people are capable of – for about two years, I would be enlightened. I would have mastery of the inner worlds. I would be a woman of power, a true Coyote Woman. Such was the content of my thinking.

Bear in mind that I had read the books of Carlos Castaneda, the man who brought shamanism to the attention of Westerners in a way no other had before, with his adventurous and romantic tales of running through the scorpion-ridden desert barefoot in the black of night, using his intuition to save him from being even scratched by a rock or scraped by a thorn. I respected Castaneda and appreciated how others revered him, and I desperately longed to receive such admiration myself. Unaware of just how strong this drive to receive external validation was, I unconsciously figured that if I could become that special, the psychological ache inside of feeling unworthy of God's love would finally dissipate. As spiritual teacher Andrew Cohen said, "What could be more special than being the Enlightened One?"

Still, something was decidedly askew. My witch friend Libia was also an acquaintance of Hozi, and I had worked hard to deny my knowledge of their sexual relationship. When Libia asked me to bring Hozi a large, stuffed brown teddy bear, I was confronted with the conflict between my mental image of myself, in which I possessed the maturity of a woman of at least 40, with that of getting off a jet in my Grateful Dead tie-dye skirt while carrying a stuffed teddy bear and looking for a 50-something, long-haired Aztec man with a feather headband and gourds hanging from his belt. The imagined scene brought a gnaw to my gut.

As we stopped off at his gallery to view the oddest blend of cosmic-perverted art I had ever seen, I told myself the source of Hozi's creativity arose from a level I simply didn't understand yet. But when we arrived at La Tierra de Maravillas, or "Wonderland" – the ethereal estate of his mystic-architect friend Guillermo – and were shown to "our" room, the master suite, with a sterling silver bowl filled with peyote buttons resting in the center of the bed – I finally had enough sense to realize that either our hosts had the wrong picture or *I* did – and more likely the latter.

Our days passed with my doing everything I could to avoid being paired up with the shaman – feigning sleep, stomach cramps, culture shock. Once I realized the nature of the game he expected me to play with him – sex in exchange for teachings – I was faced with the subtle task of avoiding any intimate contact with him while keeping him just hopeful enough that he wouldn't give up on me and send me home without the teachings I had come for. This was highly reminiscent of the classic, unconscious parent-child game, whether played out energetically or physically: the child must appease the parents' conscious or unconscious expectations enough to gain their love without selling his or her soul or essence.

You Get What You Ask For

You get what you ask for – consciously or unconsciously. You get what you are. You just do. The fact that you get what you ask for is both the bad news and the good news about the spiritual search. If you are pleased with what you have, it is less likely a stroke of good luck than it is what you asked for, consciously or unconsciously. If you feel that the path and its teachers have disappointed you, you simply have not learned what to ask for and how to ask for it. This often unwelcome philosophy suggests that if we end up with a screwball teacher who wants to take all our money away, on some level (it could be an infinite number of levels, to be sure) it either represents something unresolved within our psyche, or some *karma*[7] that needs to be paid back. The fact that we get what we ask for should come as good news, for it puts the ball back in our own court and reminds us that we can study and develop our consciousness to a point where we will know what to ask for.

There is a distinction, however, between the theory that you get what you ask for in a teacher and the common New Age slogan, "You create your own reality." The egoic interpretation of "you create your own reality" encourages us to conjure scenarios of what ego imagines would most adorn itself, and then to assume that if we play our cards right we should and will get exactly what we want on a silver platter. If we don't get what we think we deserve, we're doing something wrong.

But it is not that simple. We create our reality from all that we are on all levels of godliness and beastliness, conscious and unconscious. Or, as Ram Dass suggested in a recent lecture, "being here now" includes being with all of what is here now on every level – psychological, ecological, conscious, unconscious, past, present, future.[8] If we do not get what we think we're asking for, it doesn't mean that it's our fault and that we're bad or should crack the whip on our already wounded hearts and psyches. It simply means that in a given domain of our path we have not yet gained enough knowledge, wisdom, or healing to refine our capacity to attract what is ultimately in our own best interest. It is not about good or bad, only about learning to assess accurately where we are, and using our free will to empower ourselves to make changes.

The corollary to getting what we ask for is the importance of knowing what we want, particularly when we seek out a spiritual teacher. Knowing what we want is not altogether simple since, as Abraham Maslow suggested in his hierarchy of needs, we have needs and desires on many levels. Whereas it is ultimately true that "there is no one on this earth who is not looking for God", as the Persian mystic Hafiz wrote, we are each also looking for a lot of other things, some of which support our spiritual growth and others that thwart it.

As the Russian mystic Gurdjieff suggested when he referred to "the battle of yes and no", conscious and unconscious factors – desires both to preserve the ego and to allow its annihilation, to be liberated and to fulfill the death wish, to serve and to hoard – swirl about in the psyche on the soul's ultimate journey to self-knowledge. Self-fulfillment and self-destruction continually enact inner warfare on the battlefield of the psyche. Our only chance for peace is to show up on the scene and work out the negotiations.

When we know what we want – both on the level of egoic desire and from the deepest aspects of our selves – we are not surprised or let down when what we get does not look like what we *think* we asked for. When there is a discrepancy between what we ask for and what we are getting and we do not succumb to the temptation of self-pity, we can use the circumstance for self-inventory regarding what areas remain blind or unconscious.

If only we could say honestly and without shame, "I want a teacher who will help me straighten out my life and make me suffer less, but who won't ask me to do strenuous practices." Or "I want a teacher whom I can visit when I need a spiritual 'pick-me-up' but who doesn't require any commitment to the path they represent." Or "I want a substitute Mommy/Daddy figure because I'm determined to get the love I never got as a child." Or "I want to be with a teacher and spiritual community so I can feel like I belong somewhere." None of these motivations is a problem, and even if our own search for a teacher is motivated by one or more of them, there is a distinct possibility that we will gain more benefit than we bargained for. But our unconscious and automatic ego-based tendency is to upgrade our more mundane or primal motivations into something of spiritual meaning and import. Since transformation only begins by knowing and starting from where we are, however much we might wish to be elsewhere, being honest regarding our own motivations is a powerful stance in which we place transformational possibilities back in the domain of self-responsibility.

A related way to view the circumstance of the student–teacher relationship from an empowered perspective is to assume that we get what we need. My teacher, Lee Lozowick, received a letter from his teacher, Yogi Ramsuratkumar, which read, "My Father in Heaven blesses Lee with everything he ~~wants~~ needs," with "wants" crossed off and replaced with the word "needs". Another term for this attitude is *faith*. Ram Dass said that "faith protects you,"[9] and I believe it protects us from believing that things should be other than they are. Great saints and practitioners of all traditions have made tremendous strides in their spiritual development by anchoring themselves in the faith that every thing and every circumstance that comes to them is precisely what they *need*. It can be argued that simply holding this belief (though it is not so easy to do so), and accepting with gratitude what we are offered, bears an untold harvest of transformational possibility.

Returning to my personal story from this self-empowered perspective, the fact that I found myself in a dodgy situation with a horny shaman indicates less that spiritual authority figures are dangerous individuals who take advantage of naïve and helpless young female spiritual seekers, and more that at that time there were areas of my relationship to men and sexuality that were blind and unconscious, finding expression in and through my otherwise pure motivations for truth-seeking. It was also an indication that I was simply young and naïve and in real need of a spiritual smack in the face so that I would learn what did not work and eventually be able to help others learn the fine art of spiritual discrimination from the fruits of my own experience. We are all in the same boat in this regard. The neutral ego, as conditioned by psychology and the perception of separation, mixes with our true aspiration and longing, leaving us in the human psychological maze as we journey back to the self. It is not *bad* or *wrong* that this should be so. It is simply what is.

The Problem with Playing It Safe

I was raised on an insurance mentality. Small quantities of money were being put in the bank for my retirement before I went to kindergarten. Doors were always double- or triple-checked. Decisions were made based upon a programmed plan about what a successful human life looked like. The gas tank was refilled at three-quarters full, and the term "prenuptial agreement" was part of my vocabulary by the age of seven.

We are afraid because we know we are going to die and we do not understand our true identity. The reality of the inevitable annihilation of the body is present within every living animal and human being. We are necessarily trained to preserve the body, which is a wonderful thing since human experience is utterly precious and represents a specific transformational possibility not available in the same way on any other level or in any other form. A glitch in this fine plan, however, is the belief on the part of the body-mind identification that *it* is who *we* are, and that if *it* becomes threatened then *we* are going to die.

This fear represents a significant obstacle in our relationship to the spiritual teacher. The relationship with the spiritual teacher is not safe and it is not supposed to be safe. It is, by its very nature, the ultimately dangerous relationship, and is designed to eradicate our current (unenlightened) sense of identification, which is exclusively attached to the body-mind. The spiritual master is essentially employed on the basis of his capacity to dismantle, decompose, and annihilate the limited self-perception that keeps us suffering needlessly and unnecessarily.

There was a movement in recent years among certain groups of Zen Buddhists who wanted to make the student–teacher path more safe and secure. Their perspective was understandable. There had been a couple of major scandals; the temptation to abuse power even among learned teachers had become evident. Senior practitioners did not want sincere and potential students of Buddhism to lose faith in the tradition, and so they worked out a code of ethics with which all teachers were expected to comply. The primary difficulty with this approach is that it severely limits the range of the teacher's behavior in relationship to the student – a range that may include behaviors that are as unconventional as they are indispensable to what the student needs in order to move on to the next step in his or her growth.

We are again benefited by defining for ourselves what we want and what we are asking for from the spiritual teacher. The function of relative spiritual authority – particularly that of wise religious leaders – is to augment our wisdom gradually, without any excessive demands or risks. The function of a relative relationship to absolute authority is to be pulled slowly in the direction of greater risk, with an option to duck out through the back door at any moment. The function of absolute relationship to absolute authority is to tear apart the safety net and toss us to the mercy of God's divine piranhas, whose function it is to eat up all false perception and leave only the bare bones of naked reality.

In other words, we get exactly what we pay for both in terms of what kind of teacher we attract and in the quality of relationship we engage with any given teacher. This does not suggest that we should squander our accumulated internal riches on the first shmuru who comes our way. Only that when the rightful moment arrives, we must be willing to pay for the goods offered. In the words of Jeanne de Salzmann, a disciple of Gurdjieff, "You must pay dearly ... pay a lot, and pay immediately, pay in advance. Pay with yourself. By sincere, conscientious, disinterested efforts. The more you are prepared to pay without economizing, without cheating, without any falsification, the more you will receive."

At a recent conference I gave abroad, a man stood up on his soap box and aggressively argued the danger of the spiritual teacher for all the reasons we will consider in the following chapter.

"Have you ever had a teacher who has committed the atrocities you so eloquently speak of?" I asked him, searching for the source of his reactivity.

"No, I don't want one. I wouldn't hang out with those teachers. I see straight through them. I know myself far too well to fall for such conmen."

"Exactly," I told him. "So why are you spending all your energy protesting dangerous teachers? Be the kind of disciple who will under no circumstances attract such a teacher and you have no reason to worry."

The late Swami Muktananda, disciple of Swami Nityananda of Ganeshpuri, comments on this issue:

> *Why do false Gurus exist? It is our own fault. We choose our Gurus just as we choose our politicians. The false Guru market is growing because the false disciple market is growing. Because of his blind selfishness, a false Guru drowns people, and because of his blind selfishness and wrong understanding, a false disciple gets trapped. A true disciple would never be trapped by a false Guru. False disciples want a Guru from whom they can attain something cheaply and easily. They want a Guru who can give them instant samadhi. They do not want a Guru who follows discipline and self-control; they want one who will participate in their own licentious lives. They want a Guru who is just like they are.*[10]

Whereas a sincere disciple may at first attract a myriad of false teachers in their initial period of discernment training, over time the conscious disciple is highly unlikely to attract a false teacher, by and large because the false teacher will not be attractive to them. If we want somebody to reflect the beauty of our own ego and to urge us gently toward self-love, a good therapist or rabbi will do. If we want more, we have to be prepared to dig into the pockets of our soul and present the teacher with the currency of the concrete gesture of our willingness to give ourselves over to the process of transformation.

Spiritual life is dangerous. That is the point. It is reserved for the rare few who dare to "step off the 10,000-foot pole". To get the goods you have to put your money on the table – all of it. The people who have succeeded in spiritual life – the great ones whom the uncompromising spiritual student longs to emulate – have risked *everything*, especially who they think they are. They have also, with few exceptions (e.g. Ramana Maharshi), had one primary spiritual teacher, and respected the need for a teacher.

I contend that there exists for all of us the possibility of taking full responsibility for the current state of affairs in our life, whether that life appears to be overflowing with abundant fruits, or stagnant and screwed up. The concept of *conscious discipleship* is a powerful position, a possibility which undermines our sense of victimization by false gurus and empowers us as mature students of transformation and Truth.

John Welwood

East Meets West – The Psychology of the Student–teacher Relationship

John Welwood, Ph.D., is a clinical psychologist, psychotherapist, and long-term student of the Tibetan master Chogyam Trungpa Rinpoche. His six books include *Toward a Psychology of Awakening, Journey of the Heart, Challenge of the Heart, Love and Awakening,* and *Ordinary Magic.*

Q: I was pleasantly surprised to see how you treated the student–teacher relationship in your new book, *Toward a Psychology of Awakening.* Not many people are supportive of spiritual authority these days. It's not a popular viewpoint.

JW: Yes. I know. It is a really complex topic.

Q: Let's get the shovels and start digging.

JW: To begin with, there is cultural karma that we all participate in. We are Westerners, not Indians or Tibetans. It's not easy for us to relate to authority. It's not in our bones. It's not in our cells. It's not in our genes. It's something really foreign to us.

Q: So the fact that we are poorly trained as students should come as no surprise?

JW: It is easy to criticize Western students, but the fact is that we don't have a guru tradition in our culture. It's not that we're screwed up because we don't know how to relate to gurus. That's a cheap shot. In the traditional cultures of Asia, it was much easier to relate to a spiritual teacher. Guru devotion was more congruent with the structure of their culture and family systems. So it fit right into their ego structure. The term for that in Western psychology is *ego syntonic:* "compatible with the ego". In a culture that regards individual interests as subservient to family and group needs, it is compatible with the ego to obey authority, to do what one is told.

Q: Almost in a mechanical way ...

JW: Exactly. In fact, some Tibetan teachers I know really appreciate their Western students because we don't just go along automatically. If they wanted submissive students, they could have just stayed in Asia where they could find lots of people to follow them devotedly. I've heard several of them point out the problem in that. In Asia, many people listen to the teachings without chewing them over and really taking them in. They go along with the outer form – the prostrations, the honoring of authority – but they do not personally engage with the teachings in a way that goes in deeply.

Q: It is as if Easterners' easy acceptance of authority can be as mechanical as ...

JW: ... the Westerners' rejection of it. Yes. I think we are going through a shift where the old guru-disciple relationship has to change somewhat in coming to the West. It's not that we have to do everything democratically – I certainly would not suggest that – but there is something very interesting happening now, and there is more to it than meets the eye. When people dismiss Western students with the attitude of, "They don't know how to be students because they just want to be individualistic," it's a little too facile. My current Tibetan teacher actually says he finds Americans quite interesting because they are all so different from one another.

Q: I think you are suggesting that by bringing the Western strengths to the guru-disciple relationship, you could conceivably come up with a stronger breed of disciples?

JW: Yes.

Q: A kind of conscious discipleship?

JW: Yes. There's a potential to move to a new level. In the Asian system, the notion of discipleship is built in, and it may have gone as far as it can go there. Making a shift to the West requires a different kind of conscious discipleship. There needs to be a dialogue between the traditional Eastern model of liberation and surrender, and the Western model of individuation, where individuality is seen to have important value. Conscious discipleship in the West might include the recognition that individuality is not just some flaw, or obstacle, or resistance to the teachings, but rather that it can be a vehicle for embodying the teachings more fully. If individual development is valued as part of the spiritual path, then it can be transformed and brought to a higher octave. That, to me, is where we are going. That is actually how the mandala principle operates: All the different elements of reality, and all the different personality types and their unique contributions are brought together and included in the sacred world that constellates around a realized master. Trungpa Rinpoche called that "enlightened society".

Q: So conceivably, our individual nature would allow us to consider our discipleship more consciously and not just fall into blind discipleship?

JW: Yes, exactly. We can't just take the Asian model and say, "OK. That is what they did in Asia, and since these great teachers we are studying with are Asian, we should do it the way they did, and anything in our Western culture that doesn't fit that model, we'll just throw overboard." I don't think that works. It actually sets people up for a lot of problems. What happens is that the parts of yourself that don't fit the model you're trying to adopt get denied and come back in unforeseen ways. I've seen that a lot in spiritual communities.

Q: For example?

JW: In certain spiritual groups it is hard to have personal conversations. The members are trying so hard to live up to a certain spiritual ideal of how they should be, trying to be "good disciples", that they do not consider their personal experience valid or important. So when personal conflicts arise in the community, people have a hard time dealing with them and talking it out together because they've given up the capacity to think for themselves and trust their own experience. I've also known many people who married someone else in the community because that person was a good disciple. They would think, "You're devoted, and we share the same teacher, so we'll have a great marriage..." Then the marriage would often turn out to be a horror show because all of their unworked personal material would start to come up. But they didn't have a way of working with it, because they are supposed to be surrendering, hoping that the process of surrender and practice would take care of all their neurosis somehow. Personal relationships are where all the denied parts of us come back with a vengeance, because that is where all our interpersonal wounding shows up. In this modern world I find that psychological work is an important adjunct to the spiritual path in terms of working through material that is otherwise acted out unconsciously, becoming an obstacle to integrating any spiritual realization that you may have.

Q: I think it is clear that some things have to change in this transition from East to West, but there are also things that appear to be necessary to the path no matter what culture they are placed in, like the principle of surrender or the realization of non-duality.

JW: OK, but just to make it interesting, let's consider the issue of surrender further. Let's face it, it is going to be a lot easier for some people to be devoted, and surrender to a guru than it is for other people. But it would be naïve to say: "Those who find it easy to be devoted are more advanced spiritually than those who find it hard." You wouldn't say that, would you?

Q: Of course not.

JW: In other words, it is ego syntonic for certain individuals to surrender. It fits their personality type. In some cases, it may even serve a covert psychological agenda. For example, a person with a dependent personality structure gets ego gratification from serving someone else. Yet for others, surrender is much harder. It forces them to consider deeply what it involves and to work through all their resistances. So the ones who really have to work harder at it might turn out to be the greater students. One thing Trungpa Rinpoche said about devotion was, "Even your struggle with the guru is devotion. Your resistance and your anger can be a sign of your devotion." That helped me a lot.

Q: Given that, what do you see as the function and/or the value of surrender?

JW: One of the ways I have been able to understand devotion and surrender to the guru is that it is a way of habituating and preparing the psyche for absolute surrender, which goes beyond the teacher-student relationship. The teacher-student relationship helps us learn to put something greater above us (which goes against the democratic spirit). Since the function of gurus is to represent the Absolute principle in human form, serving the guru helps us find our rightful relationship to what is greater than us. It is like lining up the forces inside us so that they are moving in that direction. It's a kind of play, a kind of practice ...

Q: Is it entirely necessary?

JW: Yes, absolutely. The ego has to be able to surrender to the ultimate nature of reality. The separate self has to be able to let go if we are to receive the greatest blessings of life. This is a difficult path. Even though it is more ego syntonic for Asians to do that, it is probably hard for them, too, to really do that.

Q: How do we prepare the Westernized ego for this kind of surrender?

JW: It is hard for someone with a weak ego structure to genuinely surrender to a guru. For many people in Western culture, it is all they can do just to have a modicum of self-worth or self-esteem. That kind of person cannot surrender to a guru in a pure way because they want to get something back in return – approval, acceptance, rewards – that will validate them and make them feel good about themselves. But we shouldn't bash Western disciples and say, "Just because they have a hard time surrendering, they don't know what true spirituality is all about." Instead we could be more generous and say, "OK. People are struggling with their issues, and they are doing the best they can in some way." And if they have low self-esteem, maybe some psychological work could help them with that.

Q: Yes. I think that once you start getting involved in the student–teacher relationship, you see that you have to be incredibly strong psychologically to make any use of it.

JW: There is another term in Western psychology called *borrowed functioning*. Students who surrender to prop up their self-esteem see the guru as big and powerful, and get a reflected sense of self from that. The strength of the leader or the group gives them greater capacity to be able to function in their life. They are getting ego strength from the group and from the guru.

Q: I agree, but it is tricky again, because there is a higher principle in there as well: to borrow the strength of the guru or community in order to go deeper than you would ordinarily.

JW: The whole issue is very tricky, because all the low-level dynamics that we can criticize are an imitation of genuine principles that exist on a higher octave.

Q: Yes, very useful principles that you don't want to discount. I think that to project your highest self onto someone – especially someone worthy of that – is a pretty good thing. It shows that we are trying to grow into it.

JW: Yes, even trying to get the guru to love you is OK, because it is a stepping-stone to opening to the deep love that is our very nature. So we begin to see that on the one hand, it is good to have ideals and aspirations, but the danger is that we put these ideals on ourselves in a way that makes them hard to live up to. Compassion, for example, is obviously a crucial part of the path. But we all have parts of us that are not compassionate. Maybe we strive to be compassionate, but that ideal in itself doesn't make us compassionate. So then the question arises, "Do we grow in compassion by lording an ideal of compassion over ourselves?" No, that is regressive. In other words, taking an ideal of where you are not, and putting that on where you are, telling yourself you should be like your ideal, is not very compassionate!

Q: Yes. That is our self-hating culture.

JW: Exactly, it feeds right into the self-hatred that is rampant in the culture and in spiritual communities. That is why so many people in spiritual communities have dour looks on their faces. They are actually using spiritual ideals to keep themselves oppressed and make themselves feel worse.

Q: The spiritual superego will manipulate anything.

JW: But again, one of the good things about Western culture is that we are able to question these things. We can ask questions freshly, and arrive at a more nuanced understanding about what these different things really mean. We need to inquire freshly and ask, "How is this particular aspect of the practice going to work for people here? What is it that students in this culture need at this time? And how can the teachings be more oriented toward individuals" different stages of development, rather than some ideal state?" It's a big task we are talking about – which will probably take hundreds of years – and we are the guinea pigs.

Q: And if we don't do it, who will?

JW: Yes, who else is going to do it? My work has been about trying to see how these psychological understandings could be used in the service of spiritual development – so that people could work on their obstacles and resistances and use them as part of the path, rather than just rejecting them as hindrances they shouldn't be having.

Q: So somehow we need to work this notion of the individual into the process of opening to a more Absolute perspective?

JW: Yes. Spiritual teachings always talk about the Absolute – the mystery of the Absolute, the mystery of the Divine. But equally mysterious is the individual person. Since we have this tradition of the individual in the West, maybe we can contribute to the development of a new integration between absolute being and relative personhood.

Q: Do you really think something new is possible?

JW: Sri Aurobindo was one of the few Indian teachers who spoke about East and West coming together, and what this meant as a new possibility for humanity. His path was not about the human just becoming divine, but rather bringing the Absolute back down through the human vehicle. From this perspective, the spiritual view, or higher octave, of the principle of *individuation*, would involve the individual becoming a vehicle for the ultimate, beyond just being a self-actualizing person.

Q: How do you see that coming about?

JW: Now we have psychological tools, which the ancients didn't have, to work on the personal dimensions of our being. They had methods to take you to the Absolute, but not to work on your personal stuff. Now both sets of tools are available to us. This makes it possible to explore individuation in the context of spiritual development, so that the person can become transparent to the Absolute without leaving shadow elements uncooked. In this model, you are not just pursuing some divine principle on high, but actually bringing yourself along at every level.

CHAPTER 2

"Guru" Is a Four-letter Word: The Nature of Spiritual Scandals

The very term "guru" has become so pejorative that it really means "bad spiritual teacher".

ROBERT FRAGER

Orthodox and conventional scholars think that all mystics, of whatever variety, simply have no critical capacity whatsoever. We mystics, by whatever name – transpersonal, contemplative, yogic, spiritual, even new age – the lot of us are supposed to have completely lost our critical capacities. We are all looked on as phrenologists of the universe.[1]

KEN WILBER

There are gurus I have spent time with who could incontestably justify the claim that "guru" is a four-letter word. Nobody has asked me to drink cyanide-laced Kool-Aid, but plenty of other substances have been offered, and most of the other crimes of power and passion that one hears about in relation to alleged gurus have occurred both to me and to people I know. After 17 years of experience in four continents, and 10 years of research in the field, I am both personally and professionally all too familiar with the shocking abuses of power that have been committed in the name of spirituality. Yet I cannot denounce gurus in general, anymore than I can denounce all men simply because I have had some less-than-ideal lovers.

When Hozi invited me to Mexico, he was all too aware that my yearning for God placed me in a position that was as suggestible as it was vulnerable. I was gullible and credulous, so intense was my desire for transcendence. Hozi knew well that his knowledge of Aztec shamanism stirred my interest; that the exotic gourds that hung from his belt intrigued me; that his familiarity with hinted-at planes of existence whet my voracious youthful appetite for inner and outer adventure. He knew that his compelling flattery might make me willing to overlook small inconsistencies. His only mis-estimation was that I would be willing to pay for such privileges with sex.

No better was his shaman friend Guillermo, who gave us a ride home from a party high in the hills of Mexico City one night. Guillermo was already spirit-intoxicated – from tequila – well before we left for a party at still another shaman's house. As he sped down the winding one-way roads with one hand on the wheel, the other clutching a bottle, and a steep cliff just inches to the right of his beat-up Mexican-style VW bug, to say that I genuinely feared that this might indeed be the last ride of my life would be an underestimation. Terror had overcome me to the degree that I didn't care how many shamans I was trying to impress. Tears streaming down my cheeks, I pleaded with Guillermo to slow down. He responded by cracking a howling laugh and literally closing his eyes as he continued on his way, mocking me because I did not trust the Great Spirit, and telling me I had a long way to go to catch up on the inner planes if I was going to be worthy of keeping shamanic company.

As if my first two personal shamans were not enough, the third one was no better, although it took me a while to realize it. Also an artist, Aleph's paintings were not of cosmic penises and snakes slithering up the vaginal openings of goddesses, but rendered instead the precisely erotic aspect of an eggplant, a melon, a fence, a tomato; or the penetrating presence of a deer's eyes, a lion's footprint, the waiting dawn. When he invited me to El Salvador to study with him at his ranch, I was ready. Not only was I eager to apprentice to his knowledge, but the play of Eros between us was palpable and I was ready to engage on all levels. But Aleph had left out one minor detail in his proposal that I move into his studio for an indefinite period of time, and I used more than one four-letter word to describe what I thought of him when I learned that our love affair was concurrent with his relationship with his wife and three children.

Of course, my adventures with my Central American shamans were benign compared with the far greater horrors that admittedly take place when spiritual authority is abused, among the most notable instances in the past few decades being Jonestown and Heaven's Gate. In both cases, a charismatic leader convinced his followers to commit suicide through what could be labeled "magical thinking". As our inquiry into such phenomena reveals the presence of abusive authoritarian, as well as blindly submissive propensities within our own psyches, we come to understand how and why this same story-line has and will continue to repeat itself across all cultures and in every era.

"The Jim Jones mentality" is how I refer to the phenomenon by which people denounce the value of gurus by bringing up Jonestown and incidents of comparable tragedies. Whereas I always appreciate a good argument, this is not one of them. Since Jonestown, thousands of spiritual groups and leaders have risen and fallen – a few exemplary; many benign, though weak; and a fraction of a percentage truly dangerous.

Gurus Are Old-Fashioned

Many people who argue against hierarchy contend that the concept of the guru or spiritual master as imported from Eastern traditions is old-fashioned, or inadaptable to Western culture. They say that we in the West have evolved beyond such a dated system of authoritarian rule. Within spiritual circles in the United States, a simplification of the trendy spiritual perspective is as follows: The gurus came West in the sixties, we believed in them, gave them our money and lives and souls, and they betrayed us with scandals of money, sex, and power. We have passed through that immature phase, and are now ready for the new: the great return to rugged, spiritual individualism. But isn't this a classic example of American thought? We burned through thousands of years of tradition as quickly as we are burning through all the rest of the world's natural resources. While we may be succeeding in surpassing all other technological advances in human history, we are hardly outshining our predecessors in terms of widespread integrated wisdom.

We in the West are attempting a mass import of very foreign ideals into a culture that has little preparation and no matrix to support them. Claiming these ideals don't work in the West can be likened to the Jews arriving in the desert land of what is now Israel and deciding to create forests, fields, sources of water. That vision was not manifested in 10, or 30, or 100 years, but over thousands of years. To say we have outgrown the old-fashioned idea of the student–teacher relationship would be like the Israelis planting a few thousand seeds and then, after 40 years, abandoning the land, complaining that the fact that there were no forests yet meant that nothing could grow on the land.

It seems to me less that we are failing, and more that we are learning – and just beginning at that! To transplant spiritual traditions and practices from one culture to another is more than likely a job of several generations – a labor of love and patience in which we each fulfill the small part we are called to play. Whereas we will naturally evaluate the process as we go along, it is unwise to jump to quick conclusions about any aspect of the process. The traditions we are trying to import require an appreciation of the timeless wisdom they have to offer, and careful study regarding how the knowledge and wisdom they embody can best be integrated into a radically different land.

"Gnostic intermediaries", a term coined by Carl Jung, are those individuals "who personally incorporate the wisdom of a tradition and can then speak directly from their own experience and understanding into the language and concepts of the culture to which they wish to communicate."[2] In order to transplant Eastern traditions effectively onto Western soil, we are each called to fulfill the function of gnostic intermediary.

Why Spiritual Scandals Occur

If people think that a Guru is unnecessary, it is either because certain Gurus make themselves useless in people's eyes, or because people don't understand the Guru, and so misuse him and then consider him useless.[3]

SWAMI MUKTANANDA

To discuss why spiritual scandals arise, we must consider both the conscious and unconscious motivations that prompt teachers and students to become involved in them. The interesting thing about unconscious motivations is that, whereas some psychological dynamics and tendencies exist in what is truly a blind spot or latent area of the psyche significantly difficult to access due to the intensity of the individual's early psychological programming and conditioning, many other motivations remain unconscious because we simply don't *want* to see them. They are not that far beneath the surface, but we choose blindness because it allows us to gain or maintain certain advantages or comforts. In the words of the contemporary Jesuit master, Anthony de Mello, "People don't really want to be cured. What they want is relief; a cure is painful."

For example, a spiritual teacher convinces himself that he is having sex with the attractive 12-year-old daughter of his disciple in order to transfer special spiritual energies that will enhance her *kundalini* awakening, when if he looked just slightly deeper, he might discover that he is simply a paedophile. Or perhaps a married woman with a love-projection on her teacher wishes to seduce him but feels guilty about betraying her husband, so she tells herself that if she receives the spiritual energy of her teacher through sex, she could use it to heal her strained marriage. The line between what we allow to be conscious and what remains unconscious, between integrity and the lack of it, is thinly veiled. As Zen Master Jakusho Kwong Roshi said, "A crazy [man] and a sage are pretty close."

SCANDALOUS TEACHERS

It is rarely the case that a teacher consciously instigates a spiritual scandal. When this does occur, the deeply troubled individual wishes to gain some advantage in the arenas of power, money or sex by playing on other people's weaknesses. With a conscience badly wounded in childhood, usually by severe abuse or neglect, these individuals feel they have been cheated so much in life that they have every right to take advantage of others. The far end of this continuum includes individuals whose consciences appear to have been so twisted that they consider their abuses virtuous.

More relevant to us as spiritual students, or potential students, are the multitude of unconscious factors stemming from a complex combination of psychological tendencies which prompt teachers to use their position of power to enact manipulative and coercive behaviors. Many charismatic leaders who abuse their positions have notable family backgrounds that may have led them to initial greatness, but also to their eventual demise. In other cases, a family history of intellectual or artistic genius psychologically disposes them to an exaggerated vision of their own greatness.

The spiritual realization of any given teacher may be authentic and accurate on the level at which it has occurred, but there may be higher, or deeper, levels at which the individual is not realized. There may also be psychological arenas in which the person is unequipped to handle all the responsibilities that come with his or her realization.

It is at this juncture that the interplay between psychology and spirituality comes in, for whereas a balanced psychological make-up is not necessary for high degrees of spiritual realization to occur, significant psychological awareness is usually required in order to carry out the function of spiritual teacher. If one's knowledge of non-duality, for example, is reasonably stabilized, but issues around sexuality are not, when students come to the teacher with strong erotic transference (a subject to be discussed in depth in subsequent chapters), the teacher may not have a sufficiently grounded psychological matrix to see the transference for what it is, nor the strength to turn it back to the student, as is appropriate.

This is what has occurred, and still occurs, when Eastern teachers – celibate monks in particular – come to the West to share the teachings of their respective traditions. Their cultural background and their monastic training have in no way prepared them for the onslaught of explicit sexual energy they are met with in Western countries. Having spent years in celibate monasteries, and raised in cultures in which sexuality is notably more repressed than it is in the West, they often find themselves suddenly exoticized and eroticized by Western women who are culturally trained to seek power, knowledge, position, and recognition through their sexuality. Nothing in the background of these monks has prepared them for the desires, temptations, and even perversions that may arise internally when they finally come face to face with these forces (particularly as it is a common unconscious motivation for people to turn to monastic life to escape the world rather than to be more fully in relationship with it). There is clearly nothing morally or even spiritually "wrong" with these feelings, but those who have taken vows of celibacy are in a difficult bind – their reputation and vows on one hand, and their desire to know a different kind of freedom and pleasure on the other. "Scandals" commonly take place when they attempt to sustain their status as celibate monks while at the same time engaging in sexual experimentation.

Difficulties can also arise when someone who has "woken up" begins to gather a body of students – and then his or her realization fades. *Satoris*, or experiences of enlightenment, are not uncommon. They may last for a moment, a week, a couple of months, or even some years. One of the most striking examples is found in the life of the Chilean writer-sage Claudio Naranjo. Naranjo's initial experience of enlightenment lasted for three years. When several months had passed after his initial awakening and he found that it appeared to be stable, he allowed students, an organization, and a teaching system to arise around him as a vehicle to share what he had to offer. However, slowly – and at first imperceptibly – Naranjo's enlightenment began to fade. According to his own testimony, at first he fervently resisted the recognition of what was happening, until finally his own greater honor won out, and he dismantled his organization and denounced himself as a spiritual master.[4] How few people would be willing to enact such integrity in such an egoically tempting circumstance! After three years of realization, with an ego fully educated in the subtleties of profound mystical experience and the "walk and talk" of enlightenment, it would be easy to maintain one's "greatness" in the eyes of others, and even in one's own.

More often than not, individuals who have had some degree of realization or awakening and begun to teach as a result of it unconsciously use that realization as their link to power. They remain blind to the depths yet hidden within them that will not be exposed unless they are willing to surrender what they know for what they do not know.

SCANDALOUS STUDENTS

A scandalous student is someone who places him- or herself in a circumstance that is corrupt or is likely to become so, or who continues to remain in such a situation, in order to extract unconscious payoffs. In almost all cases, the sincere student is with a corrupt teacher because he or she has areas of blindness that are either getting fed or reflected by the teacher. The principle of mutual complicity – known colloquially as "it takes two to tango", and psychologically as "intersubjectivity" – suggests that both student and teacher participate in any instance of corruption. If the student is unwilling to support the teacher's corruption, the teacher has no one to be corrupt in relationship to. Similarly, many teachers may have dormant tendencies toward corruption or psychological blindness which are only awakened by a student's parallel "corruption" or weakness. The student and teacher legitimately need each other to fulfill their respective functions, but they also "need" each other to create a circumstance of scandalous behavior. The situation is entirely interrelational.

The fact is that there is usually some unconscious benefit we are receiving from negative situations, even if it is simply the comfort of what is familiar, and if we look deep enough, long enough, and honestly enough, we will eventually be able to discover the roots of our own complicit involvement in a given situation.

Maintaining the stance of victimization in relationship to a spiritual teacher is thus a strategy of avoidance on the part of the scandalous student. At the deepest level of our experience, we understand that we are never victims of anything. At the same time, our false, egoic identity thrives on victimization. The payoff in victimization is that ego gets to experience the delicious sensations of vengefulness and justification for its own weaknesses, the comforting pity of others' sympathy, the safety of separating itself by making another person wrong and itself right, and the comfort of staying in its own familiar, cozy little box of false identity. Conscious discipleship involves a commitment to learning how to step outside of the familiar and comfortable stance of perceiving oneself the victim of the teacher, or of anyone or anything else.

What's So Bad about Hierarchy?

If you want to make friends in elite spiritual circles, telling people you have a guru is not the way to do it. Walking into a party and telling someone you have a guru is like saying, "I'm a heroin addict." Dead silence.

"What's his name?" they utter nervously.

"Lee Lozowick."

"Oh ... I've ... um ... never ... heard of him," they say apologetically, as if their lack of knowledge about my teacher makes him invalid. The awkward silence that follows implies: "Oh, you're still adhering to that dinosaur model of patriarchal hierarchy. Don't worry, you'll grow out of it."

One of the main arguments used against the spiritual student–teacher relationship is that it's hierarchical, as if hierarchy itself is inherently unethical or dangerous. In progressive circles, the rule is that hierarchy is out, egalitarianism is in; vertical relationships are out, horizontal ones are in; gurus are out, mentors and inner gurus are in; God is out and either the goddess Gaia or science (depending upon your particular circle) are in; patriarchy is out, and matriarchy (in principle) is in.

The fact is, not only does culture past and present function according to hierarchical structures, but so does nature, the psyche, the process of spiritual unfoldment, and the domains of the gods and goddesses (neither Zeus in the cosmic domain, nor Jesus in the historical, were considered equals by their followers). Whether we accept it as spiritually correct or not, hierarchy occurs on all evolutionary levels and in all domains. Ken Wilber prefers to use the term *holarchy* to describe this continuum of nested spheres in which "each senior level transcends and includes, or enfolds and embraces, its juniors".[5]

An amusing example of the organic arising of hierarchical structures can be found in the "rules of the road" in India. Ironically, at the top of the structure are cows – both because they cannot be moved from the middle of the road and because in Hindu philosophy the cow is, at least theoretically, considered sacred. Next come trucks. They are massive, take up most of the road, emit generous amounts of toxic fumes which keep everyone as far away from them as they can manage, and have unrelenting horns that mercilessly warn all other users of the road that they are coming and will not change their course for any human or animal (except for cows). Next are the cars. They belong to the rich, and in all but the large cities are an indication of wealth and power – the nicer the car, the more prominent its position on the road. Next down are auto rickshaws – three-wheeled taxis run on motors. Down further are bicycle rickshaws; followed by bicycles; oxcarts; pedestrians; then animals other than cows. Whereas from a politically correct standpoint such a structure is classist, elitist and "homosapiencentric", from a practical standpoint it simply works. It provides a necessary and relatively workable structure given the chaotic structure of the culture in which it takes place.

It strikes me as quite incongruous that whereas we generally accept, though perhaps not without complaining, that corporations are run hierarchically, or that the United States government and the royal family of England are hierarchical structures, when it comes to spiritual mastery, the guru cannot be the guru. He must be a "spiritual friend', a "mentor", a "guide". He must be a "non-teacher teacher". Writers in the field of spirituality who want their books to sell often take great pains to assure their readers that when they talk about their teachers they are not talking about gurus (as if that term necessarily implies negative authority), but about egalitarian, non-authoritarian relationships between elder and younger peers.

I find this approach problematic, for wearing the clothes and talking the talk of non-hierarchy excuses both leader and followers from confronting directly the inevitable, ever-present dynamics of hierarchy. Egalitarianism is a fine ideal as well as a natural reaction to centuries of misused authoritarian power, but it has not proved itself successful in society, much less in the training ground of the soul, which requires the teacher to fill the role of head trainer.

Perhaps the source of our true concern is the recognition that *manipulative* hierarchy is dangerous; *abusive* hierarchy is unethical; *uninformed* hierarchy a source of warranted caution. Our collective rebellion against spiritual hierarchy is perhaps a crying out that we are terribly frightened that we do not have the strength and clarity to navigate intentional structures of hierarchy in a way that will help us and not hurt us, and that we fear this for our loved ones as well. Might we venture to consider that we are pissed off at God for creating a universe in which we will inevitably die and in which we ultimately have no control? That while we intuit the possibility of informed guidance from spiritual authority figures, we also know that most of them are shaped by the same forces that we are, and we do not trust that their professed mastery will help instead of harm us, just as our unconsciously projected godliness onto our parents often disappointed us as much as it served us?

I suggest it is the abuses and subsequent corruption of hierarchy that is problematic, not hierarchy itself.

Social Change in Response to Spiritual Scandals

When I encounter someone who argues vehemently against the student–teacher relationship, almost inevitably they are unconsciously trying to heal something still unsettled either in their present life or in some former circumstance (whether from childhood or from an unresolved experience in adulthood).

As supporters of social change throughout the decades have routinely discovered, and as I can confirm from my own experience, change does not
come about when those individuals espousing the cause are motivated by a
disposition of psychological reactivity, when the energy behind their cause is
fueled by feelings of pent-up anger, betrayal or outrage as a result of a personal
disappointment or disillusionment. The feelings in and of themselves are rea-
sonable, but are an insufficient base from which to educate others. The energy
of the activists' aggression estranges others in spite of the validity of their facts.

Anti-cult organizations such as the Cult Awareness Network frequently
demonstrate this dynamic. People with the best of intentions are drawn
together by the experience of having felt that either they, or a family member,
has been betrayed by a spiritual leader or group. They bond to one another
through their shared pain and anger, often resulting in a type of zealous anti-
cult cult; a dogma against dogma; a group with an assertive doctrine warning
against groups with assertive doctrines. When a family believes that one of
their members is in a dangerous cult (an estimation I would agree with in only
about 20 per cent of cases), a specialist may actually kidnap the individual and
lead them through a process of deprogramming. The deprogramming is, of
course, an attempt to remove the newer programming of the cult and replace
it with the former (i.e., the family's and culture's) programming. This type of
attempted social change almost always fails. Based upon subjective beliefs and
characterized by reactive emotionality, even when the underlying intention is
benign, feelings of mutual betrayal commonly result.

My first book, *When Sons and Daughters Choose Alternative Lifestyles*,[6] is a
guide for families about how to sustain loving relationships in the face of
ideological or lifestyle differences. The book makes the distinction between
healthy intra-familial activism and the kind that is damaging. Often, the rup-
ture between family members, the cruel words exchanged under the guise of
help, and the intensity of discrimination against the defector/betrayer create
far more damaging consequences than the imagined "dangerous lifestyle"
could ever do. When it comes down to it, many people have to make a choice
as to whether honoring their love for one another is worth more than their
ideas about what is right and wrong. If and when the individuals involved are
willing to place relationships over ideas, the psychological tools and means
follow easily.

Social-change activists work most effectively when they operate from an
assumption of oneness and unity – an understanding that others are essentially no different from themselves in spite of the appearance of things, and an
appreciation that the potential for all possibilities exists within each of us.

They recognize that the only truly effective means of serving others whom they fear have taken a wrong road is through compassion and understanding. Listening, respectfully sharing information when appropriate, and making themselves available should the person decide they want help is all they can offer.

Regardless of our degree of wisdom, can we truly feel confident that we know what someone else needs? Can we be certain that even if a situation appears unfruitful it is not just one phase of a necessary and larger process through which the individual is passing? It can be hard to watch people we love move through hardships which we imagine are avoidable, but people learn mostly from their own experience and their own mistakes.

When We Get Burned

I have met many individuals who have turned against the possibility of authentic spiritual authority because they have been disappointed by someone who was widely professed to be a world-class master or guru. One such person, when his guru died, turned his devotion to the guru's lineage-holder, as requested by his master, but found his new guru to be unworthy of his devotion and thus came to be suspect of both. Another, famed for bringing his guru to the attention of the world, became anti-authority when the guru told him he must break up with his male lover, or at least keep the relationship hidden, if he wanted to continue to represent her message. One woman's guru convinced her that he was her divine counterpart, had a baby with her, and then proceeded to enact this drama with several other women in the group. Another woman was devastated when her guru insisted that his disciples not have children, later changing his view on the matter when she was beyond childbearing age. Still another young man traveled all the way to India to meet the man he was certain was his guru, only to find he could not visit with him because he was in jail for murdering two dozen of his disciples!

In each of these instances the student felt badly betrayed, and understandably so. Such circumstances reveal how much responsibility a spiritual authority has, not only for his or her own students, but for the reputation of all spiritual authorities. Although conscious discipleship requires 100 per cent responsibility on the part of the student, the teacher is also 100 per cent responsible. The difference is that a teacher's weaknesses and mistakes affect not only all who come into his or her sphere of influence, but also the reputation of spiritual mastery in general.

Whereas ultimately we cannot know the destiny of any given student, the apparent tragedy of such errors and betrayals on the part of teachers is that potentially exceptional disciples turn away from the student–teacher relationship, effectively "throwing out the baby with the bathwater". This is where the great questions, complexities, and karmic aspects of this challenging situation come flooding in: Why did such mature and psychologically developed individuals find themselves in the hands of weak spiritual masters? Was it a karmic inevitability? Was it a result of some blind spot in the disciple? In the master? A mutually complicit need? Since the true disciple will continue to develop in spite of weaknesses in the teacher, and will even use their teacher's limitations to enhance their own understanding, we cannot, even objectively, conclude that such situations are tragedies at all.

Fortunately, in many cases the turning away from the student–teacher relationship is not a rigid and permanent stance, although it may take many years for these wounds to heal and the possibility of trusting another to be re-established. Individuals in this situation find themselves in a very tender bind. They have been touched by the master. They know the taste of that nectar and are continually reminded of it through its absence, yet remain conflicted as to whether or not they want to risk to that degree again. Their lives may feel relatively meaningless or simply empty without the master; yet they have become understandably suspicious about whether it is possible to recover the trust and faith they once perceived.

Betrayal or disillusionment between student and teacher can be particularly devastating because the relationship usually involves love – love that has not died but which the student cannot afford to continue to carry forth in the flesh of human relationship. This love, and the loss of it, do not function according to the laws of reason but in accordance with their own mandates. When I meet people in this circumstance, my deep wish is that they eventually discover the means by which to separate a bad experience with a particular spiritual teacher from the whole field of spiritual mastery, so that if it is their eventual destiny or highest possibility to find themselves again in the company of authentic spiritual mastery, they will be open enough to receive its offering.

What Is Scandalous?

Exactly what constitutes a scandal is a question that is as critical as it is unanswerable. Aside from the most extreme instances, it is not as clear-cut a line as we might commonly think. There are many contemporary examples of teachers whom some highly intelligent students and scholars consider to be indisputably scandalous, whereas other equally worthy evaluators consider these same individuals to be masters of rare capacity. In fact, most of the popular teachers of our time are met with a similar mix of adulation and demonization.

The problem with judging as scandalous the behavior of one who is considered a master is that we are judging *their* perspective from the standpoint of *our* morality or degree of understanding. Ken Wilber describes this beautifully when he says, "It is not what a person says, but the level from which they say it, that determines the truth of a spiritual statement."[7] If I grew up with alcoholic parents and was significantly wounded by the manifestation of their disease, the intake of alcohol by one who was professed to be a master would be totally unacceptable to me, perhaps even interpreted as a definitive sign that the teacher's mastery was less than complete. If, on the other hand, alcohol had never been an issue in my life, and I had a master who drank a little bit, or even a lot, but whose teaching showed integrity and consistency over time, the alcohol might be a factor of minor relevance to me.

In the West, alcohol, tobacco, and other substances have been labeled as unspiritual and addictive, yet great masters throughout the ages have used these and every other substance, at times for their work with students, and at times for no apparent reason whatsoever. In many tantric sects, such as the Bauls of Bengal, alcohol, meat, and other intoxicants are specifically employed as aids in processes of transformation and alchemy. Indigenous people of many cultures have used hallucinogenic plants and substances. Some people consider this to be totally immoral; others find it natural and of no concern. Some people have no problem with a Native American chief using such substances, but find it immoral when a Caucasian Advaita Vedantist uses them. Are such behaviors neurotic? Divine? Both? Neither?

I do not side with any of these perspectives. I suggest only that our concepts of right and wrong, moral and immoral, sacred and profane, are themselves worthy of ruthless scrutiny. Scandals are not determined in a court of spiritual martial law. It would be much easier if there were an objective source who could dictate impartially which teachers and groups were corrupt and which were not, but the subtleties of soul work can only be evaluated circumstance by circumstance, moment by moment, individual by individual.

Fool's Gold

"Fool's gold exists because there is real gold," Rumi said. While we may find ourselves outraged by the onslaught of spiritual scandals broadcast by the media, the fact is that there have been false teachers in every age and in every culture. It has been suggested that false prophets are decoys to deter the masses of less determined seekers so that only those who are serious enough to pay the price for true mastery will discover it.

Sometimes I wonder why real gold can't be made available to all. Why do so many wannabe gurus peddle false metal? I have no concrete answer, but I do know that, whether we like it or not, conscious union with God (or Truth, or Reality) does not come at a discount. Everyone is certainly *entitled* to real gold, but the rule of the game seems to be that it only comes to those who are willing to mine it.

Perhaps the work of learning to discover what a real master is – making the inner effort required to attract such a situation into our lives; coming to understand and appreciate that which the master represents and why such a function would exist – is an essential aspect of the path itself. We can either study the field of mastery and our own unconsciousness deeply enough so that we are, at least intellectually, prepared to meet the genuine master; or we can learn what genuine mastery is by meeting as many false masters as we can.

I personally chose the latter option, though for some it is less advisable, as the run-in with false masters often jades one to the possibility of there being a true master. I often wonder what makes the difference between the person who discounts all masters due to a few bad apples and the one who just keeps looking, figuring that it is due to some unconscious weakness within themselves – or even just a stroke of bad luck – that they haven't found what they are looking for. In *Spiritual Choices*, John Welwood writes, "To discount all spiritual masters because of the behavior of charlatans or misguided teachers is as unprofitable as refusing to use money because there are counterfeit bills in circulation."[8]

After two bad rabbis, three fake shamans, and a dozen other random healers, shmurus, and wannabe teachers, I had every justification to stop looking for a master altogether, and instead worship the best interpretation of the inner guru I could construct. But I had not given up, even on them. For each had revealed a hidden hole within me that had drawn me to that situation. By the time I got to India, as my story will later reveal, I was dubious about whether I could find a real master. I did not know if my true intention was strong enough to outweigh the gross unconscious forces that still dominated me, but I felt clear in what I had learned about false masters, and figured if I played the lottery long enough – lifetimes, if necessary – my number was bound to come up at some point. Will we cease to believe that diamonds exist simply because until now we have not been able to afford them, and have instead had to be content with rhinestones?

George Leonard
The Danger of Spiritual Authority

George Leonard, a pioneer in the human potential movement, is the author of 12 books, including *The Way of Aikido: Life Lessons from an American Sensei*, *Education and Ecstasy*, and *Mastery*. He is co-founder of The Leonard Energy Training (LET), and co-founder with Michael Murphy of Esalen Institute and Integral Transformative Practice (ITP). He holds a fifth-degree black belt in Aikido, and lives and teaches in Mill Valley, California.

Q: How do you view the student–teacher relationship in spiritual life?

GL: I teach people to listen to all teachers, because from all teachers you can get something, *but* to keep their own center. A good student has to uphold two ideals simultaneously: 1) respect and acknowledge your teacher; and 2) in the final analysis, keep your own judgement. One of the things that we as teachers should model is being a student.

In the book *The Life We Are Given* that Michael Murphy and I wrote, we suggest multiple mentors rather than a single, all-powerful-guru-type. The single, all-powerful guru rarely gets feedback, and it's really a question of feedback rather than a question of power.

Q: Why do you say it is a question of feedback rather than authority?

GL: It's not a question of whether you *have* authority. It's not that the teacher should lack authority, but that he or she should be able to hear, and work with, and deal with, relevant feedback. That's where it often goes wrong. The test is whether the teacher can hear feedback, or are they beginning to think that they have *all* the answers? I do believe in certain authority, certain leadership. That has to be. To do away with leadership often leads to tyranny, which is the same thing we're trying to get away from. Here in the United States we've got a pretty good model of checks and balances. There has got to be some way to check a guru who is going to lead the people to drink Kool-Aid laced with arsenic, and the Eastern model of an all-powerful teacher doesn't allow for it. I just don't think [spiritual authority] is such a good idea.

Q: In the West, or for everybody?

GL: For everybody. Period. I'm going to be radical here. I look around the world and I see the adherents of some very fine teachers – Mohammed, Jesus, Confucius – and I see them killing and slaughtering other people primarily because they are on the other side. So I'm not sure it's the greatest model we can have.

Q: But is the weakness in the teacher or in the adherents?

GL: It's within the system, which includes both. That's what I'm saying. It may go against your thesis, but this is what I believe.

Q: That's OK. Readers should hear this side of the issue as well.

GL: The greatest outrages of history have been committed in the name of the greatest religious teachers, not secular teachers. We have to look at that when we look at spiritual authority. This is not to say that authority is wrong. There should be authority. I have authority in my Aikido workshops. I speak clearly to students from my center and I want them to speak, too, but I also want their feedback. I don't want to lead people down a blind alley.

Q: What is the value of them relating to you as an authority in that domain?

GL: It shows a respect for the art and a respect for themselves. Why do we bow? Why do we bow to Morihei Ueshiba, O Sensei (our founder)'s picture? A lot of people think that's a heathen thing to do. We bow to O Sensei [Great Teacher]'s picture because he was a wonderful teacher. We are bowing for respect for him, for the art, for the community that has developed, for our *dojo,* and most of all for respect for ourselves. But this doesn't mean we're going to say Judo is bad and we have to go terrorize Judo people or Karate people. We bow as an act of respect for ourselves, ultimately. I don't think it is necessary to make yourself an exulted being. God is in every one of us. The whole idea that God is in one person, I don't like that. In my way of looking at it, God is in everything in the universe. I know that I could easily put myself in the role of guru – let my white hair grow a little longer and get a white beard. I could make my voice a little more resonant and louder in order to get the crowd to cheer and say "hallelujah" and all that kind of stuff, but I do not choose that path.

Q: I imagine there are people who try to put you there.

GL: Yes!

Q: How do you work with them?

GL: I just laugh about it. I say, "Come on. You've got to be kidding. I'm just a flawed being." The thing we've got to understand is, "I'm the center of the universe and so are you. I have God within me and so do you and so does the next person." We've got to realize God is in everybody. We don't need to have anybody as a representative of God. We're all representatives.

CHAPTER 3

The Need for a Teacher

I still don't have much interest in Buddhism, in any formal way. I bumped into a man in California who impressed me. His name was Joshu Sazaki Roshi, and he happened to be a Rinzai monk. I often say that if the man I met had been, say, a professor of physics in Heidelberg, I would have learned German and studied physics.

LEONARD COHEN

A man cannot awaken by himself.

P. D. OUSPENSKY

I never really questioned whether or not I needed a teacher. Although I had the Buddha's dictate, "Be a lamp unto thyself" taped to my bathroom mirror, I knew that I needed somebody to teach me *how* to be a lamp. I couldn't even seem to figure out how to get the plug into the socket without getting a shock.

Ringo seemed like a decent choice. The circumstances of our meeting had been anything but ordinary. I was camping out at a traditional Native American Sun Dance hosted by the Piscataway tribe in Maryland. The ritual, extending over a period of several days, included intensive fasting, dancing, sweat lodges, prayer, and a bodily sacrifice on the part of the dancers. Hour by hour, through cold rain and scorching sun, we stood beneath the sacred, circular arbor of trees as the Native brothers fasted, chanted, and prayed themselves into a visionary state, at which time they would have the chief pierce their chest with wooden pegs they had carved in preparation. Ropes would be attached to these pegs, and from these ropes they would be hung from a sacred tree that would transport their prayers to Father Sky, until the pegs burst and the men fell to the ground. A well-kept secret, the Sun Dance is a powerful indigenous rite still practiced in a few places in the Americas.

So there I was in the sacred arbor, having not eaten in three days, floating on bizarre energies and foreign ideas, lost in self-aggrandizing fantasies about becoming the girlfriend of one of the sexy Native sun-dancers, when I opened my eyes to an uncommon sight. The single Caucasian dancer came forward and, instead of having the wooden pegs put through his chest like the other dancers, he had the chief pierce his back, then attach the pegs to ropes that held an entire buffalo skull. The man whom I was later to know as Ringo pulled this skull around the arbor for over an hour, streams of blood dripping down his back and sweat pouring from his silver sideburns, until the skin finally broke and Ringo collapsed to the ground with what appeared to be a potential heart attack.

The event was so compelling, and my empathy so strong, that I formed a mysterious emotional attraction to this older man, whom I experienced not as lover but as "grandfather". Later that night, as we all settled in around the sacred fire in exhaustion, I shared my experience with Ringo. He responded with delight and gratitude, telling me that he had never had any grandchildren, and as he was getting older he was longing to pass on the fruits of over five decades of spiritual pilgrimage. During that time he had traveled as a wandering monk of no order, meeting and living with spiritual leaders and peace activists throughout the United States, Canada, Mexico and Europe, serving up the message of interfaith peace and politics. He asked if I would like to join his pilgrimage, and said he would introduce me to his friends and mentors, among them great Native American chiefs, Zen Buddhist monks and nuns, disciples of great gurus, Quaker and Amish leaders, and esoteric interfaith eccentrics like himself.

Here was my chance! Finally, I would meet so many great masters, and surely among them I would find one who was rightfully mine. I corresponded with Ringo throughout the course of my final months of university, once visiting him as he fasted for "40 days or until death" on the steps of the Capitol Building in Washington, D.C. to protest the unjust jailing of the Native American activist Leonard Pelletier. Finally, four days before my college graduation, at which President George Bush was scheduled to speak and which I had not planned to attend, as the only politically correct option was to boycott it – my poor parents! – Ringo picked me up in his '68 Ford van and we headed out to conquer "the teacher circuit".

Thus began my Summer of Torment in the Van from Hell with my Grandfather from Hades. We met some impressive teachers, and some who were far less than impressive, the one I was traveling with being among the least inspiring of all. Ringo was one of those non-teacher teachers, the kind who, when somebody refers to them as a teacher, gives them a knowing look of feigned modesty that implies: "The only Teacher is the Self. I am just a mirror." The problem with their "non-teacherhood" is that they are less likely to deal with their responsibility to their "non-disciples".

Jun Sun, on the other hand, was a noble woman. Once a radical Japanese biker (as in "motorcycle" and not California mountain bike), now turned Buddhist nun, Jun Yasuda belonged to the Nipponzan Myohoji order of Buddhist monks and nuns. They practiced peace through fasting, *long* walks (up to 10,000 miles!), chanting, and building magnificent monuments, called *pagodas*, which housed small bits of the actual Buddha's relics. Unlike non-teacher teachers, Jun Sun was a nun who only served in a teaching function when others insisted upon learning from her. Still, she took full responsibility for her relationship with those who came to be near her to partake of her wisdom.

The weeks we spent with Jun Sun were unlike any others in my life prior to that time. Our van was immobilized at a local farm to which it had been towed to get the entire engine replaced by a (literally) schizophrenic friend of Ringo who offered to do it for free. In the meantime, we stayed with Jun Sun. She was a woman who defined discipline. We got up at 4 a.m. for an hour of mantra repetition in Japanese. We weren't required to get up, rather *she* got up and pounded a three-foot high drum while she chanted for an hour and a half, and since the dorm-style open loft where we slept was actually in the temple-barn itself, we had the choice either to listen to somebody gain the merit of spiritual practice while we listened on from our toasty sleeping bags, or to join her.

Next we ate a scant breakfast of unsweetened porridge, then went out for a 12-hour day of construction on the peace pagoda, with 15-minute breaks for rice crackers. At the day's end, following a Japanese-style "bath" taken in rusty oil cans heated from beneath by a wood fire (which nearly left me with third-degree burns!), there was another hour of chanting, followed by food. By 8 p.m. the rest of us were useless, but Jun Sun, the only one who could still function, cleaned the dishes, emptied the pots in the outhouses, and answered her correspondence by candlelight. In the same way as the Hassidic Jews "went to the rabbi to watch him tie his shoes", we subjected ourselves to Japanese temple torture to watch the way in which Jun Sun worked without complaint, related to all people with fairness and concern, and served her tradition unswervingly. It would be hard to find a practitioner of greater nobility.

Jun Sun convinced me that I was actually capable of completing a 10,000-mile, 10-month peace walk from Panama City, throughout Central America, and ending in Washington, D.C. to protest some important cause I can't remember but that seemed vital at the time. To realize that I, a once-Jewish American Princess gone interfaith martyr protestor, could complete such a feat was so exhilarating that I committed to the project. I recall being *unable* to comprehend why my mother was so upset when I told her. Didn't she support *peace*? It was a full-blown case of spiritual parent torture.

Other teachers that summer were less impressive, or at least their disciples were. In one instance, we visited a fancy ashram. When we approached the *guru seva* (service) desk to sign up for our daily service activity, they took one look at me and said I was only dressed well enough to work in the dish room. Later that summer, when I was "camping" in a car I had borrowed from a friend so I could get a 24-hour reprieve from Ringo, the ashram police woke me at 3 a.m. and forced me to leave the 2,000-car parking lot, even though morning meditation started one hour later.

At another ashram I befriended a cute, barefoot, orange-robed Hindu monk, who gave me a banana and told me, "This is not a banana." He had me plenty confused, until I learned that he had given me a gift of *prasad* which was blessed by the master and contained a special blessing.

Why the Need for a Teacher?

At the end of their three-year intensive course with Buddhist scholar and teacher Reggie Ray, he told his group of students: "If you don't meet a spiritual teacher and *go all the way with them*, you are wasting your life."

"Only in a time as confused as ours could one think that the teacher-student relationship – an archetypal and sacred form – exists as an option rather than as a necessary requirement, a station on the way,"[1] writes William Patrick Patterson in *Struggle of the Magicians.*

Such statements may sound unusually strong, yet it seems increasingly implausible to me that we could believe ourselves capable of navigating the soul's unfolding without a guide. Whether the teacher assumes the traditional authoritative role of guru, or functions as a guide and mentor; whether they call themselves a teacher at all; whether the relationship lasts a few years or a lifetime, the student or disciple's unwavering and uncompromising commitment to that individual for as long as the teacher—student relationship lasts is a primary factor in the success of his or her spiritual unfolding.

There are several pragmatic reasons why the help of a teacher is invaluable for the one who dares to strive toward the fulfillment of their highest human potential.

MASTERY OF ANY SKILL REQUIRES APPRENTICESHIP

People are willing to turn to master teachers in every other arena of life. From woodworking to dentistry to philosophy to sports to music, the individual who wishes to excel in these arenas will seek out either a master or a specialist to apprentice to. Yet they maintain that mastery of the human soul can be achieved alone. Rudolph Steiner describes the situation as follows:

> *In principle, of course, self-instruction is possible. Equally, every human being, provided he reaches a certain stage of clairvoyance, can discover spiritual truths for himself, but this would be a much more lengthy path ... The teacher is the friend, the counselor, one who has already lived through esoteric experiences and now helps the pupils to do so themselves ... It is simply a question of what is required for shortening the path to the highest truths.*[2]

Returning to the consideration of hierarchy, it seems to me a quite natural movement to place oneself in the position of junior to senior if one hopes to achieve excellence in the area in which the senior has mastery. Only in the arena of the spiritual student–teacher relationship does this seem to present a problem for many people, perhaps because the individual who allows his or her ego to be submitted to someone whose function is to undermine the ego is in fact committing intentional egoic suicide. It is easier to denounce the function of the true guru than to face the fear this prospect generates.

TRANSMISSION

> *Light my lamp from your lamp, O Sadguru.*
> *Light my lamp from your lamp.*
> *Remove the darkness covering my heart.*

JYOTA SE JYOTA

Transmission may be the singularly most important function of the authentic teacher, especially if he or she serves as an absolute authority, and to a lesser extent even as a relative authority. Anything and everything else the teacher does is secondary to this function. The Eastern teachings say that the guru is the tangent point to the Divine which can be likened to a vortex that can effectively receive and direct the powerful energies commonly referred to as Truth,

Enlightenment, God. All human beings live in the Ocean of Mercy, drowning in grace, yet are so immersed in it that they cannot perceive it. The student asks the Teacher of Mercy to teach him how to see in order to know that which is already true of himself but cannot be perceived. The teacher is only transmitting the Self to the self, but until we know that in and through every cell in our body, we are missing something precious.

Another way to consider transmission is as an awakening of grace within us. The seed of Knowledge or Truth lies dormant inside every individual, and the true teacher has the capacity to water that seed through the power of his or her own awakening. As that seed begins to grow on its own, the teacher's function becomes that of attentive gardener and takes the form of feedback, guidance, and practices which will ensure optimal conditions and nourishment for the inevitable fruition of the seed.

Some traditions suggest that transmission occurs very early in the student–teacher relationship, either at first sight or even upon hearing the teacher's name for the first time. Teachers often first visit their students in dreams. The story is told that spiritual teacher Da Free John, for example, had such detailed dreams and visions of his teacher, Swami Rudrananada (Rudy) before meeting him that he flew across the country and, following solely the clues of his visions, located the tiny antique store his teacher owned on the island of Manhattan. Some people's experience of transmission includes energetic phenomena, unprecedented insights, unfamiliar bodily sensations; yet equally common are those who never experience such dramatic events. Neither the presence nor absence of such phenomena has any linear relationship to the depth or power of the transmission.

The principle of transparency is yet another means by which to consider the function of transmission. Through the purification of karmic and psychological tendencies, as well as through having learned to dis-identify with the mechanism of ego, the teacher becomes *transparent* to energies of the Divine or Truth. Through the reflection of this clean "mirror", the disciple's own obstructions are apparent.

Although transmission may well occur in the initial stages of discipleship, many commonly mistake this exchange for the end of the path itself. Instead, it is rather like a near-death experience in which we are shown the Light and the many paths and processes leading to it, but then return to our own body, obliged and gifted with opportunity to travel the arduous road to that Light on our own two feet.

AN EXTERNALIZED CONSCIENCE

Transmission is a rare and extraordinary process, for by definition the master's fire becomes ignited in the disciple. "The guru is none other than your very Self," it is said. We need the guru because we do not yet know ourselves to be one and the same as the universal Self – which is the Self of all beings. In the years prior to the conscious recognition of that awareness, the master serves as an externalized Self. We follow the master's guidance because he or she is the expression of the Self which represents the Truth in all things, including ourselves.

As a representative of the Self, the teacher instructs us regarding how we would live if we were abiding as the Self. Most of us, if we allow ourselves to be ruthlessly self-honest, know what words, actions, deeds, relationships are in integrity and which are not, but it is difficult to be that honest, and sometimes to see that clearly. Thus we use the living master as a breathing, talking stand-in for the unwavering conscience and integrity that we find so difficult to maintain without the help of an overseer.

Eventually, the externalized conscience becomes internalized, and master as conscience follows us everywhere, now alive within us. Whereas at times this can be a real nuisance (for acting in line with our conscience all the time can be most inconvenient), such clarity is the gift of gifts, and the master in this form becomes our greatest ally, companion, and protection against our own tendencies towards internal corruption.

FEEDBACK

The authentic teacher provides the disciple with a reliable source of feedback, from within as well as without. As the teacher increasingly stabilizes in our own conscience, we are progressively able to receive their feedback from a source within ourselves. Yet "the ego is hiding behind every corner," as Sufi master Irina Tweedie has said. Even strong practitioners, and teachers themselves, have blind spots and obstructions to clarity. Self-deception abounds in spiritual life as much, if not more, as in any other area of life, and long-term "do it yourself" seekers are often the ones most in need of external feedback.

In a recent lecture I gave, a man stood up and eloquently made the all-too-familiar argument that we are all enlightened. I agreed with him, then asked him if he was fully aware of that condition in himself at all times, not only through his intellect but in and through his body. He said he was. Yet, listening to him and watching him, I knew that whatever his definition of enlightenment was, I did not want to be near it. Later in the day we had a chance to talk, or rather *he* had a chance to indulge himself narcissistically in a monologue about the failure of his relationships, work life, general dissatisfaction, loneliness and depression. Although hardships visit everybody – even those we call "enlightened" – his life in no way evidenced his self-proclaimed realization. He had conducted his spiritual life in isolation, and had spent years intellectually 'dharmacizing" away his own blindness.

The external guru is a source of protection for the Self against the ego. Even for the diehards, spiritual life consists of a continual fluctuation between egoic rule and abidance in the Self – what Gurdjieff described as "the battle of yes and no". The authentic teacher is only and consistently on the side of the Self, and thus will reliably provide feedback regarding the individual's egoic tendencies toward self-deception.

A TAILOR-MADE PATH

The true teacher can provide a tailor-made path for the student. This is particularly true when the teacher has a manageable number of students. The teacher sees clearly both the students' strengths as well as their limitations, and works to empower and reinforce their strong points while diffusing their weaknesses. Such guidance may express itself in an infinite number of possibilities, ranging from assigning specific projects (such as my teacher's asking me to write my first book within two weeks of my coming to live at his ashram); suggesting that the student live in or work with particular configurations of people (an exercise which can serve anything from teaching love to mirroring the person's own unpleasant tendencies, to "infecting" them with the sensibilities of stronger practitioners); recommending specific meditation or contemplation exercises; or offering ideas about how to practice viewing a particular situation from a radically distinct perspective. The authentic teacher is like a business manager for the soul. He or she takes inventory, arranges the stock, and makes suggestions for moving things around so that the business of the Self can run more effectively and efficiently.

For teachers who have thousands of students, such personal guidance is often not available. This presents a unique challenge to the dedicated student. For even amidst singing the teacher's praises and doing the prescribed practices, it is easy to "hide out" from ego in such a situation. It is similarly challenging to work with teachers who do not talk, or who do not give linear instructions. A strong disciple will be able to discover what the teacher wants from them even under such conditions, but a less mature student may continue to perform labors of intended love under false assumptions and mis-interpreted directions.

A USEFUL CONSTRUCT

While I was living in India, there was a time in which I was sitting in the *darshan* (literally, "sighting of the master") of a great saint, and in an instant I realized the nature of the guru game from within. There he was, up there play-ing the role of exalted saint, and there were his attendants playing the role of ascetic renunciates who served the saint, and there we were playing the role of students and disciples. And it was all perfect. It was tacitly obvious that there was essentially not one iota of difference between us, yet each role was a neces-sary part of the whole process, just as the functioning of the heart is necessary to the functioning of the mind, which is necessary to the functioning of the hand. None is greater or lesser; all are beautifully interwoven into a unit of perfect functioning. The construct of the student–teacher relationship oper-ates precisely according to this principle.

In the teachings of Advaita-Vedanta, so poorly understood in the West, the non-dual reality is that there is essentially no separation between "me" and "you", and therefore there can ultimately be no teacher and no student. However, since most of us do not abide in that realization, the student-teacher relationship becomes a useful construct to engage in as we move closer to this realization. In other words, we consciously *choose* to play the role of student in relationship to one who is equally consciously *choosing* to play the role of teacher in order ultimately to realize that there is no such thing as student or teacher.

Though a unique personality in form, the guru is none other than the true Self of the disciple, for there is only one Self. The difference is that the guru knows this and the disciple does not. The disciple perceives this Self in the guru, intuits it to be true, but is stuck in the illusion of separation due to the seemingly endless baggage of karma and psychological conditioning that has left them with a view of the world and of themselves based almost entirely upon projected, subjective belief systems. And what better scenario could reveal this drama than engaging in a relationship which reflects both the indi-vidual's Self and the separation from that Self, exposing and magnifying every obstacle that blocks the realization of that Union?

The trick to "winning" this game of guru and disciple is that it must be fully engaged in in order to work. In fact, it works optimally when each player immerses themselves so fully in the game that they forget at times that there is even a game being played. A World Cup competitor doesn't get on the field saying to himself that if at half-time his team isn't winning he will forfeit the game, and an Olympic gymnast doesn't decide in the middle of a triple back-flip that she cannot continue because she doesn't trust the coach who assured her she is capable of it. Similarly, the student–teacher relationship cannot find its fulfillment if the student has one foot out the door, knowing that he or she will leave as soon as the going gets tough.

Speculation or intellectual arguments for or against the guru principle cannot touch the experience of the played game, any more than philosophies of love can create a good marriage. The student–teacher construct is a serious game in which each player, fully committed to his or her function on the "team", practices in relationship to the whole with the shared aim of winning, while knowing that it is ultimately a game. The difference is that in this game, the desired outcome is one of total loss of egoic identification, in which everything is then gained.

The Guru vs the Guru Function

> *Westerners, who are educated to be individualists, have difficulty in grasping the concept that the guru is not so much a person as a function. Of course, the guru function depends for its performance on a human being, and therefore it always occurs in the context of a particular personality. This is what is the most confusing to Western students, who tend to get caught up in externals.*[3]
>
> GEORG FEUERSTEIN

For the Western mind, making a distinction between the guru or teacher and what he or she represents is one of the most fertile grounds of misunderstanding. In *The Nine Stages of Spiritual Apprenticeship*, Greg Bogart writes: "In the Indian yogic traditions ... the guru principle is identified with the power to bestow grace. Thus, the guru is one through whom the concealed power and splendor of Shiva, the Supreme Light, is revealed and unfolded within a human being."[4]

Yet, the fact is that the external guru is a person, replete with all of the physical, mental and psychic functioning that is lawful to human nature. He or she has a personality – largely conditioned – which we may or may not like. It is wonderful if we happen to appreciate, or even adore, the person of the teacher, for it is liable to make our experience of spiritual practice, or *sadhana*, much more enjoyable. But it is in no way a requirement that our personality resonates with that of the teacher. What we need to look at is whether or not the teacher's personality gets in the way of the work of dismantling the stronghold of our ego and empowering our Self, for that is his or her true function.

The individual who assumes a guru function will not necessarily be a flawless role model, and is unlikely to fulfill the role of good mother/good father, psychologist, personal confidante or friend. If these functions should arise, it is simply icing on the cake – icing which can also become a significant impediment to the student when its appealing flavor distracts them from remembering that they came for the cake and not for the icing!

The situation becomes paradoxical when we realize that, although the guru function is entirely distinct from the person and personality of the guru, it is at the same time intricately related to it. The function always exists, but it comes into specific manifestation in connection with the physical person of the guru. Because it takes the form of a human being, the guru function will not only include that person's personality but will, under optimal circumstances, utilize that very personality – with all its quirks, eccentricities, and even psychological tendencies – as the vehicle for transmitting its teaching (the dangers inherent in this rationale being obvious).

Years after all the shamans and shmurus had passed, I found myself riding in the back seat of a car, on the way to Denver, Colorado with my teacher Lee and another of his students, who were in the front. I had not seen my teacher in several months, and I found his physical presence eliciting waves of tenderness within my body. Silent expressions of gratitude and praise for the universal, formless master arose spontaneously as I lightly chatted with him about this and that: who had married whom at the ashram, who had split up, where he had traveled, what I was writing about. The paradox of the guru versus the guru principle was mind-bogglingly obvious in that moment. What on earth did the surge of feeling arising within me have to do with the guy sitting in the front seat? How could just his presence melt my heart like hot lava?

Now, where does an individual raised in a culture of Western scientism file *that* experience? The ego's filing system allows only for measurable categories, defined by a beginning and an end, whereas the file cabinet of the Mystery is reserved for only what can be perceived *outside* of egoic logic. This is why most logical arguments against the guru cannot be refuted. The various lines of reasoning are convincing in the domain of logic in which they are argued, yet are unrelated and irrelevant on another level. Transpersonal psychology refers to this phenomenon as "state specific" knowledge, and Ken Wilber refers to the "three eyes" – the eye of the flesh, the eye of the mind, and the eye of the spirit – to describe the various levels or channels of perception from which it is possible to perceive any given experience. Both the guru and the guru function can be intellectually addressed through observable experience (the eye of the flesh), and the intellect (the eye of the mind), but can only be *understood* through the eye of the spirit.

The guru function is, in essence, impersonal. It is not *about* the personality of the guru or the personality of the disciple. This is a particularly difficult reality to wrap the mind around when the felt experience of the relationship between student and teacher often consists of the most deeply personal bond of love and reverence the disciple has ever known. Yet the impersonal nature of this bond is precisely why it produces a quality of feeling, and a possibility of exchange, that is rarely found elsewhere in the human experience. It is nothing other than God loving God. Truth loving Truth. In the words of Daniel Moran, "Absolute intimacy is absolutely Impersonal."

When one appreciates the true nature of the guru function, commonly heard statements such as "The guru model is outdated" or "I don't believe in gurus" become patently absurd. The guru as the guru function cannot be falsified or outdated. It simply *is*. It is a function that exists within the universe and which is at times embodied by a particular human being known as the teacher or the guru. It is written in the *Guru Gita*:

> The Guru principle moves and moves not. It is far as well as near. It is inside everything as well as outside everything.

The timeless function of transmission – which is what we should *really* be considering when we talk about the teacher – cannot be outdated. Instead of denouncing the concept and dismissing the possibility of its functioning in our lives, we can focus our attention instead on embodying our discipleship in such a way that it elicits the true guru function from even a would-be guru.

The ability to facilitate the soul's becoming in another human being is the greatest of skills, and the one who carries it out is worthy of humble reverence.

Ego and Annihilation

I have a growing conviction that lying deep at the bottom of even the most justified and intelligent arguments against the spiritual teacher is an all-encompassing terror of ego annihilation. So terrified is the ego of dying to its false identification, and so clever are its ways, that more often than not this fear camouflages itself under the guise of a bulletproof dharmic intellect whose classically favored target is the guru. For the authentic teacher is ego's arch-enemy.

My spiritual "grandfather" Ringo was a professional spiritual vagabond. For decades he had only occasionally settled down for a few weeks or a rare few months at a time. He would give service to whomever he was visiting; he would spread information from group to group and even between faiths; he would protest, fast, provide manual labor, or whatever was needed by the people he was visiting. He was acquainted with many of the great spiritual leaders of our time, but knew not one well. He would toast to many, but bow to none. My likeness to him blinded me from seeing the limitations of our shared lifestyle. While fruitful in providing a type of spiritual pollination, teacher-hopping and path-hopping is rarely ideal for optimal spiritual development because the self-preserving egoic dynamic is rarely exposed when an individual is not in a consistent and ongoing relationship with others.

On the outside, Ringo was indeed saintly, and it was this righteous exterior, and the benefits people enjoyed from his persona, that buffered him from receiving the feedback he required to build a saintly interior. Inside closed doors, however – in this case the doors of our beaten-up van and of our unconventional "relationship" – he was somebody else. He was ego's slave rather than its master.

As the months went by in our endlessly breaking-down vehicle, Ringo would often wake me up in the middle of the night, needing to process some interaction that had occurred between us the previous day. It took months for me to figure out that in spite of an overt agreement to have a strictly platonic relationship, in his fantasy we were lovers and he was the victim of unrequited love. It took several more years – until long after I had left his company – for me to admit that, in spite of our overt agreement, I had unconsciously been eliciting that response from him in a selfish gesture to seek validation from a projected father figure, and to then frustrate that same father figure as an act of revenge for not providing the validation I sought.

In a classic construct of mutual complicity (which I had no understanding of at the time), I was doing more than my part to sustain the dynamic. A conventional argument against spiritual authority would contend that Ringo was the person in the position of power. It was *his* responsibility, not mine, to hold integrity for both of us. And yet as fine as that philosophy looks on paper, it didn't make my life any better … in fact, it made it worse. We were two egos cleverly disguised – one under the cloak of humble teacher, unseen and unappreciated in his genius by his foremost disciple; the other donned in the garment of star disciple, both idealized and criticized by a psychologically confused master. Both of us were suffering victims, our egos having a glorious homecoming as long-forgotten childhood dynamics replayed themselves in the spiritual arena, providing the warped comfort of familiarity that only ego can fully cherish.

Ego is a neutral function that arises as a condition of incarnation. Its primary purpose is to ensure the survival of the human organism. Its programming begins some time after conception, and within the first years of the child's life it forms a set of core belief systems about who it is, what life is like, and what to expect from its incarnation as a body. Ego constructs series upon series of conceptual boxes in order to organize and manage the life of its host in an otherwise chaotic world.

Difficulties arise when the ego lawfully identifies itself with the body. Since its function is survival, it then proceeds to center all activity, thoughts, and actions based upon what will ensure the survival of the particular home (body) which it inhabits. In so doing, it separates itself from everyone else, and in a subtle and unconscious way begins to perceive the world as an adversary which is best conquered through control, ownership, manipulation. Ironically, its only real adversary is itself.

When something that existed prior to ego awakens within an individual, they often experience a tremendous shift in their inner perception. Something long-dormant begins to yearn to know and be known. Thus begins the spiritual search. Sometimes awareness of the process is fully conscious; at other times it takes place entirely beneath the surface. In the latter case, people often say, "In retrospect, I realize I was always searching for God/Truth but I didn't have the language to describe it."

When all elements are in their rightful place, the meeting with the teacher occurs. It is as if the longing of the soul finally prevails over the weightiness of ego, even if only for a short while, and the teacher comes on the scene to respond to the call that was caught in the soul's throat for so long.

However, because the teacher is simultaneously the benefactor and the nemesis of the soul, the relationship with the teacher will always include elements of push-pull, love-hate. For the teacher does not love the student's exterior or personality, but the soul itself, a soul which has been crying to be set free since its birth or before, and which knows that only a true teacher, and what he or she represents, can free it. Whereas the would-be student has been literally starving for the appearance of the teacher, that very presence represents the greatest egoic threat he or she has ever faced. This is the great bind of the student.

The teacher's job description is to conquer egoic identification while knowing very well that, at the crucial junctures of defeat, he or she will be seen through eyes of scrutiny, doubt, criticism, and mistrust. From the perspective of the student's ego, the teacher is trying to *kill* the student. Yet, when a crack manages to appear in the protective walls of ego and something of God or Truth seeps in through the vehicle of the teacher, the student experiences a quality of love that is often unparalleled in any other relationship in his or her life. Thus the drama of life with the teacher will likely be one of alternating longing and resistance, love and war, emptiness and fulfillment. It is the only way it can be.

"The Ramana Maharshi Argument"

The Ramana Maharshi Argument', as I have playfully come to refer to this rather serious phenomenon of ego, is the argument that we can reach the highest fulfillment of spiritual realization without the help of a teacher because Ramana Maharshi – perhaps the most revered Indian saint of the 20th century – appears to have done it alone. I have heard it well over a hundred times throughout my travels in India and work in the West. To say that we can do it because Ramana Maharshi did it is like saying that we can become the President of the United States because George Bush did it. Of course it is *conceivable*, for there are no essentially greater or lesser human beings on the planet. But how realistic is it?

Furthermore, it is questionable that Ramana Maharshi actually did do it alone. He maintained that the great Mount Arunachala in Tiruvannamalai, India, was his guru. It is certainly an uncommon circumstance for a mountain to actually be a guru, but the point is that Ramana's existence was singular in every way. He underwent an exceptionally rare experience in which he all but accidentally fell into a profound realization that endured, proceeded to find his guru in a mountain, and then went on to deepen his realization in ways that only one in billions is able to do.

The Ramana Maharshi argument is yet another of ego's cleverly disguised pleas for autonomy. Armed with the shield of spiritual *dharma*, ego nobly recites to itself scriptural justifications for its own position. Versions of the Ramana Maharshi argument are many. The "Advaita Shuffle", a term coined by Andrew Cohen, is the phenomenon in which the teachings of Advaita-Vedanta, or non-duality, are co-opted to relieve the seeker of self-responsibility, spiritual practice, and the need to exhibit human integrity within duality. Other people use the Buddha's "Be a lamp unto thyself" or the classic inner-guru argument to support ego's insistence upon autonomy. The fact is that, in the spiritual game, ego can and will attempt to co-opt anything and everything to maintain its own advantage and dominance. The reason we employ a teacher is to even the playing field.

As a former resident of Ramana's native Tiruvannamalai, when I hear the Ramana Maharshi argument it brings back wistful memories. When I lived there, however, it was downright irritating. There we would be at the cowshed tea shop, everybody walking around blissed out, gesturing with a subtle nod of the head toward the large hill where Ramana spent so many decades living in its caves.

"It's the mountain," they'd say, as if we all shared a magic key to bliss, "It's the mountain."

And then, more often than not, they would proceed unsolicited to expound upon their profound understanding of the Self; that the Self and the Mountain are One; that Ramana and the Mountain are One; and therefore, by implication, They and the Mountain and Ramana are One. That was well enough, save for the fact that in spite of everybody's Oneness, I knew not one individual who could convey either what Ramana or the magic mountain were able to communicate.

Prakash was a man whom I came to meet later in my search, but I will speak of him here, as he was such a striking illustration of this principle. Of Dutch descent, Prakash had lived in this same village of Tiruvannamalai for over five decades. He came to India in his early twenties in search of God. Having lived through unspeakable horrors in the concentration camps as a child, Prakash had suffered severe trauma – a trauma he never recovered from. When he set off to India looking for God, he went with an unconscious desire to be relieved of his inner torment. Born with the IQ of a genius, Prakash took a great interest in Hindu philosophy, and within a decade had a knowledge of Hindu and Sanskrit scriptures unparalleled by all but one other Western individual I have ever met.

Prakash revealed his unwavering dedication to awakening through a daily discipline that would cause most people to recoil if they were even to *hear* of it. I spent many months living in one of the cottages in the compound that Prakash had inherited from a great Vedanta scholar who'd respected Prakash's genius, and I would occasionally join him for parts of his daily schedule, which included approximately four hours of meditation, three hours of worship, three to four hours of study, and a three-hour circumambulation of sacred Mount Arunachala – barefoot – in both desert heat and rain.

But Prakash practiced in a vacuum. He had no living teacher, and not even a mentor. Having been so brutally betrayed by people in positions of authority in his childhood, he was unable to give his trust to another, and the abuses he'd endured had resulted in the creation of such complex psychological defense structures that only a teacher of supremely skillful means would have had the mastery necessary to penetrate those barricades in order to let something of God or Truth in. Prakash was a prisoner of his own fortress, and in keeping everything else out, his longed-for God was also excluded.

Again, I am not suggesting that every human being in all walks of life should have a spiritual teacher, but Prakash's single (conscious) intention was to know God, yet he was unable to open to the realization of his own Oneness without the help of a teacher.

Prakash's story is a moving one. I often felt heartbroken watching this old man practice his painstaking disciplines day after day, feeling his sorrow at his own awareness of growing into old age having not achieved his goal, yet knowing that the odds of its fulfillment were too slender to entertain as a real possibility. He had never availed himself of a source of external feedback; he had created a fortress of intellect to which no one could gain access because he believed everyone else to possess an inferior knowledge, and his distrust of human beings made him impenetrable even to the softly spoken suggestions of friends like myself. On a visit years later I learned that Prakash had suffered a severe stroke. Who knows? Perhaps it was the final gift of grace that "stroked" down his structures of brilliance in order to allow the brilliance of God to reign within him.

The spiritual teacher is not necessary if one does not aspire to the fulfillment of one's highest human potential in God or Truth. But if this is one's goal, I cannot see otherwise than to recommend the process of conscious discipleship in relationship to a true master. In the words of the late Robert Ennis:

> *The chances of someone awakening without a teacher are like the chances of getting pregnant without a partner. The spiritual teacher is the partner that is necessary for spiritual birth. Not too many immaculate conceptions happen.*

Having attempted many years of spiritual life without a teacher and spent many more as a spiritual vagabond, and having received (and currently receiving) the benefits of working with an authentic teacher, I cannot imagine why one would dare to cross the shark-infested waters of the ego without a boatman. However, if one has not experienced an authentic teacher, or has had one or more encounters with teachers who either cannot keep the boat afloat or who occasionally toss them out just to see if they can use their psychic powers to avoid being eaten, it is wholly understandable that a person would be skeptical about the possibility of finding a trustworthy teacher. Yet I remain convinced that the true disciple in search of an authentic teacher will eventually find their way to the one they seek.

As we have seen in these initial chapters, the issue of the teacher is problematic, even as it is necessary. The solution lies in cultivating those qualities in ourselves as students which will attract into our lives the presence of the authentic teacher, and will continue to evoke both our own and our teacher's growth. The next section considers how these qualities can be cultivated to optimize and fulfill the possibilities of this challenging and precious relationship.

Robert Frager

How Do You Find Your Way Through the Desert When There is No Road?

Robert Frager, Ph.D., is a Sufi Sheik as well as a transpersonal psychologist. He is co-founder of the Institute of Transpersonal Psychology in Palo Alto, California, and the author of *Heart, Self and Soul*, and *Essential Sufism*.

Q: A primary function of the spiritual teacher is to confront the student's ego. Why is that difficult for people?

RF: There is an old Arab saying, "The enemy of my enemy is my friend." The enemy of any spiritual seeker is the ego, and one of the teacher's roles is to be an enemy of that ego. The problem is, we don't see the ego as our enemy – we see it as who we are. So when the spiritual teacher says, "Stop that. Change that," the disciple thinks the teacher is *their* enemy instead of the enemy of their ego. Being a teacher is a terrible job. When I work seriously with some-body, sometimes they get it, but much of the time they think I'm attacking them. But if I let them go, I'm failing them. How long do you let someone make the same mistakes?

Q: Why would a spiritual seeker turn to a teacher?

RF: If you have a cut, you can bandage yourself, but you can't take out your own appendix. For major transformational change, you can't do it yourself. When you go in for surgery, you have to have tremendous faith in your doctor, and you must have the same kind of faith in your teacher. Check your sur-geon's capabilities, but then say, "I'm going to trust the surgeon to know enough." It's the same way with your teacher. There are problems in the student–teacher relationship, but to say that we should cease giving authority to teachers is like saying surgeons shouldn't be given scalpels because they could hurt people with them. Doctors are human, and so are teachers. To be expected to be perfect is a terrible burden for any teacher. For every one case against a teacher who has hurt a student, thousands of people have been helped. Do you fire a doctor if one operation goes wrong?

Q: Why do we give authority to the surgeon but not the teacher?

RF: We have a culture that teaches us trust for our medical profession, but we don't have a culture that teaches us to trust the spiritual teacher. Our culture doesn't teach us to support our spiritual quest. Still, there are advantages and disadvantages for Western students of spirituality. The famous Indian saint Yogananda said, "Give me a Western businessman. Their skills in time-management are the skills of a great yogi!" Westerners who are critical of the authority of the teacher often don't know what they are talking about because they've never had a relationship with a real teacher. Meeting a teacher and interviewing them is not the same as understanding how the relationship works, especially if you come at it from a Western perspective. Ram Dass used to say when a Western New Age seeker sees a saint, all they see is their New Age eyes. The very term "guru" has become so pejorative that it really means "bad spiritual teacher".

Q: Is there a distinction between self-proclaimed teachers and those who belong to a lineage?

RF: In my own experience, what is important is that the teacher is the representative of a lineage. The teacher is a link in a chain. My metaphor is that the lineage is a pipeline, and what flows through that pipeline is the blessing and energy of a tradition that connects us all the way back to the Divine. The important thing is that it is connected well to the section before it and that it doesn't leak. If a teacher is firmly connected to *their* teacher – and doesn't leak – they become a transmitter for something larger. In the Sufi tradition, the teacher is a representative. To the extent one remembers this, it moderates this absolute submission to the teacher. To submit to the *Divine* is the goal. Ideally, whatever devotion is given to the teacher is given right to the Divine.

Q: Doesn't that get distorted?

RF: Yes, it does. You'll get teachers who say, "Submit to me." Instead, the teacher needs to say, "I am only the agent for something higher. Submit *through* me."

Q: What is the role of discipleship in your tradition?

RF: It is said that a teacher is just a function, whereas to be a disciple requires one's whole being.

Q: How do you learn to be a disciple?

RF: By watching other disciples. I learned so much from the old Turkish dervishes I saw. The senior dervishes were the most humble. They were more aware of those around them. If someone ran out of water or needed a piece of bread, they would demonstrate the capacity to serve. There was an old dervish named Raji – one of the personal assistants to my teacher. Raji was one of the only dervishes our teacher would ever holler at, because Raji was the only one who could handle it. "Where's my tea?! Where are my cigarettes?!" my teacher would scream. And Raji would just smile, as if he was thinking, "Oh I have a chance to serve my teacher." He was delighted to be of service, while the rest of us were clear that if we were talked to like that, we would leave. It was a beautiful game they played to show us how a dervish should be. For most of us, just a little snap in his voice would knock us over. I learned most by watching real dervishes serve tea to each other: one of them was completely grateful to be serving, and the other was completely grateful to be served. The senior didn't say to the junior, "I've been at this 20 years longer, so *you* pour *my* tea."

Q: But how do you *learn* to be the kind of student who serves like that?

RF: You have to come into the relationship to the teacher with an empty cup. If you enter with all your preconceptions, how can you learn anything? Nothing is going to get in. One of the interesting things in Japan is that the Japanese don't look at people in terms of their skills – assessing whether they would be a great artist or a great football player. They ask, "Is this student teachable? Do they have the ability to take something in, and take it in well?" They do not say, "Are they gifted?" I want to know if potential students can empty their cup. Can they say, "This teacher is not my father. This is not my high school teacher or principal. This is my teacher," and see with fresh eyes the person in front of them?

Q: What is the most helpful thing you received from your teacher?

RF: My master's unconditional acceptance of me is what helped me more than anything else did. The critics of spiritual authority cannot know what this relationship is like. The authority I gave my teacher was out of love, certainly not out of his demand for it. One of our traditions is that you kiss your teacher's hand as a mark of respect. My teacher would say to people, "Please don't try to kiss my hand too much, because when you kiss my hand, I inwardly kiss your feet." When someone models so beautifully the ideals of the path, how can you help but love them, follow them, serve them? His love is what made him so powerful as a teacher, not by sitting on a throne. In our center in Istanbul, he would often sit on the floor and have everyone else sit on couches that were higher than he was. Of course there will always be trappings, but the more the teacher cares about the trappings, the less they are a teacher.

Q: What about personality flaws in the teacher?

RF: If a teacher lies about their flaw, that's a problem; but the problem is the lie, not the flaw. Teachers can have flaws. One of my Sufi teachers said, "When I talk to you about all of these egoic things, I'm talking about myself first. I may have been struggling longer, or at a more subtle level, but I'm still struggling."

Q: Is it possible to know the Truth without the teacher?

RF: When somebody asked Rumi that, he said that it was possible, only that the journey that would take two days with the teacher would take 200 years without. How do you find your way through the desert when there is no road?

Section Two

A Working Model of Relationship: Three Necessary Qualities for Teacher and Student

The immensity of the teacher's responsibility to the student does not abdicate the student's full responsibility for his or her own role.

"The Guru is the one who shows the right path, and the disciple is the one who walks on that path. If the two come together, God reveals Himself,"[1] said Swami Muktananda. Guru and disciple together strive to create a situation in which the growth of the other is served, and the integrity of each is preserved. The arrangement between them is designed for the fulfillment of both: the student requires the teacher as the vehicle of transmission for the teachings; and it is the disciple's genuine thirst for the teachings that activates the "pump" of transmission through which the communication flows.

This section considers three valuable, if not essential, qualities necessary for a fruitful relationship between teacher and student: basic psychological sanity, conscious relationship to power dynamics, and mutual surrender. While these qualities differ in gradation and outer form as each is revealed through teacher and student, they are essentially the same. Both teacher and student are disciples on the path, and both are required at each step to express optimal integrity for their respective levels of development.

CHAPTER 4

Basic Psychological Sanity

We have to face what psychologists call the shadow. Not knowledge of the ultimate Self, but of one's own self – of one's contradictions and unconsciousness. We cannot avoid that, but we will go through that with much more success if our aim is not only to feel better, but to find God.

ARNAUD DESJARDINS

Given the pervasive nature of commonplace psychopathology among Western spiritualists, it is fair to say that Ringo and I were both fairly insane from a psychological perspective. The primary difference was that he had already been through 50 years of psychological training and spiritual austerities and was still insane, whereas I had only done two. If ever there was a situation so stressful as to surface the broadest spectrum of unconscious neurosis in the most succinct period of time, we were in it. Not only was I cooped up in a van for three months with a lusty pseudo-grandfather who wanted my body but insisted that he was serving the evolution of my soul, I was once again unconsciously using some imagined spiritual benefactor to try to augment what was at that time a very low level of self-esteem. And to top it all off, the damned van wouldn't drive 50 miles without losing a tailpipe, snapping a fan belt, leaking transmission fluids, overheating, or contracting some previously unheard-of van virus.

Thus, more than half the time we had allotted to meeting the country's leading spiritual figures was instead spent befriending auto mechanics in garages across the United States. Our favorite hour to break the van seemed to be on Saturday evenings at about seven o'clock, just in time to be stuck in the garage parking lot until the new work week began. I would distract myself with whatever educational possibilities the local strip mall had to offer – taking resigned interest in picture-framing, doughnut-frying, commercial photo-processing, and generic haircuts (once we were so fortunate as to land near an everything-for-a-dollar store, where the rush of shopping for discount cleaning supplies and cheap nail polish was mine!) – while desperately waiting for the auto repair shop to open at eight on Monday morning. Meanwhile, Ringo would accuse me (accurately) of avoiding intimacy and turning away from a spiritually conscious relationship with him. Desperate for any company other than the man who prompted me to engage in the most twisted thoughts I had ever entertained, I would spend hours watching the mechanics with feigned fascination as I extracted some pathetic form of self-esteem from their adulterous attentions.

When we ran out of *my* money (Ringo didn't carry any because he trusted the universe to provide for us), we would canvas the local neighborhoods, knocking on doors and asking people if they needed their trees trimmed at a rate not provided by anybody but beggars. If they agreed, I would stand anxiously below as my spiritual grandfather with a weak heart tied spikes to his shoes and a chainsaw to his belt and used ropes to scale high trees and trim the branches. I collected the debris.

I knew I had descended all the way down from the upperworld when I finally found myself in the bathroom of a shopping mall taking a sponge bath with commercial brown paper towels and washing my hair in the sink with hand soap. As I squatted under the automatic hand-dryer drying my hair, a washed-out woman with two bleached-blonde braids and a Bud Light half-shirt revealing stretch marks and a beer belly walked in. A half-smile of pity bordering on compassion crossed her face upon seeing the reflected vision of her own sorry self that stood before her.

"I'd never myself have thought to use one of those things as a hairdryer – pretty clever," she said in an attempt to console me.

"It's amazing what you think up when you need it."

"You got kids?"

"No."

"Why doesn't your husband buy you a hairdryer?"

"Don't have one."

"Don't have a husband or don't have a hairdryer?"

"Neither."

"Where are you from?"

"Michigan, most recently."

"Where are you headed?"

"New England."

"You live up there?"

"No."

"Where *do* you live?"

"Nowhere at the moment."

"I really feel sorry for you, kid. Wish I could take you home with me, but I'm on the road myself. I'll keep you in my prayers." She meant it.

Ringo said that the van was manifesting the psychological difficulties between us. In retrospect, perhaps he was right, but by that point I was so nauseated by his ongoing litany of high-minded New Age psychobabble so thoroughly unmatched by his behavior that each mention of cosmic philosophy was like another bullet in my by-then fragile psychological armor.

"If the van is so expressive of our dynamic," I finally told him, "why don't we just spend our remaining savings, fix it up for good, and finally get Triple-A coverage? Then every time our screwed-up psychological dynamic empties the gas tank in the middle of the night on a desert highway because you've insisted that faith will take us as far as we need to go, I won't be stuck with an 80-dollar towing bill because you don't have any money or insurance because you don't want to 'buy into the system'."

I was informed I was being verbally abusive.

Three maddening months later, Ringo and I pulled up to the entrance of Monument Valley National Park. We had already been through two engines (one rebuilt by the schizophrenic), four fan belts, two new carburetors, two timing belts, one radiator, nine new tires, and had run out of gas a sum total of 11 times, which is to say nothing of the emotional breakdown and damage accrued. Yet one singular factor was distinct that evening, and it was to provide the very dosage of human grace necessary to finally write a new ending to a script that had been endlessly replayed in my 22 years up to that point.

At the entrance to the camping area, I encountered what appeared to me to be four dazzling Dutch nymphs whom we had seen at the most recent Sun Dance we had attended at the Big Mountain Navajo land at Camp Ana Mae in Arizona. The vision of those young women, so much like myself but with the brightness of innocence as yet unexploited, is the closest experience I have had in my life to sighting angels. No more than three minutes after exchanging names with them, I invited them to camp with us. Seeing the desperation apparent in my pleading eyes, they quickly agreed. I told them to jump in the back of the van and we would sneak them into the campground for free.

When Ringo came back from the registration office, I introduced him to the young women and informed him they were going to camp with us.

"You what?!" he began, "You told them they could come in *my* van without asking *me*?" and then proceeded with a by-then common attack of rage about how I put everything else before him, how I was always inviting people to hang out with us because I didn't want to be alone with him, how I was using him for his spiritual knowledge, what an ungrateful bitch I was, and what a spoiled spiritual whore I had become.

But this time it was different. The resident angels lent me their vision. In an instant I saw it clearly. And how much I saw! In that poignant moment of one young woman's life which had been two decades in the making, I understood the undeniable relationship between my personal psychological childhood dynamic with my father and how it had recycled itself in every other subsequent relationship with a man since then, including all shamans, professors, boyfriends, and gurus. In a moment I saw that my supposed Godlife had been cleverly and unconsciously constructed entirely around the avoidance of childhood wounds that had caused my unconscious to re-create it in endless repetition with every spiritual teacher I came into contact with. In one exacting vision, I knew the course of my future had irrevocably changed.

At the campsite we ran into two Native American men who had also been at the Sun Dance – a muscular, tattooed ex-con who had just been released from prison and had gone to the dance as an "initiation" back into the world, and an elder chief who, through his work in prisons, had escorted him there. They were headed to Oakland, California, and since my whole future – including the thrill of a future 10,000-mile peace walk – had been cancelled in a moment and had yet to be replaced with anything else, I begged a ride.

The evening came and the ex-con and the angels and the spiritual grandfather headed out into the valley to drum and chant. The temptation to feel lost and betrayed evaporated in the hot wind which carried occasional moments of their song to the campsite, where I slowly moved the full contents of my life's possessions – four boxes of clothing and a box of books – to the back seat of my new companions' twice-wrecked Edsel, a worn-down mountain bike tied to its bumper with ropes.

Internally, I placed myself on an indefinite period of probation from all future traveling until I'd successfully completed a course of therapy that I hoped would reveal to me exactly what it was I had been running from all my life under the guise of wild spiritual escapades. For I knew then, beyond the shadow of a doubt, that I would not meet the awaited master until I had gotten a basic grip on my own aberrant relationship to authority figures.

I slept outside on the ground in the center of a circle comprised of the bodies of my precious Scandinavian angels and of breathtaking rock formations, as the smoke of Ringo's fuming complaints about me seeped from the van, only to be instantly absorbed by the vastness of the valley and the clarity of my resolve. Well before daybreak I was lounging in the back seat of the Native brothers' car listening to them practice Hopi healing chants as we sped up I-5 towards Oakland. I was distinctly aware of the all-too-real fact that if I fell off the face of the earth at that moment, nobody would know where to locate me, and it could be weeks before anybody knew for certain that I had disappeared.

What Is Psychological Sanity?

My studenthood with Ringo failed because neither of us had the psychological matrix necessary to absorb the toxicity in the relationship. The concept of psychological sanity, as used here, suggests that we have some basic handle on our mommy-daddy issues. Between teacher and student (with the teacher ideally holding the greater part), the sum total of combined psychological sanity needs to be encompassing enough to keep both on track in regard to their shared aim.

When considering what constitutes psychological sanity in a student, the issue is somewhat straightforward: It means that the student knows their own psychological dynamic well enough, and has done enough healing within themselves not to impede their capacity to receive help from the spiritual teacher. It means they do not freak out every time the teacher speaks or does not speak to them, that they have some capacity to sustain tension, live in relationship with others, and fulfill the role of receiving spiritual teachings without spending every spare moment absorbed in emotional crisis. It does not mean, however, that they are free from neurosis. Nobody is. And even if the student is not sufficiently prepared to engage in a relationship with the teacher at one point, this by no means suggests that he or she will be unable to do so in the future after further psychological preparation.

Psychological sanity on the part of the teacher, on the other hand, is significantly more difficult to evaluate. The teacher should have their issues around mommy, daddy, money, sex, power, and intimacy settled enough so that their blindness in any of these arenas does not poison their relationship with students. When a conventional teacher operating from dualistic morality is balanced in these areas, we would expect them to be financially generous, to maintain honesty and integrity in the domain of intimacy, to be emotionally available to students, and not to misuse their position of power to exploit others in even the subtlest of ways. Yet the job of the authentic teacher is to undermine egoic identification in their students, and doing that job may require that they employ means which do not *appear* to be an expression of psychological soundness. In other words, once the teacher has come to terms with their own psychological make-up, they may choose to *act* in ways that are not concomitant with conventionally moralistic ideas of how a teacher should behave. Equally true, of course, is that the teacher may not act in accordance with conventional ideas of psychological sanity because they indeed lack that sanity; and also possible that a teacher whose psychological sanity is question-able may nonetheless provide tremendous service to humanity.

Whereas the fulfillment of the student–teacher relationship necessitates the basic psychological health of each, the relationship rarely begins with its prior attainment. The reality is that most students – and a number of teachers – do not start out psychologically sane. The difference is that the responsibility of the teacher implies that his or her psychological structure be steady enough not to interfere with a capacity to serve the student, whereas the responsibility of the student includes the willingness to strive actively towards psychological wholeness.

The essential factor is that since the student is still likely to be carrying around a significant amount of psychological baggage, he or she should not expect the relationship with the teacher to *feel* like it will once that baggage is unpacked, washed and pressed. If a suitable education in the art of disciple-ship were available within the culture at large, the student would ideally enter the relationship with the teacher fully aware that, whatever unfinished business remained lodged in the recesses of the student's psyche would almost certainly find its way into the relationship with the teacher in a real and imme-diate fashion.

As I suggested in the previous chapter, the dynamic of the student–teacher relationship is designed to evoke the unseen so that it can be made conscious, purified, and no longer be a barricade to the student's full expression of his or her own divinity.

The authentic relationship between the teacher and student is one of *work on Self*, not of psychological satisfaction. It is not designed to appease psycho-logical weaknesses, but instead to expose them. Yet even when the disciple knows this in principle, when their hidden psychological agendas arise, one of two outcomes will likely result: 1) because the student's agenda is totally unconscious, the teacher's response feels anything from unfair to unethical to biased to totally demented; 2) the student intellectually perceives that his or her response to the teacher is due to his or her own psychological weakness, but because the teacher's presence has pressed on such a tender psychological corn, a similar set of feelings including victimization, rage, and hurt are nonetheless evoked, even as the student's mind explains to itself the teacher's rationale.

A common example of the first principle is that the student sees the teacher as a good father/good mother figure, and longs to receive from the teacher the parenting that was missing in childhood. When the teacher does not provide this, the student is likely to feel jealous, unappreciated, angry, and/or resentful, interpreting the teacher's actions as a personal denial of his or her own needs and desires.

The second principle – involving feelings of victimization even in the face of overwhelming conscious evidence to the contrary – provides an invaluable opportunity to engage in self-observation. For example, once when I was translating a seminar for my teacher into Spanish for a Mexican audience, he told a story about me which was not only inaccurate, but made me look like an idiot – and I was the one who had to translate the message! I knew enough to appreciate the fact that he knew *exactly* what he was doing, but it did little to save the face of my ego.

Psychological Projection

The issue of psychological projections, transference, and countertransference – terms frequently used in the therapeutic context – is a fundamental consideration in the student–teacher relationship. Most simplistically stated, *projection* and *transference* refer to processes by which the student habitually transfers, or projects onto, the teacher both positive and negative dynamics, expectations, and core belief systems that were formed in utero, birth, and childhood (and conceivably karmically as well). Although these ideas and feelings are not inherent in the present situation or circumstance, the student's projections serve either to re-create the situation in the present circumstance, or to convince him- or herself that this is what is happening. *Countertransference*, as used in this context, occurs when the teacher responds to either the positive or negative transference and projections as if they were true of his or her own person, rather than seeing them for what they are. Countertransference is also used to describe the phenomenon of projections and transference on the part of the teacher towards his or her students (e.g. the need to be liked, honored, respected, seen as sexually attractive).

In the initial stages of the student–teacher relationship, transference is natural and even useful. In the same way that an infant projects qualities of Godliness onto the parent in order to feel safe and to make sense of an otherwise chaotic and mysterious world, and in the same way lovers often pass through an initial "honeymoon period" which allows them to bond and form a depth of connection which can endure future hardships, the spiritual "infant" may idealize the teacher in the natural course of bonding in order to create some semblance of "safety" as he or she enters this second birth into the great unknown world of the Mystery. Spiritual teacher Andrew Cohen describes this phenomenon as follows:

> *At the beginning stages of association and relationship with a spiritual teacher, it is reasonable for the individual to seek for affirmation of self, and in that affirmation, healing at a deep emotional level. That experience – the validation of self – is the unanticipated and mysterious event that occurs in a real meeting with a true teacher. But that event, instead of becoming an end unto itself, should serve as the foundation for the student's pursuit and ultimate attainment of final liberation.*[1]

In similar fashion, scholar Charles Tart suggests:

> *A little bit of projection, if it inspires you to actually do something real and you can later drop the projection, can work out all right. We're a culture that's desperate for spirituality. So we are going to do all sorts of projections. We are going to take somebody from Tibet who's a cook and make him into a guru because he's from Tibet and he looks exotic. If that actually gets us started moving, that's fine. As long as we develop discrimination later, and work on our loss of contact with reality, our projections, it's not all bad.*[2]

The existence of projections, transference, and countertransference is not a problem. It is what we do with them, or when we refuse to do something with them, that the situation becomes problematic. In a private interview, John Welwood described a common scenario of such projections within spiritual communities:

> *Spiritual communities can become a kind of substitute family, where the teacher is regarded as the good parent, while the students are striving to be good boys or good girls, by toeing the party line, trying to please the teacher-as-parent, or driving themselves to climb the ladder of spiritual success.*

Whereas an idealizing transference is often necessary in order to initially bond the student to the teacher, the eventual breaking of that transference is essential in order for the student to appreciate who the teacher really is and begin to take responsibility for a more mature expression of spiritual practice. (In psychological terms this process is referred to as "individuation".) As a mother weans her infant from the breast, and a robin casts her babies from the nest, a skillful teacher knows how to break the student's transference at just the right time: neither too early, so as to interfere with the necessary process of bonding, nor too late, so as to inhibit the student's process of maturation.

The breaking of transference sometimes occurs slowly and subtly, through small gestures, comments, or a shift in the quality of the teacher's attention. More often than not it is the simple expression of humanness in the one who has been bestowed with idealized qualities of godliness that breaks the transference. However, if the student persists, and the subtle gestures are not enough, the teacher will break the transference in a more dramatic fashion, perhaps acting in ways that are antithetical to what the student expects. In the instance of the false teacher, often the teacher does not consciously break the student's positive transference, but rather the student's initial fantasized projection of the teacher becomes dismantled when, through his or her own maturation as a disciple, a realistic vision of who the teacher really is becomes evident. Behaviors that were overlooked when the student was looking through the lenses of positive transference are revealed when the rose-tinted glasses are removed.

Charles Tart believes that most spiritual teachers do not understand transference:

> *The real question about transference is, "How does a teacher work with it so that the student can see what it is, stop recreating it, and enter into a more mature relationship?" But I think very few spiritual teachers really understand much about transference at all.*[3]

Tart tells about a time when he was invited to give a lecture on consciousness to 5,000 people in a human potential seminar training. As soon as he opened his mouth to say something, people would interrupt him with applause. He started to feel very high, thinking, "Wow! I'm really saying wise things here!" Fortunately, he knew enough to challenge his own spiritual pride, acknowledging to himself that it was probably a good lecture, but not *that* good. Only later did he find out that such applause was a technique used by the group to build self-esteem. Tart said that if he had not been able to "stalk" himself in that way, he would have inevitably begun to think, "Oh, these are such wonderful people. I want to work with them," and would have proceeded to get involved in their organization.

Given the dynamics of countertransference, it is not difficult to understand how even a mature teacher may enjoy the devotion and adoration of students, at times too much. The crucial issue at this point is whether or not teachers are willing and able to be conscious of their own response, and neither act out based on that response, nor take advantage of students" projections in any way. A large percentage of scandals arise when a teacher gets carried away by the positive transference of students and misuses it to his or her own self-serving, egoic advantage.

The classic example is the student who projects an erotic transference onto the teacher due to his or her own desire for power, position, or to be loved or saved, and the teacher takes this transference *personally*, and takes action accordingly. Ram Dass (Richard Alpert) told me how spiritual groupies used to approach him after talks begging for a button from his shirt or even a piece of hair. To be willing to look at what is still dark in oneself in the face of that much projected light is a tremendous challenge, but one that someone who calls him- or herself a teacher should be capable of rising to.

In an authentic student–teacher relationship, the inevitable process of projection and transference can become one of our most valuable resources to learn about ourselves. Heinz Kohut's self-psychology intentionally engages the inevitable arising of transference onto the psychotherapist as a tool for clients to understand the ways in which they are still dominated by childhood belief systems. Similarly, the psychotherapist uses the arising of countertransference both as an indication of the ways clients are projecting, and to glean ever more insight into his or her own psychological dynamics.

Whereas the teacher who is aware of the dynamic of psychological projection is unlikely to work as a therapist will, since the function of the teacher and that of the therapist are entirely distinct, he or she will empower conscious disciples to use their own projections and transference as a means towards gaining greater self-knowledge. Students do this through a process of ruthless self-honesty as they observe with sharp and penetrating detail their relationship to their teacher. Similarly, the circumstance of countertransference provides the willing teacher with an exceptional opportunity to see what areas of psychological purification remain incomplete within him- or herself in spite of whatever degree of realization he or she has attained.

Marion Woodman says that the mark of human maturity is the ability to withdraw projections. This sounds like it should be simple to do, as obviously the teacher is not Mommy or Daddy. But the sobering and uneasy truth of the matter is that most people live and die completely unaware that they are unremittingly transferring their forgotten past onto the present, abiding in a certain degree of confusion and suffering because they are unable to withdraw projections they are not even aware they have. *Conscious discipleship* involves learning to be alert to the arising of these inevitable dynamics so they inform the student, rather than take away from his or her ongoing maturation as a spiritual practitioner.

Working with Psychological Issues

Sometimes it is necessary for the student to engage in some form of therapeutic work *before* working with a teacher, sometimes *while* working with a teacher, and at other times *within the context of the relationship* with a teacher.

If and when a serious spiritual student decides to seek the help of a therapist, it is important to find one who understands, or at the very least respects, the context of the student–teacher relationship. Otherwise, the therapist is likely to pathologize the student's relationship to the teacher as neurotic, over-idealizing, or stage-specific. Such a therapist is likely to believe that when the client/disciple comes to terms with early childhood issues in relationship to his or her parents, the client will outgrow the need for the teacher. If a student who is struggling in relation to a spiritual teacher seeks help from such a therapist, he or she is likely to become very confused, as similar dynamics are likely to be at work in relationship to both individuals.

On the other hand, if the timing is right and the therapist is educated in and respectful of these principles, the therapeutic environment may serve as an appropriate forum for the student to work out certain psychological dynamics. The student can work out authority issues in relationship to the therapist, rather than getting entangled more than is necessary in psychological processes with the teacher – processes which not only interfere with the student's ability to receive the teacher's transmission, but demand that the teacher place undue attention on psychological issues rather than on fulfilling his or her rightful teaching function.

There may be specific times within the student–teacher relationship when psychological work is more or less appropriate. For example, when one initially begins work with a teacher there is a natural and almost unavoidable cycle of projection, idealization and disillusionment that occurs. Sometimes it is best to allow this to run its course and to establish a trusting relationship with the teacher before engaging in dismantling these projections.

Basic psychological sanity is a requirement for a fulfilling student–teacher relationship, yet sometimes the necessary healing occurs only by addressing the issues that arise as the relationship with a teacher deepens over the years. Even someone who has completed years of successful psychotherapy may be surprised to discover the arising of dynamics they thought themselves free of once they enter into a relationship with a spiritual teacher. The working-through of those dynamics present, but repressed, allows the student not only to fulfill his or her relationship with a teacher more fully, but also prepares the student for a fuller relationship with the Beloved, as well as with the infinite human expressions of that Beloved.

Lama Palden Drolma
Coming to Terms with Ourselves

Lama Palden Drolma is a teacher of Tibetan Vajrayana Buddhism. In addition to her primary teacher, Kalu Rinpoche, she has studied with many of the great Tibetan masters, including H. H. Gyalwa Karmapa the 16th, H. H. Dalai Lama, and H. H. Dudjom Rinpoche. Since her teenage years she has practiced in the Sufi, Christian, Native American and Hindu traditions. She is also a licensed psychotherapist. She currently practices and teaches in northern California.

Q: What is it like for you to serve in the public function of a spiritual teacher?

LP: For me, I had to make a choice between being in a public position and taking on an incredible amount of responsibility and work, and living a more private life of retreat and practice. I never entered the spiritual path with an aim to teach. Even when I was little, the only thing I felt I really received nourishment or meaning from was spiritual practice. Being a teacher is not a glamorous job at all. The only part of us that could enjoy things like other people's devotion and projections onto us is the ego, and if the ego survives while you are being a spiritual teacher you've got problems. If your ego isn't tamed by the time you're a visible spiritual teacher with the responsibility for students, you've gotten yourself in a difficult position. What I really enjoy is sharing the *dharma* with people and practicing together. I also enjoy the satisfaction that comes through facilitating other people's unfoldment spiritually. The rest of it I find awkward.

Q: What are the main difficulties of your position?

LP: It is a lot of responsibility to guide someone's spiritual path. Our spiritual life affects everything – our whole experience of being a human being – so it's a precious responsibility. There is also an incredible amount of transference – the object relations of mommy and daddy being projected on the teacher. It's not fun, and it takes skill and energy to separate oneself from all of that and not buy into the projections, the positive as well as the negative ones. When students are more mature it's easier for a teacher because they have done more of their own inner work. Then there is the joy of the shared relationship – learning together and unfolding together in our realization. I also try to never get involved in a codependent loop with students. Some teachers, who lack skillful means and wisdom in certain areas, fall into a codependent loop in which they *need* to be the teacher and they *need* to have students who think of them in a certain way. I don't feel like I personally need my students. It's not that I don't have needs, but I meet them in other ways – through having close friends, having my own spiritual teachers, having my own full life.

Q: What is your function in relationship to students?

LP: In general the way I teach is acknowledging that I'm *not* realized. I don't tell people I'm realized. I feel that I am a vehicle for the teachings. I am willing to be that. I have devoted my adult life to spiritual training and spiritual practice, so I'm sharing both what I have learned and understood intellectually, as well as the realization and understanding I have discovered through my own practice. Even the Dalai Lama doesn't say he's realized, and he's a lot further along the path than most of us.

Q: What are the particular challenges facing Western students of spirituality?

LP: People in Western culture are wounded. During a three-year retreat in the eighties, I realized that in our culture we tend to think there is something fundamentally wrong with us – a sense that we are bad that traces back collectively to the idea of original sin. We believe that there was an original flaw, and that as a result of it, we became flawed. I think no matter how you were raised, this permeates Western culture: original sin and the belief that there is something wrong with us. Several people began to understand this at the same time. When it was explained to the Dalai Lama, he later said publicly that he was so mind-blown by the fact that many people in the West hate themselves, that it took him two years of thinking about this to understand it. Then he said that he finally comprehended many things about Western culture he had never understood before. Most Western students feel there is something wrong with them, and this belief system has to be dealt with either before a student enters the path, or the teachings need to be reworked in order to tend to that as the students proceed along the path.

Q: It seems like that dynamic would apply even more strongly to women. What are the greatest challenges for female students?

LP: I think because of the male/female gender issues, it's been very challenging for many women to surrender to a male teacher if they have had negative experiences of men previous to finding a spiritual teacher. Also many male teachers have abused their position, adding further to the problem by retraumatizing women who were already wounded as children. But I don't think in an awakened being it actually makes a difference whether one is male or female.

Q: Why do you think there aren't more women teachers in the Western world?

LP: I think one reason is that women haven't felt supported as teachers. Due to patriarchy and history, I think there is an unconscious fear of being attacked if a woman steps out into a more worldly position as spiritual teacher or healer. I know for myself, even though I was completely supported by my teachers and my family, I was still very reluctant to assume the role of spiritual teacher. When I asked Kalu Rinpoche why there weren't more women teachers historically, he said that there were a lot of women with deep realization who didn't *want* to teach. Most of them couldn't be bothered. They were having too much of a good time just being yoginis – enjoying being up in the Himalayas and meditating and being with their comrades and colleagues in their communities or nunneries.

Q: How would you describe yourself, given the various roles and functions you serve?

LP: Since I came to the dharma, I often experienced myself as two distinct, separate streams of being. One as this Tibetan yogini, and one as this Western American woman.

Q: You keep them separate?

LP: No, they *felt* separate, up until a few years ago. The last few years they have come much more into integration. I don't think that process is totally complete, but much more so than before. I see myself as a Marin County woman as well as being a Tibetan Lama, a *yogini*, and a psychotherapist. I have ordinary American friends, and we share what we're going through very honestly and deeply. I'm not their teacher. I'm just one of them. One of my own particular manifestations as a woman is that I like beauty. I like the feminine. I like things like clothes and jewelry. I even wear silk shirts with my Tibetan robes. I've just always been like that all my life. So to me that's just part of the manifestation of who I am. I'm not trying to be something different from what I am.

CHAPTER 5

Conscious Relationship to Power Dynamics

Over the table there may be smiles and handshakes. But beneath the table there is the conscious demand of the teacher that the student see himself for what he is, and is not ... The student's wish for, or better, assumption of, an "equal" position relative to the teacher is in fact a psychological strategy to prevent his seeing.[1]

WILLIAM PATRICK PATTERSON

There is no sin, there is only childishness.

ARNAUD DESJARDINS

After having been burned many times over by glaringly unconscious relationships to power dynamics, I decided to play it safe. I took to practicing Vipassana Buddhism alternately under the guidance of a "nice Jewish boy" American mentor and an 80-year-old German practitioner. On the one hand, neither of my Buddhist teachers demanded practices such as obedience, absolute trust, spiritual "monogamy", sacrifice, or any other indications of a "dangerous" discipleship; on the other hand, they required so little that I could have come in and told them I was going to kill myself and they would probably have asked me just to observe that thought and return to my breath. So whereas my spiritual practice was completely safe to ego, with not even a tinge of a distorted hierarchical relationship to power, there wasn't much trace of any type of useful relationship at all. I was in a shared conundrum with thousands of other spiritual aspirants: How, in a world full of fraudulent teachers, does one decide whether or not it is worth even trying to find a good one?

The lateral student–teacher relationship is a contradictory notion. Conscious relationship to power dynamics suggests that we neither avoid nor try to equalize them. Instead, the task is to become aware of the multitude of subtle levels of complexity that are involved in such a relationship – particularly in regard to our own hidden, unconscious agendas, fears, and biases – and learn to make increasingly conscious and mature choices within it.

Returning to the issue of hierarchical relationships discussed in Chapter 2, the principle of hierarchy, or "holarchy", as Ken Wilber prefers to call it, is inherent in all things. Hierarchy is a neutral reality – neither good nor bad, right nor wrong in essence – that has gained a bad reputation because of people's own unconsciousness in relationship to it.

At first glance, the construct of the student–teacher relationship appears to imply some essential inequality. This viewpoint represents a misunderstanding of the guru principle, which is one of ultimate equality as opposed to relative equality. Many people talk about notions of equality and lateral relationships while continuing to project unconscious, subjective dynamics of "power over" or "power under" onto each relationship in their lives. They engage in a continual dance of subjective relationship, expectations, competition, and psychological games, thus engaging the very power dynamics they imagine themselves to be avoiding, through steering clear of spiritual authority.

Although it may not *appear* to do so at first glance, the guru principle is designed to bring about the realization that the Self of the disciple is no different from the Self of the guru. As I've already noted, the only difference is that the guru knows this and the disciple does not. In other words, student and teacher are precisely equal in essence, but are in different stages of embodying this realization. The construct of apparently higher and apparently lower is engaged precisely in order that the student awaken to – within the cells of his or her body and not only as a concept in the mind – the principle of non-duality: that everyone and everything is the same. Equal, indivisible, whole. Apparent inequality is engaged only in order to realize unequivocal equality.

As I mentioned in Chapter 3, the student–teacher relationship is a *construct* designed to fulfill a very specific purpose. It is a game between equals in which one plays the part of teacher and the other the role of student so that both can "win" – the student wins liberation, or surrender, depending upon the aim of the given tradition; and the teacher wins through fulfilling a need to serve that awakening or surrender.

Furthermore, as I will discuss in subsequent chapters, often the greatest gurus and teachers are simultaneously disciples. The issue is not one of equality at all, only of function. For example, my own teacher, Lee Lozowick, is simultaneously both master and disciple. In relationship to his students, he is teacher; in relationship to his teacher, he is student. Yet he is just one. The same is true of his own master: on one level he is a great saint, on another a speck of dust upon which his master walks – and the same is true of his master

... No individual in the equation holds any objective position of authority, but each serves his or her function in the given hierarchical structure, which ideally works to promote love, service, and awakening.

Understanding Our Unconscious Relationship to Power Dynamics

Our template for relationship to spiritual authority originates from three primary sources: our parents; our cultural/political leaders; and our religious models. Whereas our relationship to our parents is primary among the three, all are interconnected, as each originates from, and intersects with, aspects of the other two. When we look closely at the sources of our conditioned beliefs about authority, we will find that our models are often weak, if not highly dysfunctional.

PSYCHOLOGICAL AUTHORITY FIGURES

The most significant influence determining our relationship to all future authority figures in our lives, including spiritual teachers, is that of our parents. This influence is passed on through both the model of authority our parents exemplified, and our specific early childhood relationship to them. This influence is as obvious as it is overlooked. Children learn to relate to future spiritual authorities in whatever manner they learned to relate to their parents. Given the ever-increasing instances of emotional, physical and sexual abuse, neglect, and overall lack of strong parenting, even in the case of well-meaning parents it is no wonder we are often consciously or unconsciously suspicious of spiritual authorities.

The helpless infant perceives Daddy and Mommy as God and Goddess. Serving as representatives of the life-giving force, and functioning as ultimate protectors, the parents are unconsciously endowed with ultimate spiritual authority, a role they are destined to fail at. The particular degree and quality of that failure will influence all of the child's future relationships to spiritual authority. In conscious parenting,[2] where parental faults are acknowledged and included within the relationship, the child may come to believe that although not all spiritual authorities are respectable, he or she possesses the intuitive ability to discern those who are trustworthy from those who are not. In unconscious parenting, even well-intentioned parents leave the child skeptical as to whether or not spiritual authorities are trustworthy. Abusive parenting, on the far extreme – whether the abuse is overt, emotional, or even in the form of neglect – leaves the child with challenging imprints regarding all forms of authority, which are significantly challenging, though far from impossible, to overcome.

I would like to be clear that I am not blaming problematic aspects of spiritual authority on individual parents, for who are parents but grown children, conditioned by their own parents? The human ego is a mechanism upon which impressions are imprinted and through which categories are formed, distinctions created, and human survival skills enacted. Even the best of parents will make "mistakes" which result in the child's lack of objectivity in relationship to future authorities. It is an unavoidable aspect of human development, which if made conscious serves as a foundation for further spiritual development.

People know well that individuals who call themselves "teachers" are the product of the same conditioning that both they and their own parents were. Many are skeptical as to whether or not an individual born into a comparably challenging psychic and psychological climate can adequately fulfill an authentic teaching function, and also question whether they wish to subject themselves to the potential repetition and working through of their own childhood dynamics in the hope of discovering something different and better.

Would-be teachers should be equally aware of the influence of their own childhood conditioning, which is always present alongside whatever degree of spiritual realization they have attained. If this is not acknowledged and explored in an ongoing fashion and to a significant degree, the chances of unconscious power dynamics arising is substantial.

As an example, one of the many self-proclaimed spiritual teachers I have met told me he began teaching because his teacher had instructed him that the right time to become a spiritual teacher is when you feel you need to. This struck me as faulty, if not preposterous, thinking. There are many reasons that one might "feel" the need to become a spiritual teacher – among them narcissism, a desire to feel special, reaction to an unconscious feeling of powerlessness, and the desire to be loved and adored. Having worked as a counselor for years, it was obvious to me that this man was clearly not viewing himself from a perspective of objectivity, and was suffering a kind of humbly guised grandiosity common among would-be messiahs.

A seemingly disproportionate percentage of strong spiritual students and spiritual teachers have experienced notably difficult childhood dynamics. It is my observation that, in many cases, traumatic suffering in early childhood forces the human being to begin to "awaken" to various degrees – whether it be through dissociating into mystical domains, becoming hyper-alert and attentive to subtle energetic movements (a skill cultivated for the purposes of self-protection), or the strong desire to emerge from the suffering present within the environment of their family of origin. Ironically, the very individuals who have had challenging relationships to authority in childhood are those most likely to look to spiritual teachers for help, even becoming spiritual teachers themselves. This in itself is not a problem, only a reminder that we should not assume we have a conscious relationship to power dynamics simply because we find ourselves either in the role of spiritual teacher or serious spiritual aspirant.

As if the situation weren't complex enough, investigation into the lives of the most ardent critics of spiritual authority reveals that, in many cases, these individuals were conditioned in childhood to rebel against it. Whereas such individuals often believe their position against spiritual authority to have arisen through a process of personal reflection and contemplation, it is more commonly the result of belief systems created in their early years. Perhaps it arose when a parent taught them to never trust strangers; or when their religion forbade them to worship individuals or icons; or in the moment of disillusionment following the inevitable realization that Daddy and Mommy were not God and Goddess. In such moments, children may vow to guard themselves against future betrayal by anyone who claims any function that hints of externalized power. The fact is that what appears to be a conscious and mature choice to denounce spiritual authority is more often a cleverly and intelligently disguised reaction against any external influences.

Authentic spiritual teachers are not meant to be parent substitutes, but this expectation commonly needs to be *unlearned* within the context of the student–teacher relationship as we learn to dismantle our projections. As we mature throughout the course of our lives – ideally outgrowing the conditioned, narrow perspective on power dynamics gained from childhood – we are less likely to experience difficulty in relationship to spiritual authority. Our conditioning no longer forces either a childish relationship to authority or an unconscious rebellion against it. It is at this point that the possibility of *conscious discipleship* – either in relationship to a formal teacher or even to life itself – becomes a living possibility.

CULTURAL AUTHORITY FIGURES

Another influential source of conditioned relationship to spiritual authority occurs in the sphere of culture, most notably our political leaders and the structure of the dominant political model in general, extending to individuals and groups such as teachers, doctors, lawmakers and military figures. In each of these cases and in most countries, regardless of whether they claim to be democratic, socialist, or communist, the model is largely authoritarian and patriarchal, and is usually corrupt.

Our cultural models of authority have not been ideal role models, often overtly or covertly betraying the trust once promised or implied. The virtually unbroken chain of political scandals in all countries leaves us with an implicit understanding that even those individuals endowed with the greatest positions of political power are not trustworthy, and will ultimately choose to serve their own aims rather than those of the people they represent. Whereas many leaders in positions of power are not fraudulent, the commonality of corruption sustains an environment of constant suspicion. We have little reference for benign or genuine authority.

As we delve further into the matter, we discover that the student–teacher relationship runs in direct contradiction to political structures such as communism and democracy. The United States, for example, was settled by Europeans who left their native countries to escape spiritual and religious suppression. They fled their monarchs and religious authorities to develop a new country based upon the ideals (if not always the realities) of freedom of expression, individual rights, equality, and democracy – a system that directly opposes giving too much power to any singular authoritative source. Government was made democratic precisely because the settlers had experienced abuses of authority and repression.

Furthermore, cultural models based on "rugged individualism" are diametrically opposed to the aim of the mystical traditions which teach that there is no separate self, and that the dualistic perception of the individual – rugged or compliant – is in fact a false assumption. Whereas other Western countries may run according to models that provide a slightly stronger foundation for the precedence of the student–teacher relationship, few prepare their citizens to entertain possibilities such as conscious, informed relationship to spiritual authority for the purpose of the soul's evolution.

We can contrast this model with many places in the East which have had an array of leaders who simultaneously served a function of spiritual and political leadership. These countries were not founded upon individualism, but upon service to the collective and to God. The extent to which corruption was generally absent from these systems of authority was the degree to which citizens were provided a cultural foundation of confidence in spiritual authority. Unfortunately, such confidence has been largely lost due to both spiritual and political corruption. A parallel in the West may be the lineage of popes, who, at least in recent times, have not similarly inspired the trust or allegiance of the masses.

When we review the precedence for cultural models of authority in the Western world, we come to appreciate the fact that, aside from a few indigenous traditions, the West has largely lacked a larger context for genuine mysticism. Instead, we are taught that it is part and parcel of life that those granted the power to lead a nation will betray us. When this is the case, how would we expect it to be otherwise in relationship to those referred to as spiritual authorities, much less masters and gurus? And yet, whereas there is no cultural precedence for trusting would-be spiritual teachers, we forsake our own deeper possibilities in our unconscious adherence to the assumption that all spiritual authorities will betray us.

RELIGIOUS AUTHORITY FIGURES

> *The problem of authority is the most fundamental problem that the Christian Church ever faces.*
>
> J. I. PACKER (1958: 42, CF.44)

I was many years into both my personal spiritual search and my professional research when I nervously approached the nondescript townhouse in the hills surrounding Boulder, Colorado. I had looked forward to interviewing the renowned Jewish mystic, Rabbi Zalman Schachter-Shalomi, for months, though my curiosity was tinged with an almost cellular skepticism after decades of burnout by dogmatic and pedantic Jewish authority figures. I rang the doorbell and was greeted not by a verbal welcome, but with wide open arms by a man whose radiance was amplified by his full pink cheeks, supple red lips outlining a smile that came fully from within, and the deepest pools of baby blue eyes I had ever seen. As he took me into his loving arms with the uncommon gesture found only in the few who have learned what trust is, I found myself inhabiting a moment for which I did not have an internal reference.

"If I had known rabbis like you when I was growing up", I exclaimed while catching my breath, "I surely would have become an orthodox Jew as well!"

In the hours that followed in the humble prayer sanctuary which the rabbi and his wife had created in their basement, we delved into a winding and penetrating exploration of spiritual authority in the Jewish tradition; cultural, historical, and linguistic distortions of the original scriptures; and the pros and cons of preserving tradition versus making certain adjustments to suit the Western psychological and cultural climate.

Spiritual authority figures – particularly those like Reb Zalman who are serving within traditional Judeo-Christian models – offer sorely needed role models of beneficial and benevolent spiritual authority figures. They have become the exception in a time in which terms like "recovering Catholic" and "Bu-Jew" (Buddhist-Jew) have become catchphrases. Whereas there are unquestionably a number of mainstream spiritual authority figures who naturally elicit qualities of respect and honor, there remain few who have the capacity to serve the function of spiritual master or teacher, thus effectively guiding the aspirant toward the Godlife they long for.

More commonly, our models of spiritual authority have been anything from neutral and uninspiring to substandard. This is because, while their titles suggest wisdom, the actuality of their function more closely resembles "sustainer of religion" than that of true mystic. Such leaders serve the function of community or religious leadership – creating and maintaining an environment in which people can congregate, socialize, sustain their religious conditioning, and take comfort in familiar rituals. They have not trained to be, nor do they profess to be, mystics. Yet the absence of genuine mystics leaves us void of a template for authentic spiritual guidance.

Furthermore, our conditioned precedent for relating to spiritual authority is one of obligatory respect, good manners and lifeless agreement (or silent disagreement) – a model paralleling the typical unconscious child-parent dynamic. Thus it is fully understandable that if we don't deconstruct our conditioned attitudes toward spiritual authority we will feel wary about the possibility of finding spiritual satisfaction within a student–teacher relationship, either within the Judeo-Christian model or outside of it.

In fact, it is precisely because many of our mainstream spiritual authorities do not and cannot offer us guidance in esoteric and transformative practices that so many people have turned toward Eastern spiritual traditions, which offer both authentic teachings and practical instruction for the realization of those teachings. There is significant debate as to whether it is rightful that people turn away from their original religions in search of esoteric teachings when these teachings are available within the original traditions if the right access can be found. My personal opinion is that the specific tradition through which people find wholeness is less important than the fact that they find it. If we are able to heal the wounds of the spirit wrought by our religious upbringing, we may alleviate the need to disavow our roots. We can then make a conscious and mature choice between returning to our own spiritual tradition, or looking elsewhere.

Spiritual Childishness vs Spiritual Maturity

A conscious relationship to power dynamics naturally arises as we make the transition from spiritual childishness into spiritual adolescence, and finally approach spiritual maturity. This process is a striking parallel to that which occurs between parent and child.

Young children are at the mercy of their parents' power. Aware only of a sharp power deferential, they do whatever they imagine will draw their parents' love, protection, and regard. Children do not have a conscious relationship to their parents' power until much later in life, if ever. Neophyte students are similarly unaware of the unconscious power dynamics in play in the student–teacher relationship, and enact a range of behaviors they imagine will get them their teacher's love. All, of course, are cleverly cloaked in the clothing of spiritual *dharma*.

"Spiritual puberty" often consists of a rebellion, separation, and subsequent "individuation" in relationship to the spiritual teacher. Much as teenagers suddenly see faults in their parents as they develop their own beliefs and attitudes, disciples suddenly begin to see how they have given their power away, finding all kinds of faults in the very teacher they once idealized. Many people remain stuck at this phase of development, refusing to make the transition into spiritual maturity.

However, in the same way that children eventually become parents and realize the difficulties their own parents went through and appreciate their parents' wisdom, disciples' spiritual maturity or adulthood offers the possibility to relate to the teacher's spiritual knowledge and inherent authority from the perspective of a conscious relationship between adults.

CHILDISH TEACHERS

There are also childish spiritual masters. Though they may be sincere in their intent and even authentic in their relative realizations, they remain at the mercy of still-unintegrated areas of psychological development.

"Guruji" was a classic example of such an individual. I met him during my first week in India. Like so many teachers I had encountered before and since (only now I don't usually take them seriously), Guruji felt that we had "found" each other as master and disciple. Rather than accepting the fact that he was basically the first person I'd met during that particular trip, and that I was so desperate for human companionship and spiritual guidance that I would talk to just about anybody who would give me the time of day, Guruji believed there was a mystical karmic bond that had brought us together. Within a week he had pushed a Hindu *mantra* on me – a formalization of the relationship between master and disciple – only in this case it was forced rather than arising naturally.

In spite of his sincerity, Guruji was a baby teacher, not even an adolescent. Yet I was willing to give him a chance until the following event occurred. Guruji was the self-proclaimed lineage-holder of one of these popular gurus who have so many tens of thousands of disciples they cannot keep track of who is claiming to have received the blessing to teach. In this particular lineage, there are several documented instances of *vibhuti*, or sacred ash, manifesting itself "from thin air" when invoked by the intensity of disciples' aspiration and prayers. I did not even know if I believed in such a thing, and at the same time my ego leapt at the idea of being such a special disciple. Thus, when after a few weeks of practicing under Guruji's instruction for 12 hours a day (beginning at 3 a.m.) – a program consisting of *pranayama* breathwork, meditation, chanting, mantra repetition and so forth – I discovered a fine grayish-white substance on my bedcover, my attention and curiosity were aroused. Still suspicious regarding the plausibility of the phenomenon, for days I said nothing. I just watched it arise, always looking for possible reasons and justifications for it.

When I finally told Guruji about what had been happening, he was ecstatic. He had me collect the substance and bring it to him. We placed it on the altar, spoke about it, smeared it on our foreheads, and he boasted of it, me, and himself as my teacher to all who would listen. Yet Guruji was *too* excited about it, and I could not help but notice how good he seemed to be feeling about *himself*, rather than about God, as a result of this phenomenon. While my egoic pride basked in its newly affirmed specialness, seeing it reflected in Guruji's own feelings of specialness left me suspicious. In fact, the pomp and circumstance grew to such grand proportions that one cynical afternoon I returned from Guruji's temple, asked the housekeeper for the flimsy Indian broom, climbed up on my bed, and began to sweep the newly painted ceiling vigorously. Lo and behold, *vibhuti* rained upon me.

It made me laugh. Hard. But I was the only one. When I casually mentioned my discovery to Guruji the next morning, he did not find it so funny, but instead suffered acute embarrassment. Of course, his ego was embarrassed. Mine was, too. But I was more interested in seeing what he would do in the next moment. What he did was first try to convince both of us that even though the paint had fallen, the *vibhuti* was real as well. When, as politely as I could, I told him he was full of shit, he accused me of not having the sense to distinguish between cheap Indian paint and sacred ash. What I had sensed the moment he had pushed the sacred *mantra* on me became undeniably evident: our month-long affair of forced guru-disciple relationship had come to a close. When I told him as much, he unsurprisingly became very angry at me, and told me I wasn't ready for what he had to offer.

In the same way that spiritual students must progress through the necessary developmental stages, a spiritual "awakening" in an individual does not automatically imply that person's readiness to move into a stage of mature adult mastery. Whereas each situation clearly engenders a distinct process of unfolding, it can generally be observed that most teachers, even upon awakening, find themselves in a kind of spiritual "kindergarten" in relation to their function as a teacher. The awakening itself is not immature, as by nature it is timeless, but there remains a significant learning curve for teachers in which their own human developmental process continues to grow, as well as an organic process of learning how to transmit what they have to offer effectively. Furthermore, awakening does not imply a mature and conscious relationship to power dynamics, for such dynamics lie in the realm of psychology, not in the domain of realization. Teachers' awareness of this distinction will serve to help them protect their students from their own influence, as well as guard them from allowing their own growth-process to stagnate. For this reason it is ideal for spiritual teachers to have a network of friendships with other teachers, at least some of whom have been in the "business" longer than they have, in order to engage a source of feedback and/or mentorship as they learn the ropes of their new profession.

SELF-RESPONSIBILITY

Ultimately, both teacher and student must take responsibility for their respective roles in order for an optimal reciprocal relationship to occur.

Teachers' obligation to take responsibility for their function is, or should be, a given. To assume the function of spiritual teacher is to take into one's own hands the responsibility for guiding the student's soul to its greatest possible destiny. It is also to assume the whole of the student's *karma*, a liability so enormous many self-proclaimed teachers dare not even entertain it in their conscious awareness.[3] Although teachers must lawfully take full responsibility not only for themselves but for all of their students, a great many do not – some due to unconsciousness and blindness, others because the temptations of power and fame overpower their conscience. When teachers fall short of taking full responsibility for themselves and their function, they not only fail to provide for their students but damage the collective reputation of teachers everywhere, thus raising general suspicion regarding the possibility that authentic teachers even exist.

Whereas it is obvious that teachers must take responsibility for themselves, less apparent is the necessity for meticulous accountability on the part of students or disciples. Western translations of Eastern texts, when not recontextualized into their new culture, often serve to exacerbate this misperception. For example, the scriptures say things like, "The guru assumes the disciple's enlightenment." The individual who wants to abdicate self-responsibility might interpret this teaching to mean that all one must do is follow and love the teacher and everything will be taken care of. An interpretation that embraces *self-responsibility* would be to assume that, whereas from an ultimate perspective there is an invisible bond of transmission that provides a deep source of help to the disciple, it remains in the student's best interest to respect that fact by becoming someone whose psychological and spiritual maturity serves as a living example of the enlightenment the teacher is believed to assume.

Author Rick Lewis says that, whereas the master takes care of 99 per cent of the transformational process and the disciple 1 per cent, the disciple's 1 per cent includes everything he or she knows, and requires 100 per cent of his or her efforts. In other words, the immensity of the teacher's responsibility to the student does not abdicate the student's full responsibility for his or her own role. Both are fully responsible, only in different ways.

Students' responsibility includes the commitment to be ever vigilant in seeing and facing the myriad ways in which they childishly relinquish responsibility for their own spiritual development and for engaging in a mature relationship to their teacher. It also includes seeing the unhealthy ways in which they give their power away to the teacher – often unasked for – only to blame the teacher later for taking the very thing that they themselves offered.

Many people criticize the guru—disciple model of relationship by suggesting that the structure itself undermines the need for the disciple to take full responsibility for him- or herself. Contrary to such beliefs, to fulfill the guru-disciple relationship with integrity requires far more self-responsibility than that required by "ordinary" life, or even by religious life. The tremendous gift of transmission that true disciples receive through their relationship with an authentic guru includes the obligation to serve all of life, including themselves, the teacher, and every other sentient being.

Spiritual maturity lies in understanding and healing our own relationship to power dynamics so that we are no longer compelled to avoid or denounce power. If we should then eventually come to the path of conscious discipleship to a spiritual teacher, we will be more fully prepared to engage with it from the perspective of a mature adult choosing to engage with a source of help.

Chapter 6 will consider the possibility of a relationship of mutual surrender between teacher and student which can result not only in a bond of mutual trust, but of profoundly satisfying Love.

Charles Tart

Allowing for Human Imperfection

Charles T. Tart, Ph.D., is internationally known for his investigations into the nature of consciousness, as one of the founders of the field of transpersonal psychology, and for his research in scientific parapsychology. His many books include the classics *Altered States of Consciousness* and *Transpersonal Psychologies*.

Q: From my previous discussion with you for *Halfway Up the Mountain*, I feel that you have a solid grasp on the role of psychological projections in the student–teacher relationship. I would like to focus some of our discussion on that.

CT: We had an incident in class [at the Institute for Transpersonal Psychology] the other day. I was leading people in a Gurdjieffian-type experience that involved the students touching each other while they did some internal body sensing. There were an odd number of students, so one of them partnered with me. Afterwards he mentioned that he felt this great energy coming out of me and that it must be because I am an advanced Buddhist meditator. It made me groan. The truth is that I'm a lousy meditator. So we had to have a talk about the concept of transference with the whole class. It was very amusing. One of my students summarized the discussion as, "OK. I believe it! You're not God. All right, good."

Q: How did you explain it to them?

CT: I talked about the whole problem of projections and transference onto the teacher. When you have a positive transference relationship with somebody they are *wonderful*. They understand you, they love you, but the relationship is still built on an unrealistic basis. At any moment something can happen that will switch that transference from positive to negative and, all of a sudden, of the very same person you will think, "That bastard was exploiting me my whole life! He/she never taught me anything! They just used me!"

Q: Can transference be useful in order to build trust?

CT: You have to give a certain amount of trust and authority to a teacher if you want to learn from them. If you go to a teacher with the attitude of, "I am going to question every single thing this person says because most spiritual teachers are out to get you," then you won't take anything seriously. With that kind of emotional paranoia, you will remain suspicious and you won't try anything the teacher suggests. That means you won't get any results, and *that* will prove you were right in the first place – that they don't know anything! So you have to give a certain amount of trust, with an attitude of, "OK, I don't fully understand what this teacher is suggesting, but I assume this person knows something I need to know, so I'll put some energy into doing the suggested practice." You engage it on an "It works if I work" basis.

Q: The obvious question is when to experiment with that trust, and when not to?

CT: This is one of the murkiest areas of spiritual authority, because you have to experiment with trust while using discrimination. The obvious problem is that whenever your ego gets challenged, what is experienced at that moment as "discrimination" and "self-reflection" is probably going to be based upon egoic resistance.

Q: The prevalent attitude in the contemporary spiritual scene is to discount the value of spiritual mastery in favor of the inner guide, yet I continually question whether people have enough inner wisdom to know what the inner guide is.

CT: Yes, and how do you know that your inner guide is all that evolved? I have certainly made choices in my life that I believed were coming from some deep inner source within, that I later realized were coming from a neurotic defense mechanism.

Q: Is it a common tendency to call our neurotic choices and judgements our "deep intuition?"

CT: It is, and sometimes we may need to take our "deep intuitions" lightly. We should cultivate the attitude of, "OK. I feel strongly that things are like this, but *maybe* it is not the ultimate truth forever and ever. Maybe I'll need to check back once in awhile." On the other hand, you *do* have to put some trust in the process.

Q: It seems like we can err on either side.

CT: Yes, that's the other part of it. I might have lunch with the most evolved, enlightened being on the planet and think they are a very ordinary person because I'm simply too blind to notice their important qualities. Nevertheless, I have to constantly make decisions about what I will do next, and how I will respond based upon what I know.

Q: Given your appreciation for uncertainty, how do you proceed?

CT: I know that some people have a direct connection to God and know *the* truth. Some of these people are interesting, wonderful, powerful people, and some of them are mad fanatics. For me – and I assume some other people are like me – maturity involves having to accept a world of uncertainty. I know that I want the truth, yet if I try to *grab* the truth and make it mine and hold on to it, that very attitude is going to shut me off from the actual flow of reality. In terms of relating to a spiritual teacher, I have to watch how I open myself. Am I really paying attention and opening myself, or am I holding back too much? If I am vulnerable and listening, am I willing to try to practice some of the suggestions and see what actually happens in my life? Am I just enjoying the idea and believing I've got the idea – thinking that I've somehow *got* the actual accomplishment just because I have understood? For me it is a constant self-examination about what I am doing – with long lapses, of course, where I forget all about examining myself altogether – but then coming back again and trying to stay open to reality.

Q: What you seem to be saying is that in spite of *all* these weaknesses and possible places to fall short, there is still value in spiritual authority. Is that correct?

CT: I'd like to believe that I am so mature and intelligent and motivated that I will accomplish everything necessary on my own, but I'm too honest to believe that crap. I need someone to inspire me from time to time at the least, and occasionally I need somebody to give me a kick in the ass. Fortunately, my wife is quite a good teacher for kicking me in the ass when I need it sometimes. I will also say that there have been other times in my life when I've needed teachers to say, "Do this whether you like it or not, because you are resisting this block." And, incidentally, a teacher might not always be right about their recommendations. Again, if we project onto a spiritual teacher the idea that they must *always* be right, we are setting ourselves up to deepen our transference. Then we will have to rationalize what are their obvious mistakes, to make them seem right after all. We are also putting the teacher in danger because if we project that he or she has to be right *all the time*, that is a powerful archetype that may overtake them, giving them inflated ideas of what they can do. Then, in order to defend that, they will cover over their mistakes. And that is a very dangerous situation. The trust involves sometimes letting a spiritual teacher push you to do things that you are resisting. And with the trust you say to yourself, "This is a wise person, with good intentions, who thinks this will be good for me, but there are no guarantees."

Q: Most people cannot accept the idea of spiritual teachers making mistakes, even if they can justify it intellectually.

CT: To me it doesn't seem like such a big deal. I make mistakes all the time, and yet I'm considered reasonably competent as a teacher on the ordinary level. My humanity fits – why can't I allow other spiritual teachers that humanity?

Q: Why do most people discount the value of the teacher the first time they get their ass kicked?

CT: It takes us back to transference. The Magic Mommy couldn't *not* know. If she kissed our hurt finger and said that would make it "better" and it didn't get "better", it is because we are bad, not because Magic Mommy isn't who we believe her to be. That sounds quite silly when I say it, and to consciousness it is silly, but that is the style of primitive thinking that goes on at unconscious levels.

Q: It seems like you are proposing a modicum of moderation in our approach to spiritual teachers.

CT: I suppose I am, but I don't want to leave it at that, either, because part of me worries about that. I am giving what I consider to be very sensible advice, based on my own experience, but it can also serve as a rationalization for not trying. I think there are times in life when you need to trust much more deeply than you would ordinarily think to. Sometimes you have to get a little crazy; sometimes you have to get a lot crazy. There are circumstances in life when you have to take more of a chance, and if you take my advice too strongly and never take a *deep* chance, you may miss an important opportunity. The whole focus of our conversation is this: We are learning how to become mature and discriminating students that will draw the best out of teachers who are human beings. It is not easy. We are fumbling. We are experimenting. The big question is how can we learn from it. If only it were simpler.

CHAPTER 6

Mutual Trust and Surrender

Everywhere I go people ask me this question: "Baba, when does a person receive the grace of the Guru?" And I always say, "Only when the disciple bestows his grace on the Guru can the Guru bestow his on the disciple. If the disciple does not bestow his favor, how can the Guru give his blessing?" [1]

SWAMI MUKTANANDA

Alone in India on a one-way ticket, having dumped my wannabe Guruji, and with nothing to hold on to save a vow I had made to learn what my heart is by attempting to follow it, I found myself at a crossroads. I hadn't arrived at this juncture easily, to say the least.

The years in California, after I had left the warped security of Ringo's van in Monument Valley and before my Indian sojourn, had been fruitful on specific psychological and developmental levels, while still void of fulfillment on others. Through training to be a psychotherapist and engaging in my own course of depth-psychotherapy, I had found and named the psychological daemons that had been pulling back the reins of my spiritual life, and I had graduated from a "spiritual grandfather's" broken-down van to a problem-free new Honda Civic that was now stored in a garage in northern California and was my only remaining link to the world I had left behind. I had gotten my life together. I dated worthy men. I had a career, friends, even some *joie de vivre.* Yet although I had everything I'd professed to want, it wasn't enough. But what was it that I so wanted? And how should I go about pursuing this invisible something that was the only thing I lived for, and yet could not even begin to identify?

It was with these questions burning in my gut that I began to work with two skillful neo-shamans, Ahmed and Ariela, partaking of large quantities of "sacrament", as they called it. With the aid of bowlfuls of bitter brown mushrooms and one or two snow-white capsules, I excavated the contents of my mind further than I had been able to prior to that point. Many an afternoon I lay blindfolded in my sleeping bag on the floor of my shamans' "journeying room" as they sent sounds of sirens, symphonies, and everything in between from their stereo speakers through the canals of my ears and into my psyche, guiding me into chambers previously unknown to my conscious mind.

In spite of my general skepticism of such practices except for the rare few who use them with uncommon precision,[2] it was through one of these "journeys" that I had my first experience of the principle of surrender. I had been immersed in a study of the Persian mystical poets in graduate school, and as my body lay unmoving within the sleeping bag, my mind traveled far within, to realms and worlds I had believed were only mythical and symbolic. As I voraciously took in the cosmic smorgasbord before me, sampling from the feast of Mother Earth, devas, gods, and angels, the words of Rumi suddenly beckoned me, telling me that even when I found myself in the domains of the gods I should let go of that, too, "for even angels have mortal bodies." I listened to his call, letting go further into experiences of oneness, emptiness, finally approaching the domain of the Creator.

I realized, in a practical manner, that no matter how appealing or horrifying the vision before me was, I needed to let it go, and, in so doing, my identity increased exponentially until I could see nowhere further to go, nothing more to let go of. In this way I received an internal template for what modern mystic E. J. Gold calls "the joy of sacrifice" – the universal law that dictates that everything is "food" for something else; everything serves something else. That what we receive in the left hand we must then give from the right – indefinitely. That there is no bottom, no top, no end.

Thus, when I came into my post-journey integration session with Ariela the following week and told her that although I had every *thing* I had said I wanted in life, I felt bound by three tons of iron chains wrapped around my still-unfelt heart, she challenged me to give up everything I had found as an investment in the as-yet unrevealed.

I thought she was crazy, but knew she was right. Within two weeks I had given away everything I owned save the few possessions that would fit into my hatchback, parked it in a friend's garage for an indefinite period of time, and purchased a one-way ticket to that fabled land mass in the East that marked the destiny of so many pilgrims like myself, determined to learn at least something about this heart I was told I had. I'd been given a sneak-preview of the ancient door to surrender, and now I was left with the task of walking through it on my own two feet.

Trust and Surrender

The process and practice of trust and surrender between student and teacher prepares the individual to trust in God and Life, and to surrender to what is. This trust does not come all at once and is often learned within the context of the student–teacher relationship. Buddhist nun and teacher Pema Chodron describes this process in relationship to her own teacher:

> *Long after I became his student, and long after I began* vajrayana *practice – long after practitioners usually take the formal* samaya *vow with their teacher – I finally knew without any doubt that I could trust him with my life; no matter what he said or did, he was my link with sacred world. Without him I wouldn't have a clue as to what that meant. It simply evolved that as I followed his teachings and woke up further, I finally realized his limitless kindness and experienced the vastness of his mind. At that point, the only place I wanted to be was in the jaws of the crocodile.*[3]

Whereas trust in life and surrender to it, in this case via the master, is undoubtedly the most satisfying way to live, most people live from a context of fundamental mistrust in life from which they attempt to manipulate and control all things. Few are those who manage to grow up in the Western world with a sense of belongingness and a feeling of being loved intact.

Our mistrust occurs on two primary and inseparable levels. The Western psychological paradigm is generally mistrusting due to the emotional, cultural, and religious wounding prevalent in the culture; and the egoic mechanism, by its very nature, insists upon its separation from everything that is God, that is free, that is unknowable, that is the only Trustworthy source there is. In the words of my teacher, Lee Lozowick, "Reality is groundlessness, and the only thing we can trust is groundlessness." The egoic mechanism lobbies to justify its lack of trust through a self-sabotaging mechanism which continually projects the behaviors and beliefs that reflect back its conviction that life really is how the conditioned mind believes it to be; while the soul continues to reach out to the universe and beg to be shown that our conditioning is wrong and that the Universe/God can be trusted.

As the representative of the True Self, the authentic teacher will ideally reflect back to the student the ultimate condition of trust and love. Yet, to the distrusting egoic structure, even genuinely authentic behaviors and interventions on the part of the teacher will be regarded with suspicion. The student comes to the teacher to be shown that Love is true, that God is true – but continually defends him- or herself against that realization.

This essential dilemma of the true disciple is simply an external expression of the internal war between the ego and the soul – Gurdjieff's "battle between yes and no" – waging continually within each individual. When the "yes" becomes strong enough, the student begins to attract the teacher, but the "no," or denying force, is not easily defeated.

Testing

For most of us, trust is earned rather than given. Teachers of integrity throughout the ages have encouraged their students to test them until they are fully satisfied that the teacher is trustworthy. But we must also remember that the teacher has an equal right to test the student. In the culture of privilege that pervades the West, it is common for would-be students to feel they are automatically entitled to be the student of a given teacher simply because they wish to be. Arnaud Desjardins says:

> We take for granted that a guru is going to look after us and care for us, just because that's what we want. Westerners believe wanting to "have a guru" is all we have to do to be entitled to it ...[4] According to me, the guru must have time to guide me, to know me intimately, to give me private interviews. But what right do I have to demand that? Why on earth should a man who – through his own efforts and those of his master, through his personal karma and a whole set of circumstances – has solved his fundamental problems and reached liberation, why should such a man take particular care of me? Who am I, that destiny should grant me such unbelievable privilege?[5]

The teacher has every right to test the student. The true teacher may create either conscious or unconscious challenges for the student so that both can see clearly the disciple's intention. The teacher knows what true spiritual life will demand, and can gauge the student's degree of preparedness for the task. When the teacher either rejects or delays the would-be student's involvement, he or she is almost always doing so in the student's best interest. The teacher knows that too much immersion, or involvement, at the wrong time, may overwhelm the student on any number of levels, perhaps even causing a strong reaction that would propel the student away from the spiritual life for years to come. This later consequence has occurred frequently under the guidance of teachers who catalyze strong energetic energies, such as *kundalini*, but lack the discernment to know how much energy their students can handle. Sometimes a few years of additional preparation may be exactly what the student needs in order to engage in the spiritual life with a maturity that will be far more productive in the long run; at other times the teacher intuitively senses that the student could be better served by a different teacher.

The Teacher vs the Teacher's Personality

The traditional guru-disciple relationship, as opposed to more common Western forms of the student–teacher relationship, calls upon the disciple to surrender fully to the guru in his or her form. This type of thinking raises the hackles of skeptics of spiritual authority – understandably so, given the collective misperception regarding the function of the guru and abuses committed in the name thereof. Once again we are confronted with the paradoxical interface between the guru's form and the guru principle. Who the guru is, is not the personality, and yet the body and personhood of the guru are the vehicles through which the True Guru – who the teacher really is – is accessed. According to the scriptures, the guru serves as a living representative, a point of focus, a "tangent point to the divine".

The teacher serves as a reliable externalized icon in relation to whom we can practice the inner art of surrender.

When Trust Fails

Sometimes our trust is betrayed, our surrender apparently undermined. This can happen for any number of reasons. It could simply be random – plain "bad luck" with no hidden meanings and nothing to analyze; or spiritual naïveté and lack of discrimination; or a karmic debt that needs to be paid.

But the most common cause of our imagined betrayals by the teacher and by life in general stems from still-active core belief systems created in childhood: an egoic programming which, until fully undermined, will repeat itself again and again throughout our lives in relationship to *everything* – our parents, children, intimate partners, spiritual teachers, and even our perception of God.

A poignant example was shared with me recently by a long-term spiritual practitioner. Conceived by "accident", as a child this woman was severely neglected by her mother (who was neglected by her mother, who was neglected by *her* mother ...). She bonded closely with her father – who was neglected by his wife – in the form of a "surrogate wife". She grew up feeling betrayed by God (a common core belief for those who were unloved, or not loved well, by their parents) and unworthy and afraid of love. At the same time, her wounds propelled her into a deep quest for wholeness and a great thirst for that which lies beneath all falsity.

Her spiritual life unfolded in a series of events that recapitulated her childhood relationship to her parents. She had an affair with her first meditation teacher, who at the time she met him was married to someone else, but who eventually left his wife to marry her, then left her for another woman, suing her for custody of their daughter. Next she got involved with another married man at the ashram where she was studying, and remained his "mistress" for years until he ended their relationship in order to strengthen his bond with his wife. She became disillusioned with her teacher, who was accused of sexual scandals, then engaged in study under several other male spiritual teachers, each of whom she ended up feeling disappointed with. She finally gave up on all teachers and all lovers, unconsciously concluding that the circumstances of her life confirmed the fact that she was unlovable, and that both spiritual teachers and men in general were untrustworthy.

Until a course of therapy began to undermine this woman's false belief of essential unlovability, she continually fell in love with unavailable men whose loyalties were elsewhere, and found teachers who could not provide for her due to their own lack of spiritual, emotional, and sexual integration, thus continually proving her conviction of unworthiness and betrayal by God.

We are fortunate when we come to see all of life as a projection of our own making. Our discipleship with God or Truth works itself out through a process of increasingly refined projections and circumstances which are entirely of our own making at the same time as they are also true in life. How we learn to deal with the seeming betrayals of trust and surrender has everything to do with whether they become confirmation of our own deep cynicism, or challenging lessons in discrimination, trust, and fortitude. This is easy to say and much harder to do, but the only option is either to give in to imagined betrayal, or to open ourselves once again, perhaps this time more discriminately.

Conscious discipleship involves offering discriminating trust to the spiritual teacher. We may take as long as we need before we are willing to give our trust, but until we do we will not reap the rewards of our efforts. We wish we could get trust on credit, and receive an advance on our promised payment, but it never works that way with the teacher.

Although the conscious disciple will ultimately be served through their own trust, developing the capacity for trust may take a long time. One client I worked with left his teacher over 15 years ago after concluding that his surrender had been misused by his teacher and his community, and that he had "given his power away" in a circumstance when he should have been strengthening it. He is currently struggling as he approaches a new teacher, concerned that this will "happen to him" again. Together we considered the possibility that his 25 years of preparation has readied him to become a conscious disciple, able to offer himself to the teacher – if he so chooses – as a man of maturity, power, and direction, and not as a childish student seeking psychological reassurance from a projected mystical father. His own naïveté has taken him on an extended journey, but one he has learned from.

Though none of us would wish this process to take as long as it commonly does, when we consider it in the context of the lifetimes of the soul, we realize that if one can learn such an important lesson in just a few decades, one could consider oneself most fortunate.

The Surrender of the Master

The processes of trust and surrender are equally applicable to the teacher, only in a different way. In terms of trust, the teacher cannot rightfully expect the disciple to be trustworthy in the domains of clarity of perception, impeccability of practice, or capacity to surrender fully in the initial stages of practice, which could last several years. Most teachers know this, or learn it quickly. Some teachers need a few years of teaching experience before realizing the hard lesson that in spite of the strength and beauty of the *dharma*, and even the power of transmission, it takes time to dissolve the stronghold of ego.

The teacher must invest in the student's *becoming*, knowing well that this process is likely to leave in its wake a trail of tears, arguments, false projections, and an intense internal struggle as the teacher encourages the ego to relinquish its domination over the student's identity. Teachers cannot trust the *personality* of their student, but instead place their faith and commitment on that within the student that longs for truth and is committed to realization and union in spite of what may be decades or even lifetimes of resistance. The teacher makes a *long-term* investment in the disciple's eventual development. It is a high-risk undertaking in that the teacher is unlikely ever to see the full fruition of his or her efforts, and low risk in that the disciple's eventual surrender is assured – although "eventual" may be so far in the future that one cannot conceive how and when it will occur.

Far from enjoying a life of leisure and glory, the true teacher gives everything to his or her students. In a manner parallel to that in which a mother might throw herself in front of a moving vehicle to spare the life of her child, on the level of the spirit the authentic teacher literally sacrifices his or her own life for the needs of the student. While the false teacher takes the student's energy and uses it to augment his or her own power, the true teacher's aim is only fulfilled upon the disciple's surrender to God or Truth.

According to the great seers of karma, when the master takes on a disciple, he or she is obliged to that disciple until the disciple is fully liberated, even into infinity. The authentic teacher is wholly a Bodhisattva – a human being who sacrifices themselves for the sake of others, and agrees to an endless returning to "find" and serve their disciples. Yogi Ramsuratkumar once said, "I do not seek for happiness. I only want to do my Father's Work. If even one being has benefited from my life, that is enough. It has been worthwhile. And when this body dies, the soul that may remain, may it be born again to do my Father's work."[6]

The paradox is that at one level we are all serving the same One. It is our destiny, yet can remain unconscious for a long time. When we earn the trust of the master, it is like receiving a personal referral from the vice-president of the company to the Boss. This referral is not based upon the teacher's personal likes or a system of favoritism, but upon the quality of our work. It is this quality of work, or practice, that initiates a rigorous process of reciprocity between the disciple and Divinity/Truth. When, through the recommendation of the teacher, this force of Divinity "perceives" a quality of consistent effort, persistence, sincerity and capability on the part of its employee, it pours its energy toward that student, in effect giving them a substantial "raise" in terms of benefits as well as responsibility. This is what is referred to as the Burden of Love, the glory of sacrifice. As our capacity increases, so does our responsibility and burden, and yet that "burden" carries with it unfathomable gifts of integrity and love – the gift of giving.

Codependency vs Objective Dependence

Codependence implies a quality of grasping in relationship to the teacher based on unfulfilled and unconscious psychological needs; objective dependence is a fully conscious gesture of the recognition of one's own interconnectedness with, and ultimate dependence upon, the Ultimate Source of Truth, in this case represented or personified by the teacher. More often than not, both forces are in operation. Depending upon the disciple's own maturity when entering the relationship, early stages of studenthood (which could be brief or go on for a number of years) are likely to be dominated by a more childish dependence that will most likely later give way to gestures of autonomy and independence, which may, if the student stays with the relationship through these challenges and learns the stage-appropriate lessons of individuation, yield to an experience of objective dependence, or surrender.

Mutual surrender is a process in which both teacher and student surrender to the other, each in their own way and to the extent of their own capacity, ever deepening that surrender until the distinction between teacher and student disappears fully in essence, remaining only in form. Mature surrender is surrender between two adult human expressions of God. The master surrenders first, but the process is not complete until the disciple has followed. Surrender cannot be an act of weakness, submission, or the relinquishing of one's own responsibility, but is an expression of profound and total self-responsibility and self-salvation within the context of the student–teacher relationship. When this quality of strength and human maturity is offered as a sacrifice to God or Truth, a magic far beyond the occult begins to emerge. It is the magic of Love, found only through complete release.

The truth of the matter is that we are all surrendered to something. While we cry out about the dangers of surrender to the teacher, we forget that we are already submitting to the bondage of egoic limitation. We understandably feel more safe surrendering to the known and familiar prison of our minds rather than to the unknowable mystery of the master; it is safer to the ego to remain incarcerated within its own confines and to live and die within its own box. But in terms of the life of the soul, it is suicide never to allow the walls of limitation to crumble in the process of surrender from the self to the Self, as is expressed through the conscious relationship between master and disciple.

Ma Jaya Sati Bhagavati
Serving the Guru through Love of Humanity

Referred to by her students as "Ma", Ma Jaya Sati Bhagavati is an internationally respected spiritual leader and teacher, as well as a forerunner in the global fight for human rights and religious freedom. Ma has been teaching for more than 25 years in the tradition of her Guru, Neem Karoli Baba and the Shaivite lineage of her teacher, Swami Nityananda.

Q: What is the distinction between a teacher and a guru?

MJ: Everybody has something to teach. I grew up as a poor white girl in Brooklyn, living under the boardwalk with four black folks. As prostitutes, junkies, alcoholics, they were my first teachers. They gave me the reason to be, and from them I gained the capacity to go out in the streets and under the bridges to work, serve and teach. You can have many, many teachers, but there is only one guru. The guru is literally a teacher who would give his or her life for the *chela* (disciple). Just as the mother gives birth to the child, the guru gives birth to the disciple. That's what differentiates the guru and the teacher.

Q: What does it mean to you to serve in the function of "guru"?

MJ: In my teaching work, for over 10 years I wouldn't even use the word "guru" to describe myself because of all the associations it raised. The only way a guru can truly be a guru is to never forget he or she is a disciple. Whatever I have learned as a disciple, I pass on to my students. I always know what they are feeling because I have been there, done that, and am *still* doing that – still learning every day of my life. I learn from my guru and I learn from my students. It is not as mysterious as it is magical. If we all remember that we are constantly *chelas*, then every breath we take *in* is a learning breath, and every breath we breathe *out* has the potential to be a teaching breath.

Q: What is the primary qualification for a *chela*?

MJ: An absolute love of unconditional Love, and not just for the guru but for everyone. If the *chela* has blind love for the guru and is terribly mean to every-body else, the discipleship won't work. That is not real love for the guru. It cannot be.

Q: So just loving the guru is not enough?

MJ: There are two things I insist on for students: kindness and service. Can you be kind and can you serve? If you want to be my student and live at my ashram or help me with my projects, you have to either *be* kind, or be willing to learn to be kind. And in order to teach this, *I* have to be kind. As long as we create a space of kindness within, we are ready for whatever life has to offer.

Q: How do you deal with your students' projections onto you?

MJ: I set the table and invite everyone to come eat. I just spread out my table and say, "Come eat." I don't want conditions in my life. I don't want condi-tions for me and I don't want conditions for my students. All I want is that the table is set with love, that food is cooked with love, and the meal is eaten in the mood of love. My guru's demand was very simple. "Feed Everyone." That's what I've done all my life and I intend to keep doing that for the rest of my life. That's all I know how to do. I tell students, "Don't try to save the whole world. Just serve whoever is in front of you. Let them feel your love."

Q: As a Western woman guru, you are in an uncommon minority. Are there particular challenges for the female guru?

MJ: Female teachers and a feminine influence is vital right now in the world, because women are connected to the earth. If we refuse to care about this earth, that's the end. It's all over. If people don't accept women teachers, that's the end of everything, because the men have made a real mess of things. Woman is bursting forth like a sunrise on a very dark and gloomy day. We're too strong but we need to be strong. We're too wise but we need to be wise. As a woman feels, she acts upon what she is feeling. One of the things that I teach is equality. Women are not better than men are, but they are certainly equal. Woman feels and man thinks. You have to understand that the recognition of the *fact* of women's equality is something fresh and new and not *wanted*. It is not wanted in Hinduism, not wanted in Catholicism and not wanted in Judaism. But it will be accepted. We are coming forth.

Q: What is your primary teaching to your disciples?

MJ: I tell my *chelas* that it is a matter of making a difference and stopping that inner war within one's own being. Then one can bring peace to people while they are living upon an earth that is pretty well shattered right now. I don't have the time to make these *chelas* of mine like me. I don't have time to give them a teaching that pleases them but is not totally *real*. But I do have the time to speak of the beauty of serving another human being. And I pray they come to understand those teachings, because at this time on the planet, everybody has to serve another human being in order to maintain their own feeling of "aliveness". It's all about taking what you learn from your guru and putting it into action instead of just clasping your hands in silent prayer. Taking that silent prayer into action – that is what's needed in the world at this very moment. God is not boring. God is very, very exciting. God is extremely exciting. God is my salvation. God is where I run to. There is not one God, but many, many forms. For me, I look toward my guru as my God.

Section Three

Finding Your Teacher: The Fine Art of Discrimination

The fulfillment of conscious discipleship involves both knowing the rules and knowing when to break them.

"If the call is strong enough, unified enough, if the necessity is imperious, you indeed attract the meeting," says Arnaud Desjardins. The soul's longing ultimately calls the student and teacher together, but there may be many mirages along the way. In a culture that possesses little collective precedence for, or appreciation of, genuine spiritual authority, learning the fine art of discrimination in regard to spiritual teachers not only assists us in distinguishing strong teachers from weaker ones, but in recognizing when we have found our teacher. General criteria are initially useful in helping us sort through the morass of individuals who call themselves "spiritual teachers", but we must at some point be willing to let go of external criteria in favor of a more subtle and non-linear response to the soul's calling, and a capacity for discernment based upon an inner and mutual recognition between teacher and student.

CHAPTER 7

Meeting the Teacher: Defining Criteria for Teacher *and* Student

It is due to the previous birth's virtue that I found You;
the traces of times before followed us and showed You to me.
I called out in a language unknown to the mind,
and was drawn once again to see Thy beautiful flowering face.

S. V. BALAKUMARAN, "YOGI RAMSURATKUMAR LALEE"

"Neti, neti." *Not this, not this.* Having suffered yet another minor disillusion-ment with Guruji in Rishikesh, I was getting a very good idea of what I *didn't* want in a teacher. And so, having completed my *pranayama* exercises by 5 a.m. in my concrete cell of a room, and then bathing in the icy cold Ganges River because I was promised it would remove all my past karma quicker than any available therapy, I would sit by the bank of the eternal river and make lists. Lists of what I wanted in a teacher, and lists of what I didn't want.

"I want a teacher who speaks English, or at least some Germanic language I can learn easily. I want a teacher who is Western, or at least one who under-stands Western psychology and knows how to work with it effectively. I want to study with a woman, if possible, or a man with a hell of a lot of integrity. I want my teacher to have few enough students so he or she can work with me personally, but not so few as to make his or her credibility questionable. I want my teacher to take interest in my particular life circumstance. I want a teacher who will provide practical tools for integrated spiritual understanding instead of telling me that good and evil are illusions and there is nowhere to go and nothing to do. I want a teacher who doesn't demand celibacy for prolonged periods of time and who understands deep sexuality. I want a teacher who respects marriage and childraising. I want a teacher who is alive and who talks. I want a tradition that is juicy and immersed in life instead of just observing it. I want a teacher before I am 30."

I would make lists every day, sometimes building upon and refining the list from the day before, sometimes starting anew. I was not trying to define the ultimate criteria for authentic mastery as much as I was attempting to get clear on the criteria for *my* master. Upon the completion of the day's list, I would take the paper and float it down the sacred Ganges, praying silently, "If something other than this should be Your Will, so be it ..."

Determined to follow the guidance of my as-yet-unrevealed heart, the calling arose from within to travel to the far south, to the village of Tiruvannamalai, where the great saint Ramana Maharshi had once lived. As a woman alone, with no experience traveling in India and no reservations on overbooked and sold-out transportation options, my task was challenging. Paying fines for jumping on trains without a ticket, spending the night standing when there wasn't a place for me to sit or lie down, bribing a counterfeit ticket-dispenser to manufacture me a ticket to save myself from being stuck sleeping in the railway station, only to find I was to share my train birth with a sleazy and drooling old man, eating unknown, fly-coated foods or fasting, and traveling on crowded, steamy buses and bicycle rickshaws, I finally made my way to my destination. When I arrived three days and three nights later, I felt that there was nothing in the external world that I was incapable of conquering if I applied myself well. There was no material task more challenging than the one I had just been through, and what remained was the immaterial mountain.

For the next several days I literally sat in a mountain – the holy Mount Arunachala – believed to contain mystical attributes and powers by figures as credible as the great Ramana Maharshi. Meditating six to ten hours a day in a cave where the Maharshi had spent years of his life, I began to experience a quality of intimacy with "God" I had never felt before. My God was suddenly personalized, and near. Like a friend. "Why, if you love me and are even willing to hang out with me like this", I would ask, "aren't you bringing me a teacher who would teach me how to be nearer to you? What else do you want from me? Please reveal to me my destiny. I'm all the way over here in India on a one-way ticket and I need some help – and now would be much better than later."

I wish I could say that the very next thing that happened was my teacher arrived at my doorstep with a spiritual engagement ring and asked me to be his disciple, but instead I got involved with a final set of spiritual snake-handlers. A young male European seeker had sustained a minor awakening for a period of months and had decided it was time to collect disciples, but thus far had only courted the worship of his beautiful but psychotic girlfriend. I was lonely and pained with the intensity of my longing, and they were recruiting lost souls. In the three demented days I spent with them, disheartened by having gotten into yet another tangle with spiritual frauds, I was asked by a friend of theirs if I knew a Western man by the name of "Mr Li" who came to town yearly with a group of students to visit his teacher, the local God-mad saint Yogi Ramsuratkumar.

This piece of information struck an inner cord. A teacher who was willing to serve the function of disciple in front of his own disciples was something I had not yet come across in my seven years of searching. It suggested the possibility that someone in a position of power might actually be motivated by something other than egoic self-aggrandizement. It hinted of a promised humility, and although I was told that his guru was a madman who chain-smoked and didn't speak with anybody and probably wasn't even worth a visit, I resolved to investigate the situation.

Nothing in my life and everything in my life had prepared me for the event of meeting my teacher. Although I had been working my way toward that meeting since my birth, particularly in the seven years of teacher-hopping that preceded it, I could never have imagined the consequence of that initial meeting.

It was late morning when I staggered down from the mountain cave where I had already been meditating for five hours that day. Arriving late to the *darshan* (literally meaning "sighting of the master" but often used to refer to the meeting between teacher and students) of Yogi Ramsuratkumar, I walked in to see the Yogi holding the hand of a middle-aged Western man dressed in Indian garb. Both the Yogi and the man manifested the oddest series of twitches and erratic body movements, as if each was not in control of his expression, not to mention that when the Yogi smoked his cheap Indian cigarettes I never saw him exhale. What was I seeing, I wondered? Spiritual madness? Mild retardation? I sat wondering if I was watching some kind of healing from the Yogi to this man, who looked like any of my friends' parents at the synagogue which we attended in my childhood, while scanning the room for a character called "Mr Li."

After watching this strange healing for over an hour, it dawned on me: *this* was Mr Li! But why did he have a Chinese last name if he was Jewish-American with a Hindu guru? No matter. After the *darshan* I immediately approached him, and in the process introduced myself to the end of my life as I had known it.

"Where are you from?" he all but barked at me.

"California," I told him. "Originally from Maryland."

"At least it's only California," he sighed, "I thought you might tell me that you were a citizen of the universe."

I asked him if I could attend one of his teachings.

"Why not?" he half-grumbled.

I also mentioned to him that people who ran Yogi Ramsuratkumar's *darshan* had invited me to lunch, apparently mistaking me for a member of his group, and that when I tried to decline they wouldn't hear of it.

"Never refuse a free lunch," he said.

For some people the meeting with the teacher is more dramatic than mine was, for some less. It is not unlike the process of meeting a potential intimate partner. Sometimes the meeting includes the full set of fireworks, honeymoon period, eventual fall from grace, and then relationship-building. Other times it comes on slowly – someone you knew but had never really considered in that way, or someone you had built a friendship with and then one day you started to see them differently. Whereas it is often easier when the meeting is more dramatic, as the thrill of new romance may carry the potential student beyond the confines of excessive doubt and skepticism, it can be more beneficial for the connection to grow slowly so that the situation can be considered carefully and with discernment without being flooded by excessive emotion. For, as we all know, while sometimes strong and dramatic attraction is indicative of a magnetic affinity of souls, at other times it is a surefire sign of complementary neuroses and inevitable disaster. Knowing my own tendency to fall hard and fast, when I finally did meet my teacher, in spite of my intense rush of feeling I told myself that I would wait six months before asking him if I could be his student, just to make sure the feeling was real. In the end I waited only six weeks, but at least I was aware of the principle!

Our own psychological tendencies and dispositions are likely to play a significant factor in our initial encounter with the teacher. Each doubt, fear, hope, conscious and unconscious projection, and every bit of character strength we possess will directly influence this meeting. We can be assured that when we meet the teacher, one eye will be looking through the lens of clarity, while the other sees through the filter of mistrust and skepticism.

For example, one woman told me that she initially went to live near her teacher-to-be solely because she was in love with one of the teacher's close students. A pragmatist by nature, she found the devotional practices around the teacher to be excessively sentimental, and the teacher's tough personality not only uninteresting, but distinctly distasteful. Yet, during the first couple of years she spent living in the proximity of her teacher for the sake of her lover, she witnessed a consistency in the teacher's integrity that she had not known previously. As the years passed, she was surprised to find that a profound love had grown, a love that eventually yielded into devotion, and finally to a deep bond between student and teacher.

Another man I spoke with had been spending time moving between three exceptional teachers for 15 years, never committing to any one of them because he never had the "right feeling" – the feeling he expected and wanted to have upon meeting his teacher. When I asked him about his father, he told me that his father had divorced his mother shortly after his birth, only six months into their marriage, and for many years had affairs with a variety of women, never committing to any one of them. Furthermore, he said that even when his father was on his deathbed, he was unable to share a singular moment of emotional intimacy with him. In the light of this information, it seemed inevitable that this man would have difficulty experiencing the set of feelings he imagined he should have in order to know that he had met his teacher, as each of the three teachers in question were men and he had no internal template for emotional intimacy with men.

In my own case, when I finally met my teacher I found myself intoxicated not only by a true vision of his divinity, but also with my unconscious projected fantasies of a savior, the perfect human, the good father. My own tendencies toward extremism and zealousness prompted me to want to throw myself fully and indiscriminately at the teacher and the teachings, and had he not stopped me, and his other students not counseled me against it, I would have gotten myself into deeper waters than I knew how to swim at that time.

According to the appearance of things, it seems to us as though we seek the teacher: a friend may insist we come meet them, or perhaps a series of coincidences arises and we accidentally find ourselves in the company of a master. However, the great scriptures in many traditions suggest that the true teachers – in their highest expression and perhaps even unbeknownst to themselves – call us to them. They are callings of the soul at work – *karma*, as it is known in the East.

The coincidences are too sublime, the feeling of being "found" too precise, and the accounts of meetings over centuries and across cultures too exacting to write off the meeting between teacher and student to chance. My own teacher did not meet his teacher until three years *after* his own initial awakening, when he was already functioning as guru to a large body of students. Yet he insists that his teacher was the source of the entire process of his search, his awakening, and the eventual meeting between them, which resulted in a course of formal discipleship that lasted over 25 years, until his teacher's death in February, 2001. My own experience of receiving an inner "call" to travel across the entire Indian subcontinent in order to arrive in Tiruvannamalai five days before my teacher's arrival – just in time to meet a couple of charlatans who would lead me to him – hints to me of the same.

But while it is more likely that the teacher – or the Universal Intelligence working through the teacher – finds us rather than us finding them, the way the Great Game works for most of us is that *we* have the experience of seeking the path and the teacher, *we* have the experience of testing and being tested by the teacher, *we* have doubts, *we* work through them (or don't), and *we* engage in a course of discipleship. In the light of God, it is likely that *we* don't do anything at all, but the laws of duality must be respected, and within that domain comes the experience of free will, which we can use toward any number of ends, one of them being that of *conscious discipleship*.

Criteria for Teachers[1]

Because it is not easy to evaluate another's enlightenment or mastery from an unenlightened state, criteria for identifying an authentic teacher are difficult, if not impossible, to define. Yet, we can gain some insights into what to look for from what others further along the path suggest. In the interviews I conducted with them for my book, *Halfway Up the Mountain*, many scholars and teachers – including John Welwood, Andrew Cohen, Claudio Naranjo, Arnaud Desjardins, Charles Tart, Georg Feuerstein and Joan Halifax – set forth their criteria for identifying authentic teachers. They recommended considerations such as: Does the example of the teacher's life demonstrate what I wish to become? Is the teacher completely free? Is the teacher genuinely humble? Is the teacher free of attachment to money, sex, power and glory? What is the teacher's track record? Is this person connected to the divine level or the spiritual level? How much impurity is there? How much mixture is there of something else along with the spiritual gift? Some further, though no means definitive, criteria are considered here.

To Whom Does the Teacher Bow?

When meeting a teacher, we may be wise to ask of them: "Who is your teacher?" "Who gave you permission to teach?" Or, in the words of Arnaud Desjardins, "To whom or what do you bow?" There is a distinct difference in quality between a teacher who considers himself (or herself, less commonly) as God, and one who considers himself to be a servant of God. Even if it is ultimately true that we are all God, the angle from which we perceive this great truth is often the defining characteristic between those who are likely to abuse power and those who live in awe and servitude to the great mystery.

When we ask, "To whom does the teacher bow?" we are inquiring into the source of the teachings represented by the teacher. The lineage of mastery consists of an unbroken chain of transmission originating in ultimate truth and passed down from an initial teacher or master to his or her successor, who passes it on to subsequent successors. In non-theistic traditions, the individual may not "bow" to any one person, but will often practice in the service of a principle, such as "enlightened consciousness" or "truth as represented by Buddha nature". Such "bowing" is a position of conscious surrender and deference to a greater source of knowledge that exists without as well as within ourselves, and should not be confused with weak submission.

Of course, when we ask, "To whom does the teacher bow?" we must consider and evaluate the response. Some teachers are indeed granted permission to teach, but the individuals who grant the permission may not be a source we respect. Some teachers equate their popularity with how many "enlightened disciples" they can send out to teach. A popular teacher might proclaim 10 or 20 or 30 teachers as lineage-holders – a questionable proposition. In other cases, the individual interprets something the teacher did or said as giving them permission to teach, perhaps through some "private meeting" which may or may not have occurred, or through a dream. Or the individual receives transmission through a sacred channel, medium, or object. This may sound absurd, but I cannot recount the number of times when I was living in Tiruvannamalai that people relayed to me messages they had received from "The Mountain". Who can refute "The Mountain"?!

In my own experience, it was crystal clear from the first day I met my teacher that he bowed to his master, Yogi Ramsuratkumar. From the very beginning, the sincerity of his discipleship was evident. This renowned crazy-wisdom master in the West flawlessly assumed the function of discipleship in the presence of his guru. His deference was not feigned, but was the expression of utter attention, intelligent reverence, and mature humility. Yet, at the time, I knew nothing about his source. On my initial visits to Yogi Ramsuratkumar's ashram, all I could perceive was a crazy old man who smoked cigarettes continually, and who thousands of people seemed to agree was a great saint. It was only after I had spent the greater part of my first year of apprenticeship to my teacher under the guidance of his master, in whom I witnessed a degree of integrity and palpable majesty that I never dreamed actually existed, that I knew I would never be able to doubt my teacher's source – the genius of Love that resided at his fountainhead.

Contemporary Jewish mystic Rabbi Zalman Schachter-Shalomi says there are few instances of premature claims to power or mastery among rabbis and Jewish mystics because there is a system of checks and balances built into Jewish law. He says that if somebody happened to walk into the synagogue from off the street – particularly if he (or "she", in theory) claimed any kind of knowledge, the first thing that would be asked is, "Which Rebbe did you study with? Who is your community? Who sent you here?"

From the perspective of ego, to be the guru – the Great One – is extremely attractive. However, if we are fortunate, through our spiritual practice we will come to appreciate the nearly unfathomable responsibility that the role of spiritual master imposes – a responsibility that has nothing to do with power and self-aggrandizement but, on the contrary, demands total submission to the imposing task of directing the evolution of another person's soul. The function of the authentic teacher is an utter humiliation to the ego, entirely contrary to what the ego imagines such a role would bring. When the reality of this perspective dawns, assuming teacherhood in any circumstance, much less without a lineage to back oneself up, becomes a highly undesirable prospect.

Does the Teacher Serve the Student's Best Interest?
Is the teacher self-serving or other-serving? Look closely, as sometimes behavior that appears oriented toward others is self-serving, and behavior that seems totally egotistical and self-aggrandizing is actually profoundly humble when viewed from a deeper context.

Mel Weitzman, Roshi of the Berkeley Zen Center, says that, for him, being a priest means to serve the *sangha*, or "community of practitioners", and not to promote yourself or try to gain anything for the purpose of your own self-interest. How rare such qualities are – particularly among false prophets, whose behavior is almost entirely self-serving, though usually coated with a philosophy of "I'm doing this for you [the disciple]" or for God.

Georg Feuerstein suggests:

> *Accepting the fact that our appraisal of a teacher is always subjective so long as we have not ourselves attained his or her level of spiritual accomplishment, there is at least one important criterion that we can look for in a guru: Does he or she genuinely promote disciples" personal and spiritual growth, or does he or she obviously or ever so subtly undermine their maturation?*[2]

We can ask ourselves: Would the teacher be genuinely pleased if I surpassed his or her knowledge, or would this be perceived as a threat and met with jealousy? I know that I can unequivocally say "yes" to that question in terms of my own teacher. Nothing would thrill him more than the unlikely event that I transcended his own knowledge, and I can take refuge in the clarity of that conviction. In the non-dual world, there is no need for competition, as Truth, God, and Love are infinite, and there is more than enough available for anybody who allows themselves to partake.

What Are the Teacher's Students Like?

This is an important question, as sometimes teachers make great claims, and yet one looks at their long-time senior students and cannot see the results. If a teacher proclaims he or she has enlightened dozens of students, but I meet those people and they do not impress me in any way, it indicates to me that I should carefully consider any involvement with the teacher. On the one hand, we must be careful not to judge the teacher's students superficially, appreciating the fact that significant and enduring transformation often takes far longer to arise, and probably looks quite different, than we initially imagine upon first engaging in the spiritual path; on the other hand, we must trust our own powers of discrimination in discerning the effectiveness of the teacher's work with their students.

This was one of the primary factors that led me to leave one of my Buddhist teachers. She was continually using the example of her right-hand woman as an illustration of the fruits of mindful practice, but all I could see was a clumsy, self-obsessed and slightly paranoid (though well-intentioned) woman who was locked into a "good mother" projection with her teacher. I carefully examined this teacher's students, and found little in their spiritual development to recommend her.

On another occasion, I went to hear a teacher – one of numerous individuals crowned as "enlightened" by a contemporary Indian master – expound upon the "easy path to realization'. His articulation of dharmic principles was impeccable, but a bodily realization was clearly lacking. I told him, "I've met so many people here and abroad – 'enlightened' students of your teacher – who speak just like you do and yet their lives do not demonstrate anything that I would personally like to emulate." He told me I was not seeing clearly.

The *energetic* way the teacher's long-term students appear is probably how you will become if you choose the path of studenthood with that teacher. This could be a very good thing, as often students of strong teachers are bright, energetic, aware. Then again, depending upon the teacher, the students may be excessively intellectual, touchy-feely, provocative, passive, impersonal. You can ask yourself: Do I admire this teacher's strong students and aspire to express my own personalized vision of this tradition in the form they do?

This is not a right-or-wrong issue, and skirts the domain of personal preferences. For example, one extraordinary contemporary teacher asks his students for one or more years of celibacy, and discourages childraising within the community. This runs against my personal preference. If I felt beyond the shadow of a doubt that this was my one and only teacher, and he strongly requested this behavior of me, I would consider it, but such issues should not be dismissed lightly.

At one point, I and several other students accompanied my teacher on a visit to the community of another teacher who is a close friend of his. Although the other teacher's students were of a variety of ages, sizes, classes, and races, I was struck by an energetic similarity between them that was so distinct as to render them uncannily similar to one another. As I excitedly shared my vision with my teacher, an amused look came across his face.

"Oh no!" I exclaimed, realizing that the same was true of my own teacher and his students.

Criteria for Students

The best way to attract a teacher who fulfills the criteria for authenticity is to meet the criteria for authentic discipleship. It is so much easier to point the finger outward than inward, and yet we find no deep satisfaction until we claim the power of self-responsibility.

Frances Vaughan suggests:

> In order to choose a teacher or group with some degree of self-awareness, one could begin by asking oneself some questions. In considering involvement with a self-proclaimed master, for example, one might ask: What attracts me to this person? Am I attracted to his or her power, showmanship, cleverness, achievements, glamour, ideas? Am I motivated by fear or love? Is my response primarily physical excitement, emotional activation, intellectual stimulation, or intuitive resonance? What would persuade me to trust him/her (or anyone) more than myself? Am I looking for a parent figure to relieve me of the responsibility for my life? Am I looking for a group where I feel I can belong and be taken care of in return for doing what I am told? What am I giving up? Am I moving towards something I am drawn to, or am I running away from my life as it is?[3]

There are also other criteria that can serve as well as we take inventory of our own capacity for discipleship.

Am I Willing to Commit?
Deep studenthood is like marriage, only even more serious. It must be entered with a commitment to a serious, ongoing course of study and relationship

with a spiritual teacher, in order to fulfill the responsibilities of relationship and work through all major obstacles. However, in this case the obstacle is the *maya*, or illusion, of our own false perception. Our spiritual partner is the teacher, and the work requires a moment-to-moment willingness both to be in relationship with Truth, and to handle everything that creates a wedge between us and that possibility. True discipleship is a 24-hour-a-day, lifelong affair. The payoff is intimacy with God, but the investment is all-consuming.

Am I Responsible and Reliable?

Successful discipleship requires responsibility and reliability in a very pragmatic sense. Our relationship with the teacher is not only an affair of the heart, but one in which we must put our bodies on the line and express our commitment through practice and action. We may ask ourselves: Am I willing to participate in a relationship with my teacher with consistency? Can I be depended upon? Do I show up on time? Do I follow through with commitments? Do I tend to fulfill the agreements I make? Do I always meet deadlines, and accept responsibility? If my answer is "no" to one or all of these questions, am I willing to alter my habitual behaviors in order to become a conscious disciple?

Am I Willing to Overcome My Childishness?

In other words, am I willing to honor my teacher in his (or her) teaching function instead of insisting that he fulfill the role of good father, lover or friend? Whereas any one of these qualities of relationship *may* emerge through the course of an extended discipleship, they are gifts, and should not be expected. The teacher loves the student, and may even feel a personal fondness and affinity for him or her, but not in the sentimental way that people care for each other within the context of duality. Overcoming our childish relationship with the teacher involves a willingness to see with increasing clarity the mass of projections we make on the teacher and on God Itself.

Daniel Moran, a teacher of unquestioned integrity in the lineage of Arnaud Desjardins, speaks of the day he realized that he had unconsciously taken to wearing the same brand of pants as his teacher, and had even developed the habit of keeping his hand in his pocket and resting his weight on one leg – *just like his teacher*. This phenomenon is more common than we would like to think. Mature men often imitate even the hairstyle of their teacher, and women assume a similar taste in fashion. There is nothing inherently *wrong* with such behaviors, but they can serve as humorous reminders to us of the ways in which our relationship to our teacher remains childish in certain aspects.

What Is the Quality of My Connection with My Teacher?

There is no one correct answer to this question, but if we inquire deeply within ourselves, we may gain increasing insight into what draws us to the teacher. Do I feel that I am with a savior? Good father/good mother? Friend? Mentor? Lover? Do I idealize this teacher or am I moved to reduce him to my own level? Does my respect for him or her arise from an authentic inner place, or do I feel intimidated, swayed by others' opinions? Am I star-struck by his or her charisma and power?

The presence of an authentic teacher does not necessarily mean that he or she is *our* teacher, any more than the presence of a good man or woman means that this is the person we should marry. Nor is our unwillingness to engage with the teacher necessarily indicative of resistance, even when the qualities of relationship are generally healthy and positive. I remember meeting the Indian saint Mata Amritanandamayi on several occasions in between my various relationships with teachers much weaker than she. I was continually struck by the breadth of her compassion. I felt as though I was in the presence of a true master, and even tried to convince myself that I was her disciple. Yet in my heart of hearts, I knew it wasn't so.

"The disciple recognizes the guru and the guru recognizes the disciple. A sacred commitment is made on both sides,"[4] says Arnaud Desjardins. We are not only searching for authenticity in the teacher, but for a quality of mutual recognition that is as mysterious as the nature of love itself.

Am I Ready for the Responsibility of Discipleship?

On a recent lecture tour in Johannesburg, South Africa, a young woman said to me, "You speak so passionately about the need for a teacher, suggesting that my own longing and need will attract the teacher, yet so few teachers come here, and many of them aren't of high quality. Do you really think that principle applies to us here in South Africa as well?" Another woman came to a talk I gave in northern California and asked if I knew of a good teacher in her town, or at least in Marin County, because she loved where she lived and didn't want to move, and had a very busy life and didn't have the time to spend driving and traveling.

While these women claimed to want a teacher, they may have not yet been prepared to make the significant efforts that authentic discipleship requires. The great yogi Milarepa started out practicing black magic and traveled across land masses, endured tremendous dangers, and then had to build seven houses before his teacher would fully accept him as a disciple.

I believe that a woman in South Africa, or in the countryside in Pakistan, or in the remote regions of the Kalahari will somehow find what she yearns for spiritually, provided her intention is strong enough. True discipleship is an inward process that ultimately transcends time and space, and when the disciple is ready – now or a thousand years from now – the master really will appear!

Difficult as this may be to accept, we might consider assuming that if we have not found a true teacher, we are simply not yet fully prepared for one. Yet you should not judge yourself about this. For there are few more challenging experiences than finding yourself in the company of an authentic master and having to come to terms with the fact that you really do not wish for the life in God or Truth you believed yourself to aspire to. Better that life should take us through the full course of experiences it needs us to pass through and increase our longing to a profound degree *before* meeting the master, for the challenge of life in the company of the authentic teacher is difficult enough, and the levels of struggle pervasive enough, without having to deal with the most gross layers of resistance to the idea of the teacher and what he or she represents.

Of course, sometimes our discernment will fail. Too much rigidity in our perspective is likely to leave us safe but unfulfilled; too little and we find ourselves in a circumstance in which we feel betrayed. At this point we can decide, as many do, to abandon our belief in the possibility of authentic spiritual authority in our lives, or we can take our time to recover from felt betrayal and reconsider the unconscious aspects of our own discipleship which allowed us to support a disempowering situation. My experience is that discrimination about teachers is learned by trial and error, and mostly error! The major distinction lies between people who turn away from their mistakes in embarrassment and betrayal, and those who graciously turn toward them and learn from the experience.

Spiritual responsibility means that we take responsibility for all of our spiritual choices, including the choice to place ourselves in the hands of charlatans who then disappoint us, and including the freedom that results from the courage to accept true help in the face of ego's stormy, temperamental resistance.

I consider myself exceptionally fortunate for the way in which I met my teacher, which is not to say that it unfolded smoothly and easily. During the evening gatherings I attended in the days following my first meeting with Lee, I heard the truth about so many aspects of life in a way that I had never once heard spoken. He was startlingly frank, indulging in not a single nicety or drizzle of emotional sentimentality in his ruthless exposé of life as it is. Once in a while, in a word or a sentence, he would pierce the lie of the personality I believed myself to be disguising so cleverly. Or he would make an indirect hit, apparently addressing somebody across the room with a specific detail unique to *my* life which nobody else could possibly know.

Alongside what was happening externally, there arose in me a series of energetic phenomena – most commonly associated with the *kundalini* energy – that was as frightening as it was compelling. Through the focus of my attention on my teacher-to-be, lava-like currents of energy flowed through parts of my body; inner "wheels", which I assumed to be the *chakras*, would spin, and inner heat would become so overbearing I would drench the sheets and experience hot flashes.

When the experiences were particularly strong, at times bringing about great fear of what might happen to my body if I let myself surrender fully to them, Lee would casually respond that I should just observe them, draw no conclusions, and that if they felt overwhelming I should "put on the breaks" and relax the quality of my attention on him. My revelations of light and perception of divine dimensions were regarded with respect and treated as valid, and, at the same time, as "no big deal". The gift was that the experiences and phenomena, many of which I never experienced in the same way again, left an inner conviction of measurable strength that allowed me to endure the fire of doubts and agonizing purification in years to come. The truth of the guru principle as expressed through this Jew from New Jersey had been firmly embedded within me. I had been ruined to my previous illusions of freedom.

Jai Uttal
The Master's Grace

Jai Uttal is a pioneer in the world music community. For over 30 years he has been a disciple of Neem Karoli Baba – "Maharaji" – and an apprentice to the musical genius of Ustad Ali Akbar Khan. His musical releases include *Journey*, *Beggars and Saints*, *Shiva Station* and the new *Mondo Rama*.

Q: I would like to know the story of how you came to meet your guru, Neem Karoli Baba.

JU: I usually don't talk about my relationship with him – either in interviews or during *kirtan* [chanting of God's name] evenings or on my CDs. I feel the relationship with the guru is so private, so personal, so hard to put into words that it will be misunderstood. But for this interview, I will. I met Maharaji [Neem Karoli Baba] in 1971. I was 19. I had gone to India on a pilgrimage to see another guru. But when I got there, I found that the guru I was going to see was in prison. He was being held for murdering 30 of his monks. I was shocked. I had projected the whole teenage, guru/disciple thing on this man (whom I had never met), only to find out he was a mass murderer. Yet the miracle was that, rather than feeling disillusioned and harmed, I felt free. Somehow I knew that I had been projecting an artificial devotion to him, and suddenly it was lifted.

Q: So how did you end up meeting Neem Karoli Baba if you weren't looking for a guru?

JU: I went into a bookstore in New Delhi and they told me Ram Dass [Richard Alpert] was at a hotel nearby. I had known him, so I went to see him. When I got to the hotel they told me he had left for Brindavan to see his guru, Neem Karoli Baba, and so I went, too. At this time, though, the last thing I wanted was a guru, since I felt I had entered into the previous situation with so much naïveté.

Q: Still, you went to Brindavan?

JU: Yes. We went to visit Maharaji in the temple, and it was like entering a magical world. Everything was glistening. The sound reverberated from the *kirtan* singers, and Maharaji was glowing – his colors were radiant in the sun. He sat on his *tucket* – a little table – and started throwing fruits around and laughing and asking questions of the new people who were there. He said to my girlfriend, "Who is your guru?" And she told him the name of our intended guru, who was now in jail. "Oh, you Americans are so easily deceived!" and he was laughing and laughing. The whole scene was hypnotic, captivating, majestic. We had many, many more days like that, but I still didn't want a guru. I wasn't critiquing him as a guru, nor auditioning him as a guru. I was just captivated. When you're with someone like that, the inner fire really gets turned up. It's like being in love, though I never would have described it that way at the time. Gradually, through dreams, I began to get an incredible sense of the connection between Maharaji and me – that timeless, ancient connection.

Q: The story you describe took place 30 years ago. What happened to that relationship over time?

JU: My perception of the relationship I have with my guru really doesn't have very much to do with the relationship itself. Sometimes my awareness of the relationship is so strong that I just cry from the grace, and then two days later I am shocked to discover that I've forgotten that grace. But the grace doesn't go away; it's just my perception of it that goes, colored by my mood. My relationship with Maharaji is so conditional, but when I think about Maharaji's relationship with me, I feel it as an unconditional relationship. My perception sees the relationship as constantly changing and evolving, but my sense is that the relationship is an eternal relationship, and the change has more to do with how clear or unclear I am. I suspect that from moment to moment I go from total projection, to total receiving of Maharaji's grace, and don't necessarily even know the difference!

Q: What do you mean by "grace"?

JU: Grace is Maharaji's, or God's, blessings. It has nothing to do with what I think or feel. I'm not a great yogi by any means, or a great devotee, or a great practitioner. I do my practices. Grace comes regardless of the practices, but I continue to do my practices as an offering.

Q: Did you ever go through cycles of doubt, distrust, and distance in relationship to your teacher?

JU: I did, and still do, but it is less a doubting of who he is, and more doubting his love for me. And I've gone through periods of being angry with him. I've gone through periods of feeling deserted by him. But strangely enough, I keep doing my practices. I never really doubted the practices. I didn't doubt God's name; I didn't doubt the prayer; I didn't doubt the *kirtan.*

Q: Is there a connection between your practice of public *kirtan* in which you engage the Western public in ecstatic chanting – and your relationship with Maharaji?

JU: The practice of singing does a lot for me on many levels. The chanting is my prayer that my connection with Maharaji be made stronger and stronger in my own, day-to-day reality. My efforts can make me feel more tuned in, and when I am tuned in, it changes things I think and do. I don't know what "spiritual" means, but the chanting opens me. I can breathe better, I can eat better, I can sleep better and I can go to the bathroom better!

Q: Someone may wonder, "How can he possibly have a relationship with a guru who has been dead for almost 30 years?"

JU: I can't answer that. I don't know. I just do. It doesn't make any sense. Many things in the spirit world don't make sense, even what I choose to do with my life. For example, I ask myself, "Why should I expect people to come and sing *kirtan* with me to gods they have never heard of and probably don't believe in anyway?"

Q: Why do you think they do?

JU: Because singing in the spirit world creates transformation. It offers an incredible opening in the heart-world, in the non-intellectual world. People come to my performances to chant, we sing for a few hours, and then, regardless of whatever the individuals' belief systems are, the experience happens, and we leave completely different.

Q: In considering the topic of projections onto the teacher, I imagine that now that you are an acclaimed singer, you are in the position of knowing what it is like to be the object of those projections.

JU: What has been a revelation to me is how much I could fall prey to those projections while thinking that I'm *not* falling for them. In terms of the really intense projections people have about me, although they can be heavy and a little scary and sometimes make me uncomfortable, I don't take them too seriously. I think I've suffered and caused suffering for others by believing that adulation even a little bit. In no way do I believe I'm a guru, and in all the things I do I try to minimize the role of teacher. So I disavow that projection as much as I can, but still I have realized how much my ego has grabbed on to subtle adulation without my even knowing it. I thought I was free of it and yet I was eating the energy of people's projections up because of some of my ego needs.

Q: How did you come to terms with that?

JU: I think I got to a point where I had to look at those projections as projections, and had to feel the effects. Once you see it, it's less risky, but it is such a dangerous thing when you don't realize it is happening. Because then you are acting in so many unconscious ways, fulfilling so many different unconscious needs. You feel good when you believe in people's projections, but it is only ego that feels better. You feel like a highly adorned peacock. When you are clear about yourself, then you don't get caught. Or you watch yourself getting caught, but the caught part doesn't stay. There are so many levels of denial and self-blindness. You can't blame it on anyone else. You can't blame anything on anyone else ... except your guru!

CHAPTER 8

Breaking the Rules

Where is your sword
Discrimination?
Draw it and slash
Delusion to pieces.

BHAGAVAD-GITA

Twenty years from now you will be more disappointed by the things you
didn't do than by the ones you did. So throw off the bowlines. Sail away
from the safe harbor. Catch the trade winds in your sails. Explore.

MARK TWAIN

Had I followed the unwritten rulebook regarding how a spiritual master should talk, look, and act, I never would have become a student of my teacher. Not only did he announce at the first public meeting I attended that he was not taking any new students, but, he just didn't do the guru-thing in the way the mind imagines that one who goes by that title should. To begin with, his name is Lee and not "Ananda". He is Jewish and not Hindu. He has dread-locks and sings in a blues band. He is known to house ancient wisdom teach-ings in the guise of dirty jokes, and tells us we are trying to become *human*, not divine. From the external appearance of things, and even from the rules in the unwritten guru handbook, he just doesn't make the grade. Yet by that time in my search, I had been worn out by Divine Mothers and Advaita masterminds whose understanding – though far superior to my own – simply could not quench the depth of my thirst. The rulebook had lost interest for me.

Six weeks after our initial meeting, I walked into a nearly unfurnished room at the outskirts of Tiruvannamalai to attend a public talk Lee was giving to the itinerant Western seekers in the area. He had left India weeks before, but had returned unexpectedly at the request of his master in order to com-plete the paperwork for the purchase of some property. Unbeknownst to me, my soon-to-be teacher had already identified in me dynamics that years of psychotherapists and spiritual teachers and shmurus had either been unable to perceive, or were too unskilled to confront effectively. With such a carefully constructed psycho-spiritual resumé behind me, bearing numerous degrees documenting my intellectual knowledge, and with a litany of mystical experiences and meetings with "high beings" to back my spiritual repertoire, I had remained conveniently sheltered from the gravity and depth of my own self-deception.

Having arrived early for the meeting, I sat down across from Lee in the only other chair in a room that would soon be filled with skeptical seekers who were curious about the American crazy-wise master who had come to town. I anxiously awaited any interaction with the eccentric and unlikely individual I had already pinpointed as the most likely possibility in my life at that point to actually help me fulfill the only aspiration that really meant anything to me. I also knew that he wasn't going to make it easy – that there was a lawful "payment" that would have to be made with the currency of my soul in order for an exchange of that level to ensue.

"Do you want to know what is really going on with you?" he asked coolly and unsentimentally, before even saying hello.

"Yes," I stuttered, caught totally off-guard, my gut instantly registering a preview of the dreadful news to come.

"Are you sure you really want to know?" he challenged, demanding I be fully responsible for whatever was to follow.

"I am sure."

At that, he delivered a 40-minute personalized sermon detailing in word, gesture, and tone every overt and unconscious nuance of the false personality structure that I had effectively hidden from myself for the 25 years of my life until that point. He unveiled endless manifestations that no Buddhist teacher, psychologist, mentor or healer had ever come near reflecting with such precision. He ranted about aggression, zealousness, grandiosity, seduction: the very things that each of us most fear to hear about ourselves – aspects so seemingly repugnant that we are willing to live and die shrouded in deep lies in order to avoid hearing the bare reality of those truths. My teacher-to-be revealed them to me one by one, sparing nothing. Minute after eternal minute, one lie after the other was exposed, and with each I felt as if another strip of my inner protective skin was literally being peeled away. I was being skinned alive from the inside out, a thin layer of psychic salt raining over each fresh wound.

The truth being hurled at me was so shocking that I was only remotely aware of the room filling up with high-minded Western seekers, surely unaccustomed to the unconventional display of mastery before them, their occasional gasps and nervous laughter evidence that they were stunned just by inhaling the secondary smoke of the guru's fire of purification. But I could not be bothered with their reactions, for in addition to the egoic shockwaves frying my system, I was simultaneously experiencing something entirely unprecedented in the whole of my life until that point: I was experiencing Objective Love.

I had been loved many times before, and had, myself, passionately loved: men and countries and food and children and sex. But this was unique. It was Truth's love of Itself as yet unrevealed. A love that can only arise through clear seeing, void of motive, which expresses itself in the form of service to the other by exposing falsity. No one I had met in my life until that point had possessed the capacity to see me for who I was, as well as who I wasn't, and was willing to express it at the risk of intense reactivity. Yet to react would be to refuse the gift, and I knew it. Words that invited interpretation as insults – many of which had not even earned a rightful place in Webster's dictionary – became bullets of psychic love shattering false constructs and destroying egoic pride. The ego was humiliated by the same language that caressed the soul so famished with longing. I was utterly naked.

A few days later, I received an unexpected invitation to have lunch with several Westerners who had taken up residence in Tiruvannamalai, most of whom I did not know but was aware had been at Lee's talk. Wary of the motivations behind their invitation, I arrived to find myself the object of a thoroughly calculated intervention. Word had spread among these "spiritual tourists" that I had fallen under the spell of a teacher who was a benign charlatan at best, and an abusive patriarch at worse. Gossip had spread like wildfire regarding Lee's verbal "assault" on me days before, and these spiritually-correct aspirants were alarmed by the unspiritual vocabulary with which I had been addressed, while oblivious to the inner experience I had undergone. They had come together in a shared need to protect me – but from what?

I listened to their concerns one by one. They felt he had been inappropriate, uncompassionate, unnecessarily mean, degrading, attacking. On one level, I couldn't blame them. He was guilty of all such crimes to my ego, but this is precisely what I wanted a teacher *for*. I had been begging teachers for years to wage such an attack on the lies I had insisted upon for a lifetime that were keeping me from the very thing I most longed for: my Self. After sitting through three hours of their anxieties, insisting of myself that I listen carefully just in case I had been mistaken regarding the only thing I knew to be true in life, I thanked them for their concern and absolved them of any guilt they might feel having released their sister-seeker into the lion's jaws. I finally had a real life to begin living.

The Use and Misuse of Criteria for Defining Spiritual Authority

My teacher did not follow the rules, a fact that caused great distress not only to my family and friends, but also to other seekers who were insistent upon a more conventionally "ethical" path. The rulebook that my teacher, his teacher, and even his teacher's teacher adhered to contained only one rule: *Do whatever is necessary to serve the disciple.* The rule that absorbs all rules, and has equally been co-opted as an excuse for untold crimes. But ultimately there is little value in playing it safe. Reality isn't safe, nor is Truth nor God, and there is no way around the fact that you have to play to win.

Nonetheless, the "rulebook" – whether scribed on paper or engraved in the spiritually moralistic mind that is already replete with long lists of rights and wrongs for teachers – does have its rightful function. It offers protection to new students of the path, teaching the ABCs of spiritual discernment. Often people who have no conscious interest in spirituality will suddenly find themselves in the company of a Buddhist master, or neo-shaman, or spiritual mentor of some sort with no idea of how to evaluate whether or not they are with an authentic teacher. The "rulebook" offers some guidance in making the most basic distinctions.

Furthermore, an ethical code can serve as a useful checkpoint for individuals desirous of becoming teachers but who may not be sufficiently prepared to do so. In certain Western Buddhist circles, efforts have been made to set criteria for those serving in the function of teacher in order to avoid the most common abuses in the areas of money, power, and sex. Many would-be teachers would benefit enormously from a deep consideration of such lists of rules, particularly in the West where a pervasive feeling of deep psychological unworthiness and powerlessness has resulted in a disproportionate craving for power and domination over others in all walks of life, including spirituality.

Excellence in any field, however, always lies beyond the scope of rules and enters into the domain of objective creativity. The individual who wishes to apprentice to, and eventually attain, such mastery will eventually have to transcend all confines in order to dance with infinite possibility.

A major problem with a set of fixed criteria for judging spiritual mastery is that the student, understandably concerned with protecting her- or himself against the dangers of corrupt authority, quickly attaches to the suggested criteria as if they constituted an objective moral code, thereby limiting the student's own possibility of being able to perceive authentic authority that doesn't match up with the given definition. As Murshid Samuel Lewis said in the documentary *Sunseed*, "A concept of spirituality has nothing to do with spirituality. It has to do with concepts." The given criteria for a spiritual teacher are ultimately only criteria, whereas a teacher is a living process.

Another problem is that the *contents* of consciousness are used to evaluate the *context* of consciousness. Transmission – the greatest function of the master – is an impersonal force, as well as an indefinable and unquantifiable process. It does not choose its carriers based on their adherence to the subjective ethical code of human beings in the Western world in the 21st century. It operates according to its own dictates, decrees that stem from a source far beyond conventional reason or even ordinary time-space. This is precisely what most genuine aspirants on the path are seeking in a master – someone who embodies the *way* of mastery, not a particular form of it.

Criteria for spiritual mastery at best offer highly generalized guidance pointing in the direction of where to look when considering a teacher; a framework for making rudimentary distinctions. At worst, a set of defined criteria is a rigid and subjective moral code created by ego to protect itself from those techniques in the master's bag of tricks that might undermine its autonomy. This complex form of defense is, of course, elegantly structured by ego to appear virtuous, moral, intelligent, and honorable, always in the name of the "higher good".

Everything and Its Opposite is True

So what is the aspiring spiritual student to do? I suggest considering a few areas of generally agreed-upon criteria for evaluating spiritual mastery, as considered in the previous chapter, while cautioning the seeker that although they are generally decent ideals to uphold, as the Zen masters of old remind us: "Not always so."

LOOKING, TALKING, ACTING SPIRITUAL

Although it may not be written in the rulebook, many people have an idea of what a teacher – particularly a Western teacher – should look, talk and act like. We may be unaware of the degree to which we hold these biases until confronted with a teacher who is much younger than ourselves, has a significant speech impairment or a physical disability, or dresses in a manner we find objectionable. We may think that we are flexible regarding the language the teacher uses until we find that every fifth word out of his mouth is a vulgarity, or that he regularly tells crude jokes in public seminars, or that instead of talking about God and Truth he goes on about sex between grasshoppers or a love of gambling. We may believe ourselves to be open-minded regarding various human manifestations on the part of the teacher until we discover that she chain-smokes, wears thick make-up and spiked heels, drinks heavily, or is a lesbian. To pierce the illusion of manifestation, we must continually ask ourselves if we are certain that our ideas about how an authentic spiritual authority should look, talk or act necessarily reflect true spiritual mastery.

To the mind, if the spiritual teacher is a man, he is basically modeled after our projected image of Jesus Christ, God, or a gray-bearded Himalayan master. If the teacher is a woman, she resembles the Great Mother archetype, whether of Celtic or East Indian origin. She is large, warm, embracing, and has a voice that is compelling and melodic at the same time as it is yielding. Such masters are about as common as perfect husbands and perfect wives, whereas imitations of such projected ideals are a dime a dozen. In other words, not only is expecting conformity to such criteria unrealistic in a teacher, it may be cause for caution when it shows up!

More often than not, our ideas about what spirituality looks like are precisely what stand in the way of our experience of it. If we are not willing to see beneath the superficiality of our egoic desire for spirituality to *appear* a certain way, we are in no way prepared to enter into apprenticeship with an authentic spiritual authority.

ENLIGHTENMENT

Most people assume that having achieved "enlightenment" or "awakening" is a necessary condition to qualify one for spiritual teacherhood. But what do we mean by "enlightenment"? If there is a single issue that people in the field of spirituality disagree about more than any other, it is who is enlightened and what constitutes their enlightenment. The issue is of such importance that I dedicated a major portion of my book *Halfway Up the Mountain* to its consideration.

The teachers I most admire tend to focus less upon a fixed state of consciousness as the marker of readiness to teach others, and more upon qualities of proven reliability, unwavering commitment, and undisputed integrity. Teachers who gain the respect of both peers and students are more committed to sharing the teachings than they are to augmenting their own power and authority; they are unlikely to become corrupt in areas of sexuality, money, and power, even when such commodities are freely offered to them; and they are willing to admit to their own mistakes, even at the cost of their personal pride and reputation. Teachers I respect less grant their students permission to teach shortly after a shift in consciousness that marks the most basic level of awakening, well before it is clear whether that state will endure over time. Whereas I do believe that there is such a thing as awakening from the dream of false perception, this "enlightenment" merely marks the beginning of a new level of spiritual work – the "kindergarten" of spiritual mastery.

Beyond these, there are many qualities that comprise effective teacher-hood. For example, someone who has a solid psychological structure and the backing of a strong lineage, even when his or her realization is relatively shallow, may make a better teacher than someone who has had a powerful awakening but is not backed by a lineage. The lineage itself – the stream of transmission passed from living master to living master over thousands of years – offers tremendous protection to those who surrender to its ultimate authority and respect its lawfulness. When I meet a teacher who is self-proclaimed rather than sanctioned to teach by a master who is part of a lineage and tradition, I do not disrespect his or her function, but I am wary.

Simply to state that one must be enlightened to teach is reductionistic, as well as extremely difficult to evaluate from an unenlightened perspective. From countless trips to the spiritual marketplace, I can say with conviction that I would more readily avail myself of the teachings of those teachers who do not proclaim their own awakening, or who even claim the lack of it, before I would apprentice myself to the majority of Western "masters" who advertise their enlightenment in magazines across the world, guaranteeing to deliver enlightenment to their disciples with a metaphorical money-back guarantee.

Taking Ourselves Too Seriously

We may need to break the rules sometimes, simply because we tend to take ourselves and our spiritual lives far too seriously, and we need to see what happens if we veer off-course for awhile. As serious spiritual aspirants, we often get wound up so tight that God or Truth can't even find a crack in our shell of virtue through which to enter us. Having a sense of humor in relation to the spiritual teacher allows some space for our own humanness, as well as for the teacher's humanity, and creates some breathing room.

One time when I was attending Yogi Ramsuratkumar's *darshan*, sitting across from him about 30 feet away, my leg fell badly asleep. At that very moment he called me up to ask me a question, and without thinking twice I jumped up to rush over to the dais where he sat. As soon as I took my first step, I fell wildly off-balance, staggering toward the front of the room like a drunkard, my hands reaching in front of me, preparing to catch my fall. I looked up at the Yogi and his attendant to see the most baffled looks on their faces as I headed toward them totally out of control. Finally, I shifted my course just enough to crash into the wall just beside where he sat. The 250 people watching this event, as well as the Yogi and his attendants, were in hysterics, though it took me about a month to find it funny.

A friend of mine had a similar experience while studying at a Zen monastery in Japan. The environment was rarified and extremely formal, as is characteristic of traditional monasteries. As she stood up to bow to the master at the end of a formal meditation period, she realized her whole leg had fallen asleep, and instead of moving forward, her body went backward and she fell straight through the thin rice-paper walls of the *zendo* and ended up with half of her body outside in the garden.

One afternoon several years into working with my teacher, he called me over and asked if I wanted some feedback on my spiritual practice.

"Of course," I told him.

"Are you *sure* you want feedback?" he asked once again.

"Yes!" I repeated.

He asked me one more time and then told me, "Look. If you want to proceed on the spiritual path as rigorously and quickly as you insist you want to, you need to *RELAX*. Relax, relax, relax. You've just got to chill out. Relax. Calm yourself. Have fun. Relax ... Relax. Relax, and then relax!"

"I don't know *how* to relax!" I told him.

"That's precisely the point. I'm not talking about month-long inner vacations, but about learning to relax within yourself. As much as I abhor the inner child, when you find yourself agitated, tell yourself, 'It's OK, honey. Everything is going to be fine.' You just need to *relax!*"

Another story was told to me by author Regina Sara Ryan, who was then a Catholic nun in her twenties. Nun-like in her personality structure, as a young woman Ryan had the habit of doing everything "just so". She was the "star nun", as holy as they came. One day during a sewing period when the novices were supposed to be observing silence, they were instead chatting away, gossiping, and enjoying themselves. Just then the Novice Mistress walked in and the nuns fell immediately to their knees in acknowledgement of their sin. The Novice Mistress looked at each of them in turn, asking, "Sister, did you break silence?"

"Yes, Mother," each replied.

And on to the next one and the next she went, each one saying, "Yes, Mother."

When she finally got to Ryan, the young nun looked up ashamedly. "Yes, Mother, I broke silence," she admitted.

Pausing for a moment to take in the response, the Novice Mistress's stern face broke into a smile. "Glory be to God!" she proclaimed. "You're finally becoming normal!"

Spiritual life *is* serious – so serious that if we really want to fulfill the enormous task before us of becoming more deeply human, we must learn to laugh at ourselves, to relax, to break the rules now and then, and to be all right with it. *Sadhana* is hard work. Relating to a teacher can be difficult, if not maddening at times. So sometimes we need to laugh at the ludicrousness of our own projections, play with our own neuroses, create relationship with others around our shared absurdities in relating to the teacher, bring a little bit of laughter into the intensity of our discipleship.

If we are going to risk a relationship with authentic spiritual mastery, I suggest we realize that we are entering into the sphere of Limitlessness, in which narrow definitions and rigid criteria are like blinders that restrict our capacity to see the range and depth of possibility that the master offers. Then again, if we want to play it safe (which is particularly common when we have been scorched by corrupt teachers or corrupt parents), criteria might be just what we need for a time until we are able to trust our own intuitive sense more fully.

The fulfillment of *conscious discipleship* involves both knowing the rules and knowing when to break them. When we know the rules, we are informed seekers with an increased capacity to detect fraudulence and deception, and are more likely to find ourselves in the company of teachers worthy of our attention. When we know how to break the rules, we do not suffer the limitations of our own spiritual morality and intellectual rigidity.

Vimala Thakar

The Compassion of the Cosmic Intelligence

Vimala Thakar is a meditation teacher and close companion of the late J. Krishnamurti. After serving as a renowned activist in the rural land-reform movement in India, Krishnamurti asked her to begin to teach and set the world "on fire". She has taught meditation throughout the world for several decades. The author of over a dozen books including *On an Eternal Voyage*, and *Being and Becoming*, Vimala is now retired, spending time at her two ashrams in India, at Mount Abu in Rajasthan, and Dalhousie in Himachal Pradesh.

Q: How did you meet Krishnamurti?

VT: I was traveling with the land movement. I had no idea who Krishnamurti was. Life brought Krishnamurti and Vimala together. All this is due to the compassion of the cosmic intelligence.

Q: How does one magnetize that cosmic intelligence to oneself in order to attract the teacher?

VT: Through your inquiry, which itself becomes understanding. The guru doesn't give anything but *love*, and the light of his or her own life. When your inquiry is genuine, as opposed to empty intellectual theory, then life is love, and life brings you to the person who can be of help to you.

Q: It is my understanding that Krishnamurti abdicated the need for the teacher, though he still taught. Could you explain that?

VT: Krishnamurti communicated his own understanding. He shared it because that was his role. It helped *many*, but *he* did not consciously help. He communicated, he responded to questions, he had some healing powers. Krishnamurti lived his life, and thousands came to be helped through his communication and the presence of his person.

Q: You have taught both East and West. Do you think the student–teacher relationship has a place in Western culture?

VT: Western culture is changing. Eastern culture is changing. All cultures are a melting pot. When this form comes to the West, it can be very difficult to cultivate the correct inner attitude and approach in the one who claims to be a guru, and the one who tries to be a disciple. The student and teacher must meet as friends. They must share – the student shares inquiry and the teacher shares understanding.

Q: Why is it difficult to cultivate the correct inner attitude?

VT: In the West you see more of a student–teacher relationship rather than a guru-disciple relationship. A disciple, in the traditional sense, lives with the guru under the same roof, and learns by observing every action of the guru. The guru-disciple relationship is something very sacred. Unless a person is willing to devote himself fully to the guru, the relationship cannot happen. Such intimacy is a *fire*. For those who take the path of devotion, the melting of the ego takes place. The Hindu songs say, "I'm related to *It*. Let me remember that in my daily relationships."

Q: Can you be more specific about the challenges for the Western individual who seriously engages in the student–teacher relationship?

VT: In the West, students have to go beyond the mental. They understand the words, they get the concept, but understanding the concept is not touching the understanding beyond the concept. When it comes to uncovering the mystery of reality, the sophisticated brain has no relevance. Spirituality is quite different from philosophy, theories, concepts. If a Westerner would like to get to the secret of *bhakti* yoga [the path of devotion], he must go beyond logic. In spirituality, the guru–disciple relationship has no limits. In a traditional guru–disciple relationship, if the guru observes that you are overwhelmed by your ego, the guru will point it out in a simple, straightforward way. Will the disciple in the West – who is primarily an intellectual animal – be able to hear it?

Q: How, as a single woman in India, with all odds against you, did you manage to sustain your search for truth?

VT: My love of life and the urge to discover the truth firsthand sustained me. I had read so much, but I could not be satisfied in borrowing anyone's version of truth. I would probe and probe until the light dawned on me. Living here in India, a woman unmarried – it was not a path of roses. There were many difficulties and handicaps. But a revolutionary cannot have the luxury of defeat – pessimism, negativity. Never. Difficulties can be converted into opportunities, challenges into the call for more creativity. Everything in life has two aspects: If you know how to use it, it becomes an advantage, and if you don't know how to use it, it becomes a disadvantage. That's what I have done, my dear. For every challenge I received, I would say, "This is a love letter from the Divine, and I must find an answer from within."

Section Four

Hot Issues

The eyes of mistrust see one facet of the diamond; the eyes of faith see another. We must keep our eyes wide open, but it is the eyes of discrimination that are the most indispensable of all.

The sizzling fires that blaze intermittently through the student–teacher relationship cannot be avoided. The authentic student–teacher relationship is not safe. It is hot, dangerous, and brimming with unforeseen possibility. Whether through avoidance, rebellion, or embrace, the serious spiritual aspirant *will* be propelled into dealing with provoking questions that have no clear-cut answers. For example: What are the advantages to having one teacher rather than many? When my teacher acts in ways that make no sense to me, even bordering on the socially unethical, do I abandon my trust in him or her, or am I open to a teacher who works in unconventional, and even socially unacceptable, ways? How do I distinguish between madness and "crazy wisdom"? Is it beneficial, or even safe, to practice obedience to the teacher in Western culture? How do I come to terms with actual weaknesses in my teacher? Can he or she have blind spots and still be an effective teacher? Where do I draw the line?

Understanding the nature of these spiritual fires does not shield us from the heat they inevitably bring, but it does provide guidance in how to burn consciously and with minimal damage.

CHAPTER 9

Spiritual Monogamy vs "Sleeping Around"

*We cannot "fool around" if we really want our teacher to take us seriously.
In spite of what may be strong emotional feelings toward one master or
another, we must look clearly at our own personal history in order to see
where we are likely to err in our approach to the spiritual teacher.*

LEE LOZOWICK

If only I could say that I met the master, was enlightened shortly thereafter,
and we lived happily ever after. But the story is not so simple. Meeting the
master is the end of one story, but only the beginning of another. For the lies
constituting my personality structure had been revealed, but neither undermined nor replaced. I had fallen wholly and spiritually in love with Truth in
the form of my master, determined for the first time in my life to enter into a
"spiritual marriage" between student and teacher, yet he was insistent that he
was not looking for new students. He said that the sacrifices involved were far
greater than most people are prepared to handle, and repeatedly warned me,
"If you are wise, run the other way as fast as you can."

Meanwhile, one of the local Westerners, upon realizing I would not be
talked out of my vision of the guru, decided that I should at least be given a
good education on the topic, and thus gifted me a copy of William Patrick
Patterson's book, *Struggle of the Magicians*. I opened it and read the following:

*Awakening through the grace of vision, born usually of deep disappoint-
ment with ordinary life and himself, the student is magnetized to seek.
Influences, conscious in origin, enter his life. A book, a poem, an image,
an impression, a person – some representation that transcends the personal, the ordinary, speaks to him. There is a flash of awakening. He
responds, resonates, the world suddenly appears greater, more mysterious.
Jubilant, inspired, he identifies, imagines himself a spiritual being, and
seeks a teacher. His expectations are as great as his "spiritual" dream of
himself, his capabilities. He doesn't see that aligned against his permanent
awakening are massive mechanical forces, both personal and collective,*

societal and natural, all of which contrive to keep him "in place". Nor
does he see that only a very small part of him, his essence, wishes to
awaken; his personality has no desire to awaken. And so it obfuscates,
lies, and defends.[1]

I didn't doubt that *other* people's personalities didn't want to awaken, but
surely mine did. I was a maiden disciple blinded by spiritual infatuation; so
resolute, in fact, that I made a vow to be Lee's student for the remainder of
my life even if he never once acknowledged himself as my teacher. I had heard
a famous Zen story about an archer of low caste, who, upon being rejected as a
disciple by the master archer, took a stone and placed it on an altar in the
forest and worshipped it as his master. Through the intensity of his devotion,
the "stone master" transmitted to him the secrets of mystical archery. If need
be, I was determined to do the same.

Meanwhile, totally unbeknownst to my conscious self, I initiated an intricate plot to win his affections. Accustomed to getting what I wanted if I was
clever enough, I had somehow decided that since the thing my master loved
most was *his* master, if I endeared myself to Yogi Ramsuratkumar and proved
myself deserving of his affections, my teacher would see that I was worthy and
necessarily accept me as a student.

When learning to swim, it is more clever to begin in a shallow pool than to
throw oneself overboard into the sea, but my naïveté knew no bounds. And
how could it, as not only had nothing in my cultural upbringing prepared me
for such an event, but for exactly the opposite? I had learned to control,
manipulate, overpower, and assert my authority and independence. Yet,
beneath all manipulations was a hungry heart, sincere at bottom, and the masters wasted no time capitalizing on my aggressive sincerity to teach me a critical lesson.

The first part of my plot – to win Yogi Ramsuratkumar's affections – succeeded, though through no doing of my own. He not only offered me his
affections, but lathered them upon me until the cloud of bubbles surrounding
me was so thick it would have taken a cannon to burst through them. He drew
me into his inner circle, bestowed upon me a special place by his side, and
gave me the job of chanting for him every day. He allowed me to drink from
his water cup, which left me so intoxicated that at times the sacred *mantra*
would run through me without stopping for days at a time, my absorption in
God rendering *everything* – including much-needed sensibilities – dormant and
ineffectual. He provided me the status and recognition that had dominated
my egoic ambition for decades, if not longer, inflating it to such extremes I

could not help but see the absurdity of it and experience the futility of its emptiness. In a way that only a true master could, he saturated my soul with benediction while simultaneously deep-frying my ego.

There was only one problem with my plan: it didn't work. When Lee got wind of what I was up to, he congratulated me sincerely enough on having gained the attention and affections of one the most renowned living masters in south India – and let me know in no uncertain terms that as long as I was working under the guidance of Yogi Ramsuratkumar, he would have nothing to do with me. He said that even if master and disciple are ultimately One – as in the case of him and his master – they are still two in form, and each works in a highly refined and specified energy field which must be respected. He had no intention of interfering with his master's work with me, and told me that if I wished even to be considered as a student of his, I would have to get Yogi Ramsuratkumar's full permission to leave, without a single gesture of control or manipulation on my part. He added that since I had gone to the trouble of making such a mess, I may as well cash in on the benefits and stay close to Yogi Ramsuratkumar, both in order to receive the personalized grace that was being made available to me in spite of my manipulations, and also to learn the lesson I needed to be released by the Yogi. Lesson Number One: One Master Only – unless otherwise specified.

To appreciate fully the extent of the bind I found myself in, and why I would expose myself to this test of faith under such unusual conditions, requires some background information.

Yogi Ramsuratkumar was so uncommon, so far off the spectrum of my previous comprehension of what can arise within the container of a human body, that after six months of spending at least four hours a day with him, seven days a week, it finally occurred to me that he was indeed a *man*. If, after being by his side for hundreds of hours over many months, I hadn't seen him as a man, what had I seen him as? He was more like a ghost – the shell of where a human being once was. A nearly transparent figment of the imagination. I experienced him as a fluid process rather than as a person: like a geyser of compassion, a continual outpouring of radical and obscure blessing oozing out from and through this porous frame of a human being look-alike.

I respected his authority because it wasn't subjective. It is said of his teacher, the southern Indian saint, Swami Papa Ramdas of Anandashram, "Ramdas plays football with the planets." Yogi Ramsuratkumar was no different. He played human beings with the precision that a world champion chess-player moves pieces on a board. At the same time, he was innocent to the point of expressing himself in the purest of childlike mannerisms. Yet the moment you doubted his mastery, it would come out and cut you like a sword. To question whether or not he was enlightened is as irrelevant as asking whether or not Picasso ever got a degree in Fine Arts.

Yogi Ramsuratkumar showed no sign of being willing to release me. A few days after Lee's departure, he called me up during his public *darshan* to speak with me, asking me how long I intended to stay in India. I told him I wasn't quite sure, but that I had thought perhaps another six weeks. (Surely I could learn my lesson by then, I thought.)

"Mariana is not going to stay here for six weeks," he exclaimed in his inimitable squeaky voice. "She is going to stay here for six years!"

At that, he waved his hand to motion me back to my seat among the crowd, and began to laugh madly. When Yogi Ramsuratkumar laughs, the whole world laughs. Whatever it is, it's funny in the truest sense of the word. We both laughed, hysterically, myself in a mindless stupor, tears streaming down my face for no apparent reason, until *darshan* was over an hour later. Then I went back to my room and sobbed for much longer than I had laughed.

There I was, having found in a Jew from New Jersey the master I had been seeking for seven years, and now I was about to be held spiritual hostage by one of the greatest living masters on the Indian subcontinent – only he was not *my* master. Did he really mean I would be there for six years? What about Lee? Was I willing to endure six more South Indian summers with heat so intense that boils erupted on my body? To endure physical and spiritual conditions in which even a 25-year-old woman was likely to turn wrinkled and gray within a couple of years? To search amidst a dreadfully limited pool of eccentric spiritual tourists for the man I had not yet met but so desired to be the father of my unborn child? And that was just the beginning! What about the teacher I longed to be with across the ocean? Would he take me after six years, and would I even survive the *sadhana* ahead with an individual so powerful that his laser glance could burn a hole in my soul such that I could physically perceive my body being scorched? What if he didn't allow me to leave the country to renew my tourist visa and I became an "illegal alien?" How about my friends and family? They thought I was strange before, how was I to now explain that I was captor of a god-mad saint who rarely spoke and explained nothing, but was so potent that I implicitly knew beyond the shadow of a doubt that if I even tried to escape that the cosmic forces he commanded would crash a bus, make my passport disappear, create an avalanche to block the road?

Within weeks I had gone from being a naïve young seeker, fully in (perceived) charge of her life – confident in her capacity to control, achieve, succeed, and seduce – to a still-naïve young woman, but one who had been taken at her word by two of the most radical and powerful masters of the respective oriental and occidental continents. I was now a marionette whose strings were held by two, but whose free-will was paradoxically the key factor in determining the form in which her destiny would unfold.

The question of spiritual monogamy is a topic of significant interest to most serious students of the path, and the subject of frequent scorn among committed spiritual tourists. A useful, though not definitive, means by which to explore this topic is to consider the relationship between lovers as a metaphor for the student–teacher relationship. We model our relationship to God, or the Beloved, or the teacher based upon the template we learn from our human relationships. If we want to learn to be lovers of God, we can discover our weaknesses by looking at our patterns in intimate relationships, and we can deepen our capacity for intimacy with the One by practicing it with human beings and with the teacher.

The Problem with "Sleeping Around"

In California and other New Age centers, the term polyamory ("many loves") is widely used to indicate a lifestyle choice in which a person chooses to have many lovers instead of one. Sometimes the individual has a "primary relationship" accompanied by additional relationships; at other times it appears more as free love; and in still others the individual may not be involved in a relationship at all, but adheres to a philosophy of open relationships.

There is an interesting parallel to spiritual monogamy here, because while there is the occasional individual who manages to live a polyamoric lifestyle in a clean, honest, and conscious manner, in many, if not most cases, one who chooses such a lifestyle does so as an escape from the challenges of ongoing commitment and intimacy. In Western culture, where our conditioned psychological template for authentic intimacy and healthy sexuality is fragile and confused, it is difficult for most people to manage even one intimate relationship successfully, much less many. The same principle applies to the question of "monogamy" in relationship to a spiritual teacher.

When people hop from teacher to teacher, they may have an experience of striking intellectual or bodily intoxication, but the relationship usually remains limited in its breadth and dimension. A great teacher for a day is like a dharmic psychedelic that yields profound inspiration and insight – then fades as quickly as it arose. The experience is real, it just doesn't last. Many people are nectar junkies, and who could blame them? The first taste of the master's nectar is often sweet and intoxicating. But if we stick around long enough for it to hit the bloodstream of ego, we may find that the divine medicine tastes like poison. Rather than endure the often unpleasant process of digesting the teacher's full transmission, many people unconsciously opt for a series of mini-transfusions of nectar which temporarily satiate ego's belly but rarely satisfy the soul.

Most commonly, people who hop from teacher to teacher stay with one until either the teacher, or the process instigated through the presence of the teacher, begins to threaten the ego in a significant manner. The unconscious fear of egoic annihilation, which is the eventual destiny of any individual who commits to a solid and rigorous path of spiritual discipline under the guidance of an authentic teacher, creates too much pressure for the psyche to endure. Of course, the individual in this position does not think, "My ego is threatened." That would be far too vulnerable a stance for ego to admit. Instead the mind may suddenly give rise to thoughts like, "I'm not quite sure I agree with the way this teacher talks about men/women," "I don't like the way this teacher plays favorites," "Maybe the teacher is not as great as I imagined him to be." Or ego's discontent may simply be experienced as an inner itch – the need to move on.

The difficulty in learning discernment, of course, is that any of these thoughts may reflect ego's escape plan, or may indeed be accurate and indicative of very real underlying issues, with the individual's growing capacity for spiritual discrimination finally allowing them to see the deep cracks in the teacher's structure. I experienced this personally on a number of occasions, such as the time when I told one of my pseudo-gurus that I had a dream that he was not a real teacher, and he told me that if such dreams ever came again, I must instantly wake myself up! There is no clear way to know whether such doubts are symptoms of egoic resistance or not. However, if one has been teacher-hopping for many years and is confident that one's preferred teachers are indeed good teachers, then the failure to commit to any of them is likely to be more a sign of hidden egoic resistance, and less of intuitive knowing.

Returning to the consideration of the intimate relationship between partners as a metaphor for the student–teacher relationship, one of the greatest possibilities of such a relationship is that of giving birth to one's own "spiritual child" (not to be confused with the inner child!). If we take one or two metaphorical "sperm" from several masters, the chances of getting "pregnant" are far more slim than if we take tens of thousands through the ongoing transmission from one teacher backed by a whole lineage. From the appearance of things, as well as from the perspective of egoic gratification, the more spiritual "lovers" one has, the better. However, as Robert Ennis suggested regarding those who claim to be serious about the spiritual path but choose not to work with spiritual teachers, "Not too many immaculate conceptions happen." Furthermore, if an immaculate conception should arise, we must ask ourselves if we really want the full responsibility of being a single "spiritual parent" with no child support. Full engagement with a genuine guru, or spiritual authority, is likely to result in the birth of one's own true spiritual self, and to raise oneself into spiritual maturity requires as much constancy of attention and dedication as raising an infant does, albeit in a different form.

The Value of Monogamy

In the domain of human love, there are qualities of bonding, surrender, and depth that cannot be known until they are experienced through years of devotion and commitment to one's personal beloved. The same is true of a relationship with an authentic spiritual teacher. I have read books by people who deconstruct the value of the monogamous and committed guru-disciple relationship with razor-like clarity. I have listened to discourses refuting the value of the guru that were delivered with such charisma and intelligent articulation that even one who knows otherwise is impressed by such intellectual savvy. Yet the fact remains that most of these individuals have either been badly burnt one time too many by a would-be spiritual authority, or they have unhealed wounds from a parent (or some other authority figure in their early life) which express themselves as an intellectual opposition to the principle of spiritual authority.

In spiritual monogamy, two primary processes occur: one, the teacher comes to know in great detail the nature of our personalized resistance to Truth and the habitual antics we perform to shield ourselves from it, thus enabling him or her to work with us effectively; and two, the transmission provided through the medium of the teacher penetrates our psyche with increasing depth and potency, finally penetrating its way through the nooks and crannies of our psyche.

In the first process, whether we see the teacher as an individuated expression of the divine itself or as a finger pointing to the moon, the student–teacher relationship is very intimate, even if ultimately impersonal. The teacher observes the student over many years, making suggestions and giving directions according to the teacher's increasing awareness of how the student is best served in light of the nature of the student's resistance. Meanwhile, the student learns to trust the teacher to the degree that confidence in the teacher's direction overrides the convincing assertions of the arrogant ego. The relationship becomes co-creative, as teacher and student work together not only for the purpose of the student's ultimate adherence in Truth or God, but so that the fruits of their relationship are used to serve and heal humanity.

In the second process, related to transmission, the context of enduring spiritual monogamy allows for the full benefit of the subtle and invisible forces of Truth eventually to penetrate the fortress of the student's psyche. In the same manner in which a canyon is formed by what begins as a small stream of water flowing over the same land over millions of years, what is once felt as but a hint of transmission flowing from teacher to student gradually wears down the hardened rock of the false identity structure as the stream of benediction and clarity passes unceasingly over it. With enough time and consistency, the hardened ground will eventually crack. As long as the disciple continues to make him- or herself even the least bit vulnerable to the teacher and the teachings, transmission will have its way.

It can be extremely difficult to trust this process when, sometimes for years at a time, no visible results can be seen, but the absence of concrete and linear evidence does not imply a lack of progress. In a lifelong marriage there are years in which the deepening of love can be felt, and other periods in which it seems as though little or nothing is happening. This is equally true of the committed relationship with the spiritual master. During these "dry periods", we are carried along by faith, conviction, commitment, or whatever other force of will and willingness we can muster.

Whether students court transformation in the context of Buddhism, Sufism, Christianity, Judaism, or potentially even an unknown or obscure tradition, they link themselves to a force so powerful it has the potential to give birth to an awakening to Truth and surrender to God. No one tradition is superior to another. The transforming potential is the student's committed intention and loyalty to that source, which can initiate a powerful alchemical process that no amount of spiritual "promiscuity" ever can.

Spiritual Affairs

It should be noted that, in the context of spiritual monogamy, "affairs" almost never work. The spiritual affair happens when a student who is committed to one teacher begins "flirting" with other teachers. Because the student–teacher relationship is not a sexual one in the physical sense, such affairs are easily justified by the mind ("After all, I didn't *do* anything with him/her"). In the same way that flirting with other men and women generally deflects energy away from one's primary relationship, the misdirection of attention away from one's own teacher toward a beautiful spiritual stranger can disrupt the energetic flow of transmission from teacher to student.

One interviewee told me that after 20 years with her teacher she "fell in love" with another – younger – teacher who readily acknowledged her spiritual strength and offered her the seductive attention commonly shown to new students. The validation showered on her by this new teacher, like the thrill of new romance, was far more interesting to her than the slow wearing-down of barriers that had been occurring with her steady and faithful teacher over the previous two decades. Her older teacher supported her in this affair for a time, as she clearly needed to find out for herself if this new love was real, but eventually asked her to make a decision between the two either way, as by remaining on the fence for too long her progress in either tradition would suffer.

This was the very position I found myself in at the point in my story where I was "involved" with both my own teacher and *his* teacher. I had found the spiritual love of my life, but the other was intoxicatingly beautiful as well. "Maybe I could get away with this affair for just awhile?" I unconsciously thought to myself. Although I knew that to seduce another teacher when trying to court the attention of my desired master was probably a very bad idea, I justified it by telling myself that, since Yogi Ramsuratkumar was the very individual my desired teacher had surrendered to, availing myself to him was the same as availing myself to the other. I learned otherwise. The intricate manipulations of ego are merciless!

The conscious disciple is wise to take full responsibility for all such spiritual affairs, but it is important to know that teachers themselves – even highly respected and powerful ones – are not always trustworthy in this domain, particularly in the West. Every authentic teacher who knows the full power of the force they represent, and particularly those who believe that their access to this force is superior to that of other teachers, would like strong students to benefit from what they offer. Yet some teachers feel justified in spiritually "seducing" other teachers' students, while others do not. The distinction between those who court other teachers" students and those who do not has to do with the degree of psychological and cultural conditioning and purification in the teacher. In Western culture, the lack of integrated development of the emotional and sexual centers can leave even impressive spiritual teachers with confusion regarding power and seduction which extends into their teaching work.

If a teacher has not developed a solid psychological foundation in these areas, either as a result of a healthy childhood or through psychological healing, this blind spot, or psychological hole, may manifest in parallel domains in the spiritual sphere. Such teachers are likely to be less conscious regarding how they throw around their power, and are more likely to "spiritually seduce" other teachers' students. It is a great challenge even for a strong student to resist such a temptation, as the forces of both transmission and seduction are extremely potent, and together they are tantamount to atomic energy. For this reason it is vital that one who assumes a teaching function in the West deeply examines his or her own relationship to personal intimacy and sexuality, even if following a celibate lifestyle or believing him- or herself to be far beyond this level of psychological work. I am personally struck by how common it is for otherwise extraordinary teachers to be blind in this area.

Exceptions to the Rule

Every aspect of the student–teacher relationship will include exceptions. Even once-extraordinary human romances sometimes end in divorce, and vows meant to last into eternity are interrupted or severed. The same is true of the student–teacher relationship.

Sometimes student–teacher relationships end in divorce – either pleasantly or less so. In most cases, the strong student needs a teacher who is at least a few, if not many, paces ahead of his or her own development, and some students outgrow their teachers. Other times – though not nearly so often as most people presume – either the student's needs or the forces of the universe shift in a way that a transition from one teacher to another is required. One woman I interviewed, for example, was with a great Western master for nearly a decade when her teacher invited another teacher to speak at a conference he was hosting. The moment the other teacher walked into the room, the woman knew he was her true master. She consulted her teacher on this matter and received his full support in "changing partners". A rare pleasant divorce.

Teachers also die, and sometimes the rightful response on the part of the student is to remain with the teacher even when he or she has left the body, while another student may need or desire a source of ongoing feedback and transmission from a living master and must make the necessary energetic shifts to adjust to the new situation. This can be a difficult decision for the student to make: correctly assessing whether he or she has reached a sufficient degree of spiritual maturity to interpret feedback correctly from the now-disembodied master, living as a spiritual "widow" or "widower" of sorts – or whether, in spite of an inner loyalty that does not die, it is time to move on.

And if the student chooses to look for another teacher, the transition from one Beloved to another can be tremendously challenging to navigate.

Another variation on traditional spiritual monogamy is found in Hindu culture, where it is not uncommon for an individual to have a root guru accompanied by various other respected teachers who serve to support the function of the main teacher. Tibetan teachers operate similarly. Depending upon what the student ultimately wants from the relationship, sometimes this works effectively, other times not.

Sometimes teachers send their students to study with other teachers. This is particularly common among Buddhist and Sufi masters. Perhaps there is some area the teacher is unable to break through with the disciple, or another teacher may possess a particular quality or skill that the teacher would like his or her student to learn from. Sometimes the reason remains unknown, such as in the case of a woman I interviewed whose teacher not only continually sent her to spend time with other teachers, but would never acknowledge himself as her teacher in spite of her unwavering certainty of this fact and two decades of dedicated discipleship. Then there are rare cases, such as that of the Sufi sheik Llewellyn Vaughan-Lee, who carries forth the lineage of Irina Tweedie. "Mrs Tweedie", as she was called, came to understand that Vaughan-Lee was not an immediate disciple of herself, but of *her* master, Bhai Sahib. But as Bhai Sahib had long since left his body, Vaughan-Lee's rightful access point to his master was through Irina Tweedie. Both willingly adjusted to the needs of this situation.

The essential distinction is whether the student is *sent* by his or her own teacher to study with other teachers, or at least given approval by his or her own teacher to do so, or whether the student crafts his or her own eclectic spiritual program. When a teacher sends a student to apprentice with another teacher, or at least offers his or her full support, the teacher is still orchestrating and overseeing the student's progress, maintaining a global perspective of the student's overall needs.

When the student creates an individual program, the danger is that ego is once again craftily creating *its* strategy – a plan designed to undermine a deeper dismantling of egoic self-reference. Proponents of the independent, do-it-yourself camp cringe upon hearing this perspective and react by saying it is disempowering to the student to give the teacher so much control over the process. But it is only disempowering to ego. In making recommendations to a student, a *good* teacher takes into account the range of the student's egoic needs and desires as well as the true longing of the soul for re-union.

A further exception to the rule of spiritual monogamy is that seekers may "sleep around", even for decades, because they simply have not found their true master. Some people live their lives without finding their teacher, or find them only late in life. There are classic stories of those who travel East and West in search of their master, eventually giving up their search entirely – only to find the teacher at the equivalent of the local laundromat. Irina Tweedie, who was to become one of the greatest Sufi masters, met her teacher when she was 52. Who could second-guess such forces?

Lastly, there are those who really enjoy the game of teacher-hopping, and are content with the gratification they receive. They are like spiritual hummingbirds who make a life out of nectar-sucking, and may even catalyze some useful cross-pollination in the process. Vishnudas, a German by birth, was one such individual I came to know in my various trips to India. It seemed that whatever teacher I went to in order to conduct my research, there was Vishnudas. He had worked out a one-man musical performance, with bells on his ankles, guitar in hand, harmonica and microphone attached to a head-piece. He sang traditional Hindu *guru bajans* (songs of praise to the master) to American rock and folk melodies, filling in the name of the "guru of the hour" in appropriate spots. He had been doing this for years, and I often wondered if in his ecstasies he sometimes mistakenly sang the wrong name. I suppose he would chuckle, "They're all one anyway."

Regardless of the validity of the exceptions, it is my conviction that, in the majority of instances, "sitting around" with a variety of spiritual masters is in principle no different from sleeping around with different men or women as a lifestyle. An endless stream of physical love affairs will bring a lot of excitement, emotional "highs", and some profound encounters (as well as a healthy dose of cynicism), but we are unlikely to learn much about the depths and possibilities of love. Similarly, sitting with many masters is likely to bring about a heady dose of ecstasy, some deep dharmic insights, and leave us with the impression that we are going somewhere, yet we are likely to end up with very little aside from a bag full of spiritual trophies.

In spite of the potent possibilities of monogamy, it is wise to take as much time as one needs before jumping in. A committed relationship to a teacher not only bears similarities to marriage, but is infinitely more serious, as the implications of such a commitment conceivably extend even beyond the life of the body. Many teachers will wait a long time before asking their students for a monogamous commitment, and some may never ask at all, but sooner or later the conscious disciple benefits from making a firm decision. Whereas ego may interpret the teacher's call for the disciple's commitment as an expression of the teacher's personal greed or hunger for power and dominance (and, in the instance of the false teacher, this may well be the case), the authentic teacher is committed to the student's best interest, courting his or her commitment so that the student may receive the benefits of the vow of ultimate surrender. Still, the decision must come from the student, and in its rightful time.

Arnaud Desjardins
Master as Disciple

Arnaud Desjardins is one of the most widely respected spiritual teachers in the French-speaking world today. Renowned as a filmmaker for French National Television, at the suggestion of his teacher (Swami Prajnanpad, 1891–1974), Desjardins left his television career to open his first ashram in 1973. Today he lives and teaches at his Hauteville ashram in southern France. He is the author of over a dozen books, including two English translations, *The Jump Into Life* and *Toward the Fullness of Life.*

Q: How can someone distinguish authentic authority in a teacher?

AD: The *disciple* gives the authority (regarding who is a real master and who is not) when they are convinced that a given teacher is authentic. When I first met Ma Anandamayi and Swami Ramdas, I was sure that they were authentic – their being was fully convincing. But the fact is that many admired people have sooner or later proved to be fake gurus. My feeling on the matter is simple: If I want to learn to play piano, I will accept the authority of the teacher. If I want to become a classical singer, I will accept the authority of the teacher who says, "Use breath like this," or "Make the voice vibrate in this part of the face." And if I go to the doctor, I accept his authority.

Q: Many people will accept the doctor or the music teacher, but not the spiritual master.

AD: I would say that that is *their* problem! For thousands of years, the authority of the spiritual master has been accepted. Yet to accept a specific teacher, we must feel: "He knows. I don't know. He has the experience that I do not have, and I *need* his help." Many years ago my teacher, Swami Prajnanpad, wrote to his group of students in France: "You must be asked the fundamental question once again, 'What do you want?'" We were to ask ourselves if we truly *felt* that he could be of help to us. From that point on, it became clear to me that if I wanted to proceed further in my work with him, I needed to do what he asked of me. I needed to follow his advice and not take what I like but refuse what I didn't like. It took some time for me to be ready to surrender to the guru in that way.

Q: A lot of people want to surrender to the teacher like that, but have great difficulty in doing so.

AD: Complete surrender will only come little by little. One day I started telling Swami Prajnanpad, "Swamiji is Hindu, but has French disciples ..." He interrupted me and said, "Swamiji has no disciples. Swamiji has only candidates to discipleship!" That was a grand lesson for me. I understood that to be a disciple is much more than being an ordinary student or devotee of a master. So my aim from that day on was to become a disciple – to have complete trust and confidence in the guru. It does not mean that the guru cannot be wrong or that he or she knows all and everything, but when he or she gives an instruction, we have complete trust in them. But this comes little by little.

Q: In the West, obedience and surrender are considered weaknesses.

AD: The question is not one of obedience. The question is, "How can I expect to be helped by someone to see what I don't see, to understand what I don't understand, to awaken when I am asleep, if I don't follow his or her advice completely?"

Q: Many people come to the guru with great sincerity, and want to follow what is asked in order to receive help, but they are acting from a childish position of looking for approval and salvation.

AD: There is no sin, there is only childishness. All sins are manifestations of our childishness. Be childlike but not childish. It is a very important distinction. A sage is an enlightened child – simple, but never childish. The great temptation is to go to the master with the attitude of, "Father, Mother, love me!" thinking that if we remain a child, a good child and a nice child, that this true adult will take care of us. But that's not the businesses of the guru. It's not a question of remaining a child – putting my small hand in the big hand of a perfect father or a perfect mother. It has nothing to do with childishness or dependence. We go to the master because we intuit that the master is not other than ourselves. If he is a genuine guru, he is my Self. It is said that if the guru and disciple are together in the same room, there is not two in that room. There is only one: the disciple. The guru is not other than the disciple. He or she is the disciple already enlightened. *We* are the proof that the guru is one with us.

Q: Does the individual who is serious about the spiritual path *need* a teacher?

AD: You cannot progress on the way without recognizing the authority of a master and following his instructions. That is my 100 per cent conviction. Of course there are some geniuses – very, very few – who become fully enlightened without a long and deep relationship with the master. But it's not the rule.

Q: What is the distinction between a guru and teacher?

AD: In your first book, *Halfway Up the Mountain,* it was clear that there are two kinds of teachers: those who have studied with a master or masters, and those who have not. They may have a personal gift, and be a person of very high human quality: noble, generous, and deserving of respect. I know such people, and have even supported my son and wife to go to them for further study. But they are on their own. They lack the backing of a teacher, a lineage, a tradition to follow. Of their heart I would ask, "To whom do you *pranam* [bow], from within?" They say, "Oh I have great respect for all the sages. I fully agree with what the Buddha said." But it is not the same. In most cases, there is need of the human master. God is the ultimate Guru, but who is able to give themselves completely to God? Very, very few.

Q: How about those people who would like to have a teacher but haven't found one?

AD: First comes the inner urge to change – to go beyond the limitations of ego. One must cultivate *Being.* One must feel, "I want to have this experience and I am ready to pay the price for it." Even if he or she is weak, lost, and far from the goal, one who seeks has a chance to be found. The guru will come if the disciple is convinced that some sort of realization is possible.

Q: After finding the teacher, how does a student then progress?

AD: Those who are inspired by the highest goal will be in a far better position to go through the first stage of fears, desire, neurosis, contradictions – the whole domain of psychotherapy. First we have to face what psychologists call the shadow: not knowledge of the ultimate Self, but knowledge of oneself – one's contradictions and unconsciousness. We cannot avoid that, but we will go through that with much more success if our aim is not only to feel better but also to find God.

Q: Whereas I once believed all I wanted was God, my experience through years of practice is that there is more than one strong desire in me – one is to find God, but there are many other desires for personal fulfillment.

AD: You have this strong desire, and you have to pay the price. What is the price? To take into account all the sides of yourself. All the *vasanas* and *samskaras*. How do you reach the other shore? By crossing the ocean of life, of experience. That is very important for most of us – not only the monastery, the prayer, the meditation, but to express consciously within limits. Until we can really say, "I've done what I have to do. I've got what I have to get. I have given what I have to give," we will not be really free. You can accelerate the process, but you cannot jump.

Q: So we move into the expression of desire as a way to become of the attachment to it?

AD: There is great freedom in "knowing that I know". You may wish to believe, "Money will not bring me happiness." So get some money; see if it brings you happiness. Or you try to convince yourself, "Ooh, success and fame will not give me happiness." Get some success. Get some fame. Does it give you lasting happiness? It is a rather dangerous way because it is true that desire increases desire, yet we have to experience life as consciously as possible, not repressing anything. Then we can be free to fulfill our spiritual destiny. When we have done this, we are ripe, fit for the ultimate *sadhana*, because we have lived.

Q: Did you go through this process yourself?

AD: Swamiji was always tempting me to see if I was *really* ready. When I complained to Swami Prajnanpad that I was still so interested in pleasure, and becoming a famous film director, and doing so many things, he told me, "Be faithful to yourself as you are situated here and now." "But that has nothing to do with *atmadarshan*," I told Swamiji. "Leave *atmadarshan* for the time being. Be what you are. Do it with awareness and with open eyes. See and accept all. You want pleasure? Go ahead and find pleasure. With pleasure and happiness will come other things. Take both." So it was my good fortune to meet very rich people, famous French movie stars and performers, and to experience that pleasurable lifestyle. At one point I fell in love with a very famous singer in France – a woman with thousands of admirers and a woman of depth and sincerity, different than the others. And she was in love with me. It felt so wonderful. And yet I saw that my five-year-old son could not understand what was happening. The atmosphere at home was not the same. His mother was weeping. I could not have one side without the other. This is how Swami Prajnanpad led me, by teaching me through experience. Still, sometimes the temptations were so strong. I would be in a French restaurant, beautifully dressed, with a lovely, famous film star, leading the high life. Somebody would come up and say, "You are Arnaud Desjardins. I saw your program yesterday on television," and I would swell with pride. And then I would remember the great saints I had known – Ramdas, Ma Anandamayi, the great Tibetan masters – and I would have to ask myself, "What do I want?"

Q: Until we know what we want, do we remain candidates to discipleship?

AD: A candidate to discipleship feels, "I want God – that's for sure – but I also want great love, sex, fame. I want to meet bright, fascinating people, to travel, to enjoy the seashore." A disciple is no longer interested in these things. The thought and accompanying attraction for various things may arise, but there is no inclination to follow it. To be a disciple means that the goal is One. Freedom, God, and compassion are one's only interest. Once you are a disciple, and God is most important, the way will go fast. This is my experience for myself, and also for many people I have known.

Daniel Moran
Living in the Shadow of the Master

Daniel Moran is a senior teacher at Arnaud Desjardins' Hauteville ashram in southern France. He is known for his piercing clarity and his uncompromising approach toward self-knowledge. He has been a disciple of Desjardins for over 30 years.

Q: What is the function of the spiritual master?

DM: The master is not someone who gives. The master cannot give anything. He or she can only be transparent. The master is not something that contains, but is only a channel. He receives from his own master, keeping nothing. He transmits, but he does not give.

Q: You are a highly respected teacher within your tradition. Many people say, "Daniel could leave and still have many disciples." Yet you stay here and live and work closely with your master.

DM: I stay because this experience with my teacher is still getting better and better; it is still moving. I am always seeking to be in alignment with the master behind me, while focusing on the person in front of me.

Q: I have heard that you said, "The greatest disciple lives in the shadow of the master, not the spotlight." What do you mean by that?

DM: One meaning of "living in the shadow" is to respect the lineage. It is not for the son to wish to put down the father. It is logical that the master remains the master, because he or she is the disciple's link to God. If my ego desires to outshine the master or to show him how great I am, I lose my link with God. So one meaning of "living in the shadow of the master" is that we serve the master without trying to take his or her place. You can be in the spotlight and still be very humble, or you can wash the dishes with false humility. The worst kind of pride is to be falsely humble. It's not very easy to find the balance between false humility and true humility.

Q: That's a good point. So what does it mean to be invisible?

DM: It means not to interfere in the space of the master – not to be a parasite on the energetic charge that he emits. It is to serve the master, and not use the master to serve oneself.

Q: Again, that is a helpful distinction, because the common egoic strategies are either to become a big, important student, or a humble, submissive disciple, but both are self-serving.

DM: Those strategies are widespread. From the moment one considers oneself as an ego, or separate entity, the other, in turn, is also a separate entity. In the relationship between master and disciple, when we look from the point of view of the master, the relationship is already perfect, but the same relationship as seen from the view of the disciple is troublesome. It comes back to the dance between the Divine and the human. From the point of view of the Divine, there is no difference between the Divine and the human; but from a human point of view, in that same relationship with the Divine there is a difference.

Q: What is the most important quality of a good disciple?

DM: Obedience. He or she has to take the *risk* of being obedient. But we don't want to obey because we fear that the master won't nourish us on a spiritual level, just as our parents were unable to nourish us on an emotional level. We are afraid, because we see this "other" as holding power over us, and we feel imprisoned, confined. We fear obedience will keep us in a prison so we decide not to obey. We think that if we obey we will lose our freedom, but in fact the opposite is true. The more you obey the master, the more you have your own life. Because in fact, the master is not an "other". The master is none other than our own self.

Q: What is the difference between blind obedience and conscious following?

DM: If we take the words of the master as being the truth – "the master said it and therefore it is" – it is pure blindness that leads nowhere. So to follow the master is to listen to what he says, but we need to really work to make it our own understanding. For it to become our own experience, we need to have a turn of mind in which we become quite critical and look for the weakness. If we look for the fault but can't find it, only then can whatever is being communicated become our experience. There is only one thing that can make us at ease and free – our *own* experience, not the teacher's experience. In other words, we cannot live from the food we have simply swallowed. We can only live from the food that we have digested. At the moment of digesting the master's words, they become alive in us. They become part of ourselves. What is being asked of us is to take what he or she says and make it our own. It must be incorporated into the body – the head is in agreement, but the feet must express it. If we simply repeat the words of the master, it will be an exact copy in terms of the words, but completely false in terms of the actions. It is only at that moment, when we have made the master's words our own, do our actions become useful for the general good.

Q: Many students feel it is a natural progression to "graduate" from the master and move on, presumably to a circumstance in which they themselves become the master.

DM: If we forget the master, we will lose something, because the master is the link. We arrive at this foolishness when we pretend to reach a state with no conditions, and at the same time say that the condition of the master is a barrier. The master is the bond and the link to that light. He represents "what is". Each time I say no to "what is", I deny the master – the link that connects me with the light.

Q: So you are not talking about a submissive stance, but something more "lawful" perhaps?

DM: Wanting to be in the spotlight means wanting to be in the place of the master and that is disrespectful toward the Divine Order. It is not in alignment with God's order. We pretend that we are God and then we tell God to go to hell!

Q: Swami Prajnanpad, the head of your lineage, said, "You can follow Swamiji, but you cannot imitate him." Would you discuss that statement in terms of learning to be a mature student?

DM: My teacher, Arnaud, asks us to always be ourselves. The way that my teacher expresses himself and the way I express myself are completely different. I can never become him, and I dare say he cannot be me. But that doesn't prevent the sense of our expressions from being exactly the same in essence. In our desire to be one with the teacher, we often mistakenly imitate the *personality* of the teacher. Students will demonstrate the same expressions as the master, the same commentaries, and the same affectations. I noticed within myself that even after many, many years of discipleship, without even realizing what I was doing, I was wearing the same kind of clothes my teacher wears. I even had the same ticks and the same gestures! I think we want so much to be like them – who they *really* are – that we unconsciously do anything we can to try to be in communion with them. We even imitate true practice.

CHAPTER 10

Guru Games and Crazy Wisdom

The real function of the spiritual friend is to insult you.

CHOGYAM TRUNGPA RINPOCHE

With the torrential flow of grace that now gushed over and through me without rest due to Yogi Ramsuratkumar's benediction and unwavering commitment to my liberation, I began to drown. And drowning wasn't pleasant. I was going down gasping, sputtering, calling for Mommy, begging Moses to part the sea and let me feel the dry lands of egoic security once again. When I hear neophyte spiritual seekers asking for annihilation, to drown in grace, to die into God, I find myself wondering how many have had even a glimpse of what they're asking for. I, too, once believed that all I wanted in life was to drown in an Ocean of Love, and I still do – but who among us willfully allows ourselves to be thrown overboard into the ocean with a boulder tied to our feet?

One evening during this part of my story, I sat on the stone wall outside of the local Arunachala temple, the rocks still steaming from the 120-degree day which had by then cooled down to a "moderate" 112 degrees. All 18 feet of material in the traditional Indian *sari* I wore were sweat-saturated many times over as I poured out my woes to my friend Astrid. Originally a secretary from Denmark, Astrid had come to India 25 years earlier on a two-week guided tour, met Yogi Ramsuratkumar, realized he represented her greatest transformational possibility in this lifetime, renounced a life of materialism and greed, and had not once since stepped outside of the Indian subcontinent.

I lamented to Astrid that her beloved Yogi Ramsuratkumar had taken to severely messing with my mind. For several days, or even weeks, at a time he would shower me with his personal attention. Out of a sea of thousands of disciples, he would single me out, ask me to sit by his side and sing to him, give me blessing-saturated bananas or oranges to eat that would expand my state of consciousness exponentially, and visit my house to bless my room or give me special messages. To receive the master's personal attention in this way is to be viscerally reminded that each of us, personally, is totally and unequivocally embraced by God, ultimately held in the lap of the Great Mother, sucking the breast of Grace at all times.

Then, in a seamless and unannounced transition, he would ignore me –
totally. The desolation I felt at such times was in exact proportion to the exul-
tation I had felt when he had showered me with his attention. Not only would
he no longer garland me with his *malas* of literal and metaphorical roses, but I
would cease to exist to him. I would watch him as he directed his penetrating
eyes in my direction, but instead of seeing *me* he would see through my body
to what was *behind* me. I had never known such feelings before. Through the
simple withdrawal of his glance and acknowledgement, not only would the
bubble of my egoic inflation be instantly popped, but I would feel reduced to
literally *nothing*.

When I finally fell low enough, I would begin to grovel, telling God that I
was willing to trade in my narcissistic demand to be acknowledged and important for His mere acknowledgement of my existence – some small sign that I
was not essentially hollow and nonexistent.

Whether it had taken days or weeks to get there, at *precisely* the moment I
was willing to bow down internally in humility and acknowledge the false
identifications that separated me from all of humanity and from the cosmos,
Yogi Ramsuratkumar would call me to him and once again shower me with
the personal affections of the Divine.

And so it went for months, with not even a faint sign that I would be
allowed to leave India in the foreseeable future. The nature of this dynamic,
combined with whatever other notes the Divine was playing on the splintered
keyboard of my soul, was such that I slipped into what I much later learned
was a mystical depression. Divine joy intertwined so intimately with divine
sorrow that both became forms of despair. For to allow myself to get drunk on
divine nectar was to agree to experience unbearable emptiness when the
nectar was withdrawn.

I shared my aching heart with Astrid, the only person I thought might
understand what I was saying without reducing it to some psychological issue
that would require further inner child work. When I finished my story, she
smiled sympathetically. "I know it feels personal," she said, "but it's the oldest
guru game in the book. They've been doing it for tens of thousands of years
precisely because it works. It doesn't matter what you tell yourself, when the
master plays that card, it works. Don't be too upset with yourself for taking it
so seriously," she added. "It takes most people at least a couple of decades to
come to terms with it, and, besides, it's good for you."

By this point I was in regular correspondence with Lee, giving him blow-by-
blow accounts of my antics and tribulations with Yogi Ramsuratkumar. Though
the two of them lived 6,000 miles across the ocean from one another, it was

completely predictable that when Yogi Ramsuratkumar adorned me, Lee would strip me; and when Lee encouraged me, the Yogi would ignore me. Lee would do things like write me a letter telling me what a great boon Yogi Ramsuratkumar's blessings were for himself as my teacher, and when I wrote back telling him how delighted I was to hear him say he was my teacher, I would receive a letter telling me how presumptuous I was to call him my teacher before Yogi Ramsuratkumar had agreed to let me go. Or he would write to me about how strong my practice appeared to be, then follow it with a letter about how I was flushing diamonds down the toilet through my childish antics.

And so the months passed. With pristine clarity I would remake my vows to the path, only to be immediately beset with an animosity toward God that is still embarrassing to admit to. Fortunately, I had come across Sufi master Irina Tweedie's book, *Daughter of Fire*, in a local ashram library. It had literally tumbled off the bookshelf as I walked by, dried flowers mysteriously falling from its pages onto the library floor. The book detailed Mrs Tweedie's daily trials with her master, which not only bore many similarities to my own, but actually seemed more unbearable than what I was experiencing and thus provided me with a strange sort of relative comfort.

I am hardly suggesting that everyone who gives themselves wholly to the student–teacher relationship will experience such dramatic duels and agonies as I did. Most people won't. Many Buddhist teachers, and most teachers who function in the role of mentor or guide, do not intentionally confuse and disrupt the ego in this way, perhaps trusting that spiritual practice itself, or the influence of the lineage, will eventually provide the necessary disturbance to knock egoic identification off balance. Still, the ego is the same for all, and I have come to appreciate that in the vast majority, if not in all instances, the process of dismantling egoic identification is at best difficult in moments, and at "worst" (from the perspective of ego, not the soul) can be outright agonizing for even extended periods of time. According to an old Persian saying, "The self will not go in gladness and with caresses, it must be chased with sorrow drowned in tears ..."[1]

While even someone with no psychological or spiritual orientation could see through the simple ploy that Yogi Ramsuratkumar used on me, through its use he revealed to me the fickleness of ego, the tendency toward a conditional relationship with God, the experience of God's glory and God's heartbreak, the simultaneous reality and falsity of duality. He knocked the Humpty-Dumpty ego straight off the wall so that even "all the king's horses and all the king's men" couldn't put it back together in quite the same way again.

The legendary story of Marpa and Milarepa is a classic illustration of a crazy-wisdom teacher playing guru games.[2] Once a black magician who came to realize with great remorse the nature of his misdeeds, Milarepa found his way to the renowned master Marpa, offering him everything he had in exchange for the great teachings of liberation. Though Milarepa was eventually to become his greatest successor, Marpa could never outwardly acknowledge him as such. Instead of giving Milarepa esoteric teachings, Marpa would ask him to build houses of weighty stones with his bare hands. When Milarepa had laboriously completed a house, hoping finally to have earned the teachings he had come for, Marpa would find some fault with it, or realize that he had asked for it to be built it in the wrong spot, then tell Milarepa that in order to receive the teachings he would need to rebuild the house in another place, disassembling the stones and transporting them one by one. Milarepa built seven houses, stone by stone, his body ever bruised, his hands torn, his back half-broken, his mind distraught, and his will nearly shattered.

If that were all there was to the story, one might assume that Marpa was an exploitive, domineering, patriarchal, uncompassionate teacher. But the story is told by Marpa's wife that whereas by day Marpa would make demands on Milarepa that seemed ruthless and cruel, he would return home at night teary and distraught by having to kindle the painful fire of purification that was so necessary for his most beloved disciple to endure.

By the time Milarepa had built all seven houses and had "earned" the teachings, he had already received the transmission he sought through the intensive purification process he had undergone as a result of his trust in and reverence for Marpa, and his unwavering desire for ultimate surrender.

Crazy Wisdom

"Crazy wisdom" ("wisdom gone wild") – the English term coined by Chogyam Trungpa Rinpoche – refers to a quality of inner freedom that knows no bounds. A term commonly misunderstood to represent, and thus defend, spiritual teachings and practices that err on the edges of moral behavior, crazy wisdom teachings are instead always designed to serve the disciple's freedom from the insidious rigidity of egoic identification. Crazy wisdom is ruthless and raw in its insistence on uncompromising freedom, and thus at times its outer expression is cutting, confrontational, or simply bizarre. Still, at other times it is mild, ordinary, and even invisible to the eye. Its priority is to undermine the stronghold of ego identification, and if necessary, the crazy wisdom master will employ unconventional means to effect that outcome.

Arnaud Desjardins points out that true wisdom is always crazy to the ego. Since the ego does not understand authentic wisdom, even a mild intervention that cannot be absorbed by the ego's conceptual framework is quickly labeled as "questionable," or even "crazy," when instead it is simply outside of ego's capacity to classify and file into its system. Thus is it important not to mistake the inner wildness of crazy wisdom for a set of external behaviors, as to do so reduces crazy wisdom to a concept of extreme behaviors, rather than an expression of unrestrained freedom born from within.

Disciples of the great Indian mystic Mother Mayee, for example, would spend countless hours walking the beaches of Kanyakumari with her, carefully searching for particular types of garbage that were of interest to her, which they would collect, carry with them in sacks throughout the day, and then burn in a fire in the late afternoon. Many people had theories about why they did this, but none could be sure. They knew only that they basically trusted her, did what they were asked, and in a seemingly unconnected and inexplicable manner, their lives were transformed.

As it is unconcerned with conventional morality, the expression of crazy wisdom can be disturbing to the mind, challenging conditioned notions of ethics and morality. It is wise that this is so, as far too many self-proclaimed messiahs have incorporated highly questionable behaviors in the service of so-called awakening. Unfortunately, such behaviors on the part of charlatans have created skepticism regarding the field of crazy wisdom – a manner of teaching that has been in existence for thousands of years. In a culture full of dubious spiritual authorities, few Western crazy-wisdom masters today are afforded the privilege of making use of their full bag of tricks. They are well aware that a single lawsuit brought against them by one unhappy ego could result in their losing the opportunity to continue their teaching function, and thus they choose to accept the "oppression" of their mastery in service of remaining available to their students.

There are three major spheres in which crazy-wisdom teachings and guru games regularly raise questions for most people: sex, money, and drug and alcohol use.

SEX

Having seemingly committed every other error in the book, I can say with great pride and amazement that I have never had sex with a guru. Not that all sex with gurus leads to negative or difficult consequences, for in many cases it doesn't, but it certainly raises a red flag of caution, as it should. As anyone who has seriously engaged in spiritual life in Western culture knows, the issue of sex is a big deal.

In ancient Tibet, sexual intercourse was an accepted means of spiritual transmission from teacher to student. If we consider the powerful process of union that occurs in sexual encounters, it seems conceivable that when one participant abides in conscious dynamic union with Truth, God, or the All, a spiritual explosion of inestimable value could result. It is not far-fetched to believe that transmission from teacher to disciple might more readily occur through physical union with the master. It involves the same principle as a contemporary Zen master conveying the final transmission to his successor by having both himself and his student locked in a closet together for two days, forehead to forehead, their heads bound together with string.

One of the early Dalai Lamas was particularly known for his love of women. It was common practice for households in which a daughter had received the honor of the Dalai Lama's transmission through sexual union to raise a flag over their home. It is said that a sea of flags floated in the wind over the town.

Not only is Western culture totally unprepared to accept, much less approve of, such behavior, but the vast majority of most Western and Eastern teachers are equally unprepared to embrace the full responsibility of providing "transmission" in this form. I raise these points not to endorse regular sexual encounters between students and teachers, but instead to release the consideration from a "spiritually correct" perspective based on conventional morality, and to suggest that we consider evaluating the situation from a "context-specific" perspective.

Often in Western culture it is difficult to know whether teachers' chosen sexual practices – for themselves and for their students – are a function of their spiritual work, of their personality preferences or of their psychological weaknesses. What appears to be important is that teachers be honest about their sexual practices. Then it is up to the student to decide whether or not these behaviors are acceptable to him or her personally.

Criteria which might be useful in evaluating a teacher's sexual practices include whether they involve us personally – either because we are personally intimate with the teacher or because the teacher's suggestions affect the sexual relationship with our intimate partner in a negative manner; whether they involve children – ours or anyone else's; whether the results seem to be helpful or harmful; whether the teacher appears to have integrity, both in sexual relationships and in his or her teaching work in general.

Sexual relationships between teacher and student are usually, though not always, the result of a mutual process and agreement. It is rare that a teacher will engage a sexual relationship with a disciple without his or her full and willing consent. Of course, the teacher has power and influence in the situation, and he or she should take full and complete responsibility for how this power is used and misused in terms of seduction and eroticism. But we disempower ourselves when we place the full responsibility on teachers if sexual liaisons with them, should we choose to become involved, do not turn out how we imagine they should.

As spiritual apprentices, we should be aware that erotic transferences onto the teacher commonly arise at some point in the student–teacher relationship. If we can see these erotic transferences for what they are without judging them or taking them too seriously, we can use them to empower our conscious discipleship.

MONEY

Guru games might seem interesting to those of us who are attracted to intensive spiritual practice but who still crave playing the wild card that characterizes crazy-wisdom teachers and traditions. Interesting, that is, until the teacher asks us to tithe 10 per cent of our precious income, or more, to the *zendo*.

Although he was a penniless renunciate, the late Indian master Swami Nityananda used to employ large crews to build temples and roads. At the end of the day he would routinely direct them to the side of the road and have them lift up a rock, under which they would find the exact sum of money they had earned according to the amount of work they had completed. A suspicious tax collector, perplexed by how a master who wore only a loincloth could generate such sums of money, approached Nityananda one day demanding to know where the money was coming from. In response, Nityananda brought him to a nearby swamp, opened up the jaws of a resident alligator, and pulled out a large wad of bills. The tax collector never challenged the master on financial issues again.

A senior student of a great Zen master left the monastery with his master's full blessing in order to build his dream house. He worked at it laboriously for three years, and when he had completed the final details of his mansion he invited his teacher for a housewarming party. His teacher arrived, made a full survey of the house, thanked his student for building him such a fine estate, and moved in!

When some curious, skeptical guru-seekers came to a weekend seminar to check out my teacher last year, he spent the first two lectures speaking little of spiritual topics but instead making one sales pitch after another for books, tapes, T-shirts ... telling people that the way to his blessing was through his wallet. That he wasn't there to offer the teaching, but to make money. The curiosity-seekers were scandalized and shortly left. He did not speak that way for the rest of the weekend.

G. I. Gurdjieff kept his students always at the edge of financial ruin, generating one financial disaster after another. When questioned about why he kept his students in this state, he said that it was absolutely essential because if people feel too comfortable they don't grow.

The crazy-wisdom master will employ the use of money, or any other available commodity, to offer students an opportunity to free themselves from the attachments or aversions that keep them bound to their illusory perceptions. Even though in essence money is only symbolic, it is also *very real*. It is instructive to observe ourselves supplicating God to grant us ultimate liberation, then cringing at the thought of donating a hundred dollars to buy some new *zafus* (meditation cushions) for the meditation hall.

In a psychological sense, the act of trading money for teachings is symbolic of the energetic exchange between teacher and student. In many cases it actually helps people to pay financially in exchange for immaterial goods. It is classic psychological economics that when we pay for something, in our desire to "get our money's worth" we are more willing to pay attention, apply ourselves, and make ourselves vulnerable to whatever "service" we have purchased. When something is free, people don't trust it. After moving to a small town in England, I tried to attract a clientele for my massage practice by setting up a chair at the local market and offering free 10-minute massages. Not only did people not sit down, they walked around me. But when I put up a sign offering 10-minute massages for 3 pounds (5 dollars), I was busy the rest of the day.

Material riches are a metaphor for true power and objective wealth. The only true power and wealth are internal, but most people will settle for money, fame, or relative power, or at least for the fantasy of it. Of course, the unconscious belief is that the material wealth will somehow miraculously translate itself into ultimate happiness, which can only be found through that which we could refer to as Union, Objective Compassion, Surrender, God. It is interesting to entertain the possibility that all the corrupt, patriarchal dictators in the world are actually seeking union with God, even if they are totally unaware of it.

On the reverse side, many people in spiritual circles operate with the idea that money, power and fame are inherently corrupt, negative and unspiritual. This limiting belief is primarily the result of Eastern philosophies and practices of traditional renunciation that have been poorly translated to contemporary Western culture. In the development of contemporary spiritual culture in the Western world, we must come to terms with money, power, and the constellation of conditioned belief structures that surround these forces. It is our relationship to money, the teacher's relationship to money, our relationship to money in regard to the teacher, and what we do with all of that, which determines whether material riches and power are an asset or a detriment to our spiritual process. If we are conscious in our discipleship, we can use our relationship to money to gain valuable information about ourselves. To truly renounce is to renounce false relationships to all things, and our relationship with the teacher will either overtly, or simply in the natural course of things, challenge our attachments to money.

Of course, it is also important to recognize that, in a very real way, money is needed to support the teacher and his or her work. In traditional Southeast Asian Buddhist cultures, the townspeople and lay practitioners would financially support the local monastery as an expression of their acknowledgement of its essential function in the community. They knew that the monks and nuns were practicing on behalf of the welfare of all, engaging a rigor of practice that they could not or did not desire to engage in themselves. They also knew that the way they could contribute in a practical fashion was through their financial support. Each student must come to terms with his or her own response to the specific situation encountered in relationship to a teacher.

Every time I see the ads for "enlightenment intensives" (courses charging hundreds of dollars in exchange for promised enlightenment), my third eye rolls. Even so, I cannot help but wonder whether or not the intention behind their enthusiastic longing really goes unheeded. In most of our lives, money comes and goes in waves, and powerful lessons can be learned by putting our money and our bodies on the line.

For a few years I spent time with a guru who was jokingly referred to as a teacher of "yuppie yoga". She attracted the rich and famous, and at her *darshan*, gifts of diamond rings, gold necklaces, stacks of bills, and property deeds would be offered. Perhaps the students' generosity served *them* in some way, and perhaps these wealthy individuals needed to create a literal kingdom in order to entice them to worship.

It is impossible to create rules about teachers and money. Once again, what is true in one circumstance is false in another; or what is true in one situation may even be false in that *same* situation just a day or a week later, or for a different individual. All we can do is empower our own conscious discipleship by becoming aware of the variables, the dangers, the possibilities, and the necessity of risk.

ALCOHOL AND DRUGS

A great Chinese Zen master was known for drinking a cup of whisky every night before bed, and for decades it remained a great mystery to the monks why he did so, though nobody had ever asked him. When he was on his deathbed, the monks realized they could not allow him to die without discovering the meaning of this practice, so one of the senior monks approached him and begged him to reveal its purpose.

"For many years I have had difficulty sleeping due to the pain of my arthritis," the master told him, compassion in his tired eyes, "and several years ago I discovered that if I drank a glass of whisky I could sleep much better."

Chogyam Trungpa Rinpoche drank heavily, and was widely criticized for his alcoholism. When the Naropa Institute, the Buddhist college he founded, was first initiated, a fundraising event was planned and wealthy donors from all over the country were invited. Trungpa Rinpoche was expected to give the keynote lecture. Starting in the early morning on the day of the event, he began to drink. To the concern of his students, he consumed such extensive quantities of Japanese *sake* throughout the day that by the time he was scheduled to address the donors he was doubled over and unable to speak. Infuriated and embarrassed, a close student glared from the audience at his drunken teacher, doubting his mastery and watching his behavior with scorn. At that very moment Trungpa Rinpoche opened one eye, stared directly and soberly into the eyes of his distrusting student, and closed it again.

Many Zen and Tibetan masters and their students are known for consuming large amounts of alcohol. Many yogic, native indigenous, and shamanic traditions involve the use of psychedelics and other drugs. In some cases drugs are used as a sacrament; at other times their use is a distraction or addiction justified with a spiritual rationale. Yogi Ramsuratkumar was known for chain-smoking a particular brand of local cigarettes. When I lived by him, visiting skeptical Westerners would often challenge me, claiming that Yogi Ramsuratkumar couldn't be a true master because he was a nicotine addict, and one who had controlled his senses would never engage in such self-destructive behaviors. I did not know the reason for Yogi Ramsuratkumar's behavior, but his implicit mastery had revealed itself to my satisfaction again and again, and I thus found it easy to allow such choices to be his own business. Once again, we continually impose contemporary Western moral standards upon a wisdom that has no convention and no bounds.

As conscious disciples of any tradition, our task is not to make moral and rigid judgments about whether the intake of drugs and alcohol is "right" or "wrong" for a teacher or his or her students. What we are called to consider is whether or not the teacher's relationship with us is compromised, and whether we can or cannot personally tolerate the behavior. The likelihood is that we may never know whether the teacher's drinking or intake of drugs is fully in the service of his or her practice or of neurosis – or perhaps unrelated to either.

Furthermore, we should be wary of falling into the trap of imitating the teacher, indiscriminately deciding, "Well, he drinks two bottles of sake each day, and *his* practice seems to be going all right, so I guess that means I can, too." Many teachers gain poor reputations because of their disciples' imitation of their habits, rather than as a consequence of the teachers' actions themselves. Are we willing to act in accordance with our own integrity and discipline irrespective of whether or not the teacher practices in the exact same fashion? The process of conscious discipleship is about empowering and taking full responsibility for our *own* practice, not morally evaluating the teacher's practice. Thus we must be ever-cautious of the tendency to compromise our own practice through unconscious mimicry.

It took me over six months to solve the first crazy-wisdom *koan* my teacher gave me: to obtain Yogi Ramsuratkumar's permission and blessing to leave India with no manipulation or control whatsoever on my part in order to assume a life of practice with him back in America. With my foreign entry visa nearly expired, I was aware that at the very least I would need to get permission to go to Burma to get an extension. I also knew that if I did get that extension I was going to have to stay in smoldering India, far from my teacher's physical presence and for a *long* time. I became desperate to gain my release from the Yogi.

When we are desperate enough, the universe responds, though admittedly not always in the form requested. This time, the universe kindly sent a wall of mirrors in the form of people and circumstances that revealed just what I was up to. Among the messengers was a four-year-old girl who was jealous of the attention her twin sister received from Yogi Ramsuratkumar, and proceeded to perform all kinds of antics just to receive a morsel of love so that she, too, could feel special.

Though it had taken six months to arrive at, in a moment I saw clearly that it was not the quality of Yogi Ramsuratkumar's attention on *me* that was responsible for my divine "jail sentence", but of mine on *him*. I had begged for the Kingdom of Heaven, and it was his obligation to see to it that I obtained those riches by any means necessary. I saw plainly that whereas I had been clear within myself about who I wanted for my teacher, I had not *acted* clearly because my ego was unwilling to forego the delicious attention it was being fed by Yogi Ramsuratkumar in favor of spiritual monogamy with my teacher. The ping-pong match the two masters played, with me as the ball, created a demand for me to take full responsibility for my own conscious discipleship. I was finally willing to cease the childish behavior that had made me feel like a prisoner when, in reality, I had handed my captors the keys to my own cell.

In that moment of insight, I knew Yogi Ramsuratkumar would allow me to leave India to proceed in my life with Lee. He did not have to let *me* go; I had to let *him* go. When I did, he responded in kind *almost* immediately.

Almost ... but he wanted to be sure I had learned my lesson, or perhaps see if I wanted to play for the bonus as well. The next morning, no sooner had I stepped into the *darshan* hall when Yogi Ramsuratkumar called me up to speak with him. Earlier that morning he had received my one-sentence, non-controlling, non-manipulative request to leave India. I had told him in the note that I would like to return to California, pick up my car, drive to Arizona, and ask Lee if I could become his student.

"This beggar [which is how he referred to himself] doesn't understand Mariana's note," he told me – he who understood the English language better than I did. I knew we were in another game: the game of "Playing Dumb". It was one of his favorites.

"I would like to go back to California and then go visit Lee and ask to be his student," I repeated, just as the note said.

"What?" Yogi Ramsuratkumar turned to his attendant, telling her, as if I were speaking Atlantean, "This beggar doesn't understand."

"Mariana is asking you if she can return to California, at which time she will collect her car, drive to Arizona, and ask Lee if she can be his student," the attendant repeated. No good.

"What do you want?" The Yogi turned to me again, growing apparently frustrated by my seeming inability to communicate the simplest of messages.

Entirely at a loss, I sputtered, "I want to go back to America and do whatever Lee suggests I do!" – at which he raised his hands high in blessing, laughing in a way that makes the whole world joyous. This time, however, his laugh symbolized the end of the game, not the beginning.

"My Father blesses Mariana to return to America!"
The deal was sealed. At least that one ...

We must continually remind ourselves that whether we are talking about the controversial aspects of crazy wisdom – sex, money, or drugs – the real "craziness" is the paradox that exists within the dualistic perception of the human mind. Some force of Intelligence or God or Truth has opted to manifest a wisdom as crazy as human incarnation, complete with its mental madness and utterly distorted perception of reality, yet has also provided human beings with a longing to understand their condition. Who is the ultimate crazy-wisdom master?! "There is no one on this earth who is not looking for God," said the Persian mystic Hafiz. We are all students of crazy wisdom – persisting in our studies of money, relationship, sex, self-knowledge, disillusionment, confusion, personal and collective unfolding. Some of us choose to work with a teacher in relationship to this madness, having understood that the task is too intricate to teach ourselves, and the chances of self-deception too high.

Georg Feuerstein
Understanding the Guru Principle

Georg Feuerstein, Ph.D., is founder-director of the Yoga Research Center in northern California. He is the author of over 30 books, including *Holy Madness, The Shambhala Encyclopedia of Yoga, Tantra: The Path of Ecstasy*, and *The Yoga Tradition.*

Q: How can one tell if the guru's work with the disciple is effective or not?

GF: It takes a long time for the changes made on the subtle level to actually show up in self-expression on this level. But you *would* see certain changes. If someone who has been part of the scum of the earth engages a guru who is acting compassionately, it is not possible for that person to remain the same. But how much of the person's behavior will change in the course of one life-time? It's really dependent entirely on how hard that person works on himself or herself. The guru can only put the light in them. That is why teachers always say, "I cannot make you enlightened." If they could, they would have done so with everybody. Instead it depends upon the individual's free will. The guru can put enough energy into the system to say, "OK, now run with it." But if you don't run with it, the energy has to come again the next lifetime. You start all over again.

Q: You seem to be saying that even if a person doesn't work as hard as they conceivably can, even if they relate to the master over time and do at least some work, something will change.

GF: You never just "hang out" with a teacher like that. You always have to over-come yourself to be in the presence of a great adept. Even if you don't do the meditation as he tells you to, and you don't do this and that, just being in the presence of a person like that will always challenge your ego. It will inevitably make profound inner changes even if those changes are not completely obvious in all aspects of your personality now. But once you are only the subtle system, you will shine. You will be different. We must assume that anybody who is in the company of a great master like that was very likely with that master before. Because what gives a person the capacity to hang in with such a person? Each destiny is so unique. You may only see the master once in your lifetime. You may see him or her at a distance. But already the change begins.

Q: What does it mean to be a good disciple? How does someone new to the path learn to be a good disciple?

GF: The first thing is the student's qualification, which in Sanskrit is called *adhikara*. And this is where I think Western students are very ignorant because they don't understand that traditionally it wasn't just the disciple checking out the guru, but the guru *really* checking out the disciple. When the guru takes on the disciple as a *disciple*, not just a student, it is a major commitment that goes beyond this lifetime. So, traditionally, a guru will test a student. The potential disciple says, "Please teach me!" And the guru will perhaps ignore him for the first year, or make them do all the donkey-work on the ashram and never give them the time of day otherwise. Then the potential student may start complaining and walking away. The guru knew they didn't have the stuff necessary to stick it out for the rest of their lifetime. Disciples had to bring a certain determination, and they had to have the stamina to be constantly tested. But also, traditionally, part of the game is that the guru completely accepted that he would be tested too. The disciple was expected to look at a teacher and ask: "What is this guy made of? Where is this authority coming from? Is it just scriptural learning, or is there realization, too?"

Q: Could a student have more than one guru?

GF: Guru-hopping, and being sent by your own teacher to another *lama* to receive teachings, are, of course, totally different things. The serious Tibetan Buddhist student is already established in relationship with his or her root guru – which means there is already a relationship of a devotional nature to the guru – before going to study with other teachers. The tradition prescribes that the guru be looked at by the disciple as a Buddha – even if he is not enlightened. You have to look at your teacher as a Buddha, as a fully awakened being. Because if you don't, you already have lost the game. But in the West, we don't have that capacity. We are intent on our own greatness. Once you have accepted a teacher as your guru, after testing that person carefully for however long you need to for your satisfaction, you have to stick with that guru. If you don't, that's when everything becomes turmoil inside. The moment we accept a teacher as our guru and that movement is reciprocated (which the guru, if he's clever, won't do lightly), a point is made at the most subtle level of our existence. If we casually throw that away, we can do great damage to our spiritual practice. And people don't usually understand that.

Q: What is the cost of discipleship?

GF: Being a disciple has nothing to do with social life. It's the end of social life. It's the end of your own personal ideologies. It's the end of your own dreams. After that, there is only the dream of waking up.

Q: The guru-disciple relationship seems to be a particular construct, which some people choose to engage while others don't.

GF: Yes. It's an artificial situation.

Q: Why do people take it on?

GF: It helps us grow. We can't understand the mechanism of the ego in a vacuum. The ego can only be reflected back to itself when it looks in the mirror. We are blind, and so the guru puts up all these mirrors around us. And wherever we look, we see our own chaos, which of course has to do also with the chaos of society, the arbitrariness of the arrangement. We realize the ego is a just a product of all of this craziness of mind. When we really, really see it's a convention, a device that was reinvented in order to make meaning out of nothing, we can step beyond it. So the guru constantly undermines meaning. And then you let go. And then there's freedom. Genuine freedom, not just a vacuum within the chaos.

Q: Why can't we do it alone?

GF: The process requires a being who stands outside the stream of *samsara* and activates a different function, which we call *the guru function*, in order for you to see the craziness of your own bondage. You can analyze your mind till kingdom come, but unless somebody stands outside and obliges you to continue to look deeper and deeper and deeper, you don't see all the links that you make in your mind to explain away your confusion.

Q: So you engage in this artificial construct because there's an element of that construct that's not bound?

GF: Yes.

Q: And in order to do that you need an element that is outside of your control?

GF: Yes, and that element is the guru.

Q: Yet you have to choose to fully believe in the construct and go through it in order to *really* be taught to see that it is a construct?

GF: Yes. That's the paradox. The guru goes around your artificial world and cuts all the bonds slowly. It's a very skillful dance, because if it goes too fast, you go crazy. You literally go nuts. If things are taken away before their time, you don't know who you are anymore. The guru is a very skillful physician. The teacher, *if* he or she is skillful, knows the limits of your construct and what you're able to let go of.

Q: How does the earnest disciple deal with apparent imperfections in the teacher?

GF: It's a simple answer, truly. If a teacher's behavior causes you more conflict than you are capable of practicing with, it's better to leave. *It's better to leave.* There has to be a fit between a teacher's behavior and your capacity to handle and negotiate that behavior, while still seeing it as a transformative tool.

Q: How do we recognize the true teacher?

GF: This is really the challenge for disciples. Real teachers are chameleons. They can be anything. They are in all forms. Why not activate all possible forms of the human being? For a disciple, it's really more a matter of determining whether you can trust. And if there is no trust in the ultimate goodness of the teacher, you had better not even start. There may be moments of doubt, but if you sit back, apart from the situation that has arisen and you still conclude, "No, I trust the teacher," then go ahead. If we can engage the process by saying, "Yes," then we have won! It's a game. The teacher can tell you, "I'm enlightened," and you say, "Oh, great! I want to study with you!" And then it turns out he's a rogue. But you could benefit tremendously, even from a rogue, if you trust him or her.

Q: Do all disciples come to the guru with the same potential?

GF: The scriptures are very clear that there are three types of disciples. The first are the really lowly ones that are constantly obnoxious, arguing, refusing. Gurus have them because they are compassionate and they recognize that people have to start somewhere. The second category, which includes most disciples, are people who are generally committed to the teacher and have a basic interest in the teaching. There is change in them over time, but there is not a lot of capacity. But then there's the third type that comes with a burning impulse to liberation that is not neurotic. In most cases when people come to the teacher and say, "Oh, I want to be enlightened in this lifetime," it's just an illusion. An illusion! It has nothing to do with what is possible for them in this lifetime. That's the first illusion to drop away when you are with the guru. You realize that it's a lot harder than you thought it was. But there are disciples belonging to the third category who are genuinely manifesting this deep, deep impulse to be liberated. We need to make peace with our present capacities as disciples, assuming that there's grace at work. If we hang in there long enough, making whatever effort we can, we will change and our capacity will increase. But we have to be patient.

Q: It's a frightening time in our culture now, and easy to be impatient.

GF: It's a great time! Truly. No better time to practice! Wartime and this kind of social, cultural, environmental chaos creates a great opportunity. We see the world all possibly disappearing in front of our eyes, so what is it we are hanging on to? It motivates us to practice if we look clearly enough. You ask yourself, "What is it all about? Why am I hanging on to this and that? Where will I go with it all?" It makes for great spiritual practice.

CHAPTER II

Obedience

You must pay dearly, pay a lot, immediately, in advance, with yourself.
The more you are prepared to pay, the more you will receive.

JEANNE DE SALZMANN

The Sanskrit word for "obedience" translates as "listening to the guru".

At this point in the story that is my life, I had been sent by a God-intoxicated Indian saint to visit a crazy-wise Jewish teacher in Arizona in order to "do whatever he suggests". Most people, including my poor family, thought I was crazy. I am, by conventional standards. But true wisdom is crazy, authentic spiritual life highly unconventional, and the game of radical transformation one of fundamental risk.

I hadn't been at Lee's ashram for two weeks when he asked if I would like to do a writing project for him.

"Sure," I said, having always done a lot of journal-writing and scribbled out an occasional sappy poem to a lover or a god.

"Great. Go talk to Sarah and she'll tell you the idea. I've been wanting someone to do this for years but nobody has been willing."

Only two weeks in and I had my first test of obedience from the master. I was elated – once again, foolishly so.

I returned to him an hour later highly agitated, certain a misunderstanding had taken place that he would clear up for me. "Sarah said you wanted a *book* written."

"That's right."

"I don't write *books*. I've never taken a writing class and wouldn't have a clue where to begin. Books take years of work, and before that decades of accrued wisdom to even get to the point of envisioning oneself worthy of writing one in the first place!"

"Do you want the project or not?" he asked, apparently indifferent to my argument.

"Sure," I gulped.

How the hell do you write a book?! I pondered half the night, the summer monsoon rain beating on the tin roof of the kitchen-table-sized trailer I had been loaned to live in.

In the morning I asked Lee if I should take a class at the local community college.

"Nope."

"Private tutoring?" I was still hopeful.

"No."

"Interview writers?"

"Negative."

I guess you write a book by writing a book, I thought with resignation, and went about engaging in my preliminary research.

Though moving along at a snail's pace, I was rather proud of myself for doing it at all. But that wasn't enough for the master, whose job description includes enticing the disciple to fulfill his or her highest potential in the least amount of time without demanding more than is humanly possible.

The day before Lee was due to travel to India for five weeks, I found myself in the uncommon circumstance of driving him in my car to a bar in town to watch a gig being performed by our ashram blues band.

"So, are you going to have the manuscript complete when I get back from India?"

His question sent my mind and body into temporary shock, and the car nearly veered off the road.

"Watch the road!" he yelled.

I swerved back. "I haven't even begun the actual writing. Are you serious?!"

"Of course, I'm serious."

To say that the following five weeks were hell in a Siberian winter would be a significant understatement. I slept about three hours a day, wrote 16 to 20, and used the rest of the time to fit in my various spiritual practices. I ate while I wrote, jogged to a nearby building when I needed to use the bathroom, did not engage in idle conversation. When I felt so mentally deranged that I couldn't bear it any longer, I would break down in tears of exhaustion, at which time a merciful *sangha*-mate would insist on driving me to the movies to watch a dumb comedy so my mind could rest. I would then return home to resume work until my eyelids could stay open no longer, wondering whether I was being tortured or liberated.

The mere mechanics of writing one's first book in five weeks was not the most difficult thing that I was dealing with. Far more confrontational was battling the 10,000 daemons that were preventing me from *believing* I could complete such a task – that I was smart enough, talented enough, worthy enough. But somehow I managed. In five (admittedly miserable) weeks of obedience to my teacher, I had surmounted obstacles that years of therapy and meditation practices had not neared scaling. For over a decade Emily Dickinson's quote, "I dwell in possibility," had hung on my wall, but now it was finally far more than a distant romantic idea that belonged to another. When I finally let out my first exhausted sigh of relief after turning in my manuscript upon Lee's return, I found I had surpassed so many self-effacing belief systems about myself that I was disoriented regarding who I was. Freed through book torture!

As if the personal benefits to my transformational process and the overwhelmingly gracious response of readers were not enough, my very own family, after years of tolerating the outrageous adventures and bizarre ideas of their Buddhist-shaman-Hindu-anthropologist-therapist daughter, finally thought that this strange spiritual thing I was doing just might be a good idea. Not only were they impressed with the content of the book, but their outlandish spiritual daughter was now published, and even appearing regularly on radio and television programs. The book was called *When Sons and Daughters Choose Alternative Lifestyles,* and my mother's first comment after she read it was, "You should have written that book years ago and you would have saved us so many problems!" We both laughed in recognition that it was precisely those years and problems that had taught me everything I knew about the subject. Even more surprising was my orthodox, Jewish, cult-fearing father's suggestion that my eldest brother might benefit from "spending some time at that commune of yours with that guru-fellow. It's sure done you a lot of good."

Exactly two weeks later, Lee gave me my second book title ...

If you really want to crash a spiritual cocktail party, all that's required is to raise the topic of obedience to the spiritual teacher. Obedience is poorly understood in the field of contemporary spirituality, conjuring up images of "power over", control tactics, manipulation. It is no wonder this is the case, as countless abuses have taken place in the name of obedience, and those who argue against it are doing so primarily in order to protect the innocent from untrustworthy influences. Furthermore, not all student–teacher relationships – particularly among the various Buddhist traditions – require obedience, certainly not at all stages along one's path. Teachers who warn against obedience should be listened to, and those who demand blind following should be scrutinized, but many teachers of impeccable integrity in all traditions still choose to work within this model because of its overall benefits demonstrated over many centuries.

Obedience is not a moral issue, but a pragmatic practice – the primary purpose of which is to facilitate the aspirant's relationship to truth with optimal efficiency. Thus, I strongly encourage the reader to suspend preconceptions about obedience to whatever degree possible, and bear with me as we travel step by step through a consideration of the labyrinth of obedience to the spiritual teacher. If your particular tradition does not suggest obedience, I encourage you to respect and follow that, using this chapter to augment your own understanding of this complex issue in general, and to appreciate why individuals in other traditions would choose to engage in this practice at certain junctures along their process of unfoldment.

Obedience to Whom?

The highest expression of human incarnation is ultimate and unwavering obedience to a force which some call the Divine or God, and others refer to as Truth. This force, "unborn, undying, never ceasing, never beginning, deathless, birthless, unchanging forever",[1] can be expressed through an individuated form known as the human being. The principal reason why an individual should even consider obedience to a spiritual teacher is to practice obedience to the Divine or Truth within oneself via one who lives as a more transparent reflection of it. Ultimate obedience to God or Truth cannot be expressed with unwavering constancy until the human being has been purified of obstructions that permit access to that already-present force. We "borrow" or "rent" the guidance of the true teacher as a temporary stand-in for objective obedience in our lives until we ourselves are rightfully prepared to assume that function.

To place obedience to the teacher in its rightful perspective requires understanding the distinction between the guru and the guru principle, or the personality of the teacher versus the Teaching he or she represents. The guru principle expresses itself through the personal form of the guru, who expresses the Teaching through his or her personality and culture. But objective obedience is only and always to the Ultimate.

As students striving toward the expression of our highest spiritual possibility, we are once again dealing with two seemingly opposing forces: one that longs for the true heart's release and will gladly do anything required toward that end; the other being the egoic insistence that the former should never occur. Ego, fully identified with the body and programmed to believe that it can and must preserve the life of that body, will, under ordinary circumstances, obey only itself. Obedience to the teacher creates a circumstance that allows the student to learn the distinction between egoic demands and the objective commands of truth; what it is to let go of control enough to allow something unknown to emerge; and the experience of trusting something beyond one's own limited mind. The spiritual student in obedience to the teacher is in "surrender training", preparing for the ultimate surrender to Truth, Life, the Will of God.

Reasons to Obey

Modern Western culture was founded upon values of independence, freedom, autonomy – values which its members are taught are superior to all others, only to be confused and disillusioned when the proponents of those values act in a hypocritical and untrustworthy fashion. Women especially, who even in our "liberated" culture are subject to discrimination and marginalization, are likely to feel betrayed and oppressed. Given this cultural background and experience, to suggest that obedience to spiritual authority has value for true liberation to occur may be heard as a preposterous suggestion.

The fact is that few human beings have ever consistently experienced the guidance of the objective authority of the Self – either as expressed within themselves or in the form of another – much less the possibilities of living in obedience to that Self as temporarily mediated by one in whom it is expressed more fully, one who has no investment in the deeply engraved defense structures that keep the individual aspirant from expressing that Self consistently in his or her own life.

TO PRACTICE LETTING GO OF CONTROL

Those who are happiest in life are that way not because life gives them everything they want, but because they have learned to let go of trying to force life to be other than it is. Instead of resisting life, they turn toward it in its full expression, continually letting go of the endless stream of conditioned egoic demands and expectations in favor of a mature acceptance of life and of their own humanity.

It is hard to trust that the universe has an Ultimate Intelligence that is greater than the intelligence of the separative mind (perceived by most of us to be "who I am"). Yet those who have even touched upon this revelation through mystical experiences or altered states of consciousness attest to its reality, and most of us intuitively sense that Love ultimately and mysteriously conquers fear, hatred, resistance.

We should not underestimate how difficult it is to truly let go of the illusion of separation. Whereas the ego can generate convincing impersonations of letting go, and imitations of freedom (as is readily exemplified in New Age spirituality), each authentic letting-go – a true feeling, a moment of absolute Presence, an unmotivated "yes" without personal agenda – represents to ego a miniature jump off a cliff. To make such a jump requires tremendous fortitude. Since ego is convinced that even a small letting-go means death to the individual it has been put in charge of protecting, we must convince it that it can survive these leaps without incurring its ultimate demise. We do this by providing it with experiential evidence that it can, in fact, survive our small experimental leaps into the unknown. Our trust in and obedience to the teacher offers assurance that our "radical experiments" in letting go are ultimately useful and productive, and that our egoic mechanism is not, at source, once again asserting its own agenda.

When we finally begin consciously to allow the intelligence of life to move us, the universe within and without opens. Imagined limitations are replaced with lived experiences of unlimited possibility. Others benefit from our contact with an energy which now fills us. We are more open and generous because we are no longer continually defending ourselves from engaging in relationships that once felt so threatening to the protective ego. When we release our limited control and embrace the unknown, we become privy to previously hidden secrets of the universe (though some can and should remain forever mysterious). Life opens radically, and true Self-expression begins.

PREPARATION FOR DEATH/THE BARDOS

We need to learn to let go not only to be able to experience life in its infinite range of possibilities, but to prepare us for the process of dying, for death itself, and most likely for what comes beyond death. According to most Eastern mystical traditions, the moment of death is the most crucial moment of our lives. It is in that moment that our capacity to surrender fully to the Universe, Enlightenment, the Source of All is tested. So important is the moment of bodily death that many branches of Tibetan *vajrayana* Buddhism focus an enormous amount of energy on practices to prepare for it.

In the moments just prior to death, the individual is forced up against the final wall of his or her resistance, and intuits facing the final opportunity to let go in this lifetime. Even earnest practitioners, however well motivated, rarely appear to be able to let go fully at the moment of death. A lifetime of conditioned mental habits and unconscious patterns live in and through the very cells of the body. The cells themselves, conditioned by the protective ego to ensure survival, are programmed not to let go. Although this concept may be difficult to understand, it is relevant to each of us: Conditioned egoic functioning believes itself to be real, and believes itself to be the body of the individual in whom it arises. The human being misidentifies with this force, forgetting his or her essential nature and believing that when the body dies, he or she dies. However death comes – accompanied by overwhelming physical and/or emotional discomfort; with great fear and exacerbation of attachments; when we are highly medicated and despondent; unsuspectingly while we're asleep – if we have not trained ourselves to let go in life, we will be *unable* to let go in death, in spite of the best of intentions.

This principle becomes evident when we care for someone who experiences a difficult death process. I cared for a dear friend during her final months of life as she was being consumed by an aggressive and extremely painful cancer. In the final weeks, it was obvious that her body could go on no more, that it was time to die, that every further day she hung on was a day of agony, defeat, and refusal to accept the task of death that life had set before her. But she could not let go. Through long, agonizing nights we would lie on her bed while she, unable to talk or open her eyes, grasped at life as if she were a hungry ghost that refused to accept the reality that it was already dead. For this reason alone, I told myself, it is worthwhile to learn to let go while alive. Obedience to the master – misunderstood as it is – offers unparalleled instruction for this process.

It is highly likely that death is not the end of the life of the soul. According to sages in many traditions, who for millennia have studied states of consciousness beyond the life of the body, when the individual dies, the Soul or Essence enters into a series of realms of consciousness in its journey of reincarnation. Tibetans refer to these realms as the *bardos*.[2] The individuated soul passing through the *bardos* is said to pass through any number of illusory distractions – both hellish and heavenly – as well as a variety of strong attachments and the reliving of difficulties in one or more former lives. The individual's greatest possibility lies in his or her capacity, developed in life, to be swayed neither by attractions nor repulsions, but to let go and allow forces of consciousness larger than egoic attachment to dictate the direction of the soul's unfolding.

Many people who have engaged in significant experimentation with deep meditation techniques and psychedelic drugs have had experiences that lead them to conclude that the only way to pass through difficult states is either to let go of them through detachment, or more powerfully, to allow them to transform themselves by surrendering into them. The ability to let go in this way requires tremendous presence, consciousness, and psychic strength.

The practice is the same in life as it is in death: to let go. Many people can learn to do this to a great extent through their own inner process and the circumstances life provides them with. The advantage of working with a spiritual teacher is that the teacher can provide instruction in seeing and dealing with those attachments that are the most obscured in us and may therefore be the hardest to let go of when the body dies.

Letting go in obedience to the teacher is a risky form of practice if there are doubts as to the teacher's integrity, but within the context of practice under the supervision of a trustworthy guide, it is particularly effective. With the exception of circumstances in which dangerous and unethical acts are committed, obedience can teach discrimination and help conscious disciples (as opposed to victimized subjects) learn something about how they tend to relate to forces greater than their own ego.

THE TEACHER HOLDS OUR HIGHEST POSSIBILITY

The authentic teacher literally holds the space for our highest possible manifestation in the face of the limiting self-concepts we were taught by our parents and culture. The teacher, not bound by our limited self-concept, sees a possibility that often exceeds anything we had imagined for ourselves.

The authentic teacher is always watching for unexpected openings in which skillful intervention may catalyze a profound shift in the student. He or she is like a personal (spiritual) trainer, providing the willing student with exercises that strengthen the spiritual muscles necessary to the student's progress in Self-development.

There may also be areas of potential development that the student has neither considered nor desired, but that nonetheless offer opportunities for both gratifying self-fulfillment and for service to others. In my own case, a request by my teacher to write a book in a highly condensed period of time, combined with my willing obedience, allowed a series of books and articles to be produced that have seemed to be of benefit to many people. At the same time, it provided me with a work vehicle for confronting false belief-structures that had kept me from fulfilling a childhood dream of being a writer. Such limited self-concepts keep us from expressing greater freedom and flexibility in all aspects of our lives and relationships, and deprive others of what we might otherwise offer.

One student was asked by her teacher if she ever sang. She responded, "Never." Three years later she was showcased at the Nice Jazz Festival – a high-profile event – still emotionally insecure, but now singing blues to the masses and feeding thousands of hungry souls. For most students the process is less showy, but equally powerful. Perhaps the individual has a great capacity to serve others selflessly but has always been too afraid to express her warmth, and the teacher provides a circumstance in which the disciple can practice giving what she has to offer; or somebody is deeply desirous of an intimate relationship but is too full of self-hatred to allow one to develop, so the teacher arranges circumstances in less threatening arenas in which the student can slowly build connections that pave the way for the possibility of a future relationship. The point is not *what* the specific exercise is, but breaking past preconditioned limitations that restrict us and keep us from our highest potential as human beings. It often takes someone outside of ourselves to perceive this for us and direct us so we can work through "stuck" places.

On our own we rarely engage in behaviors that are beyond our range of familiarity and comfort. The reason that accidents, death, illness, war and other tragedies are so powerful is that they are outside of our domain of control and propel us into new domains of possibility. Conscious obedience involves a voluntary agreement to allow more of those opportunities to be created for us.

Ultimately, our highest possibility is that which some people refer to as enlightenment, surrender, God. The spiritual path is the roughest road there is, strewn with obstacles and ever-deepening disillusionment, as the depth of our own falsity, suffering, deceitfulness, and perceived separation is revealed. Under such circumstances it is difficult to remember our soul's deepest longing and to align our lives in accordance with that longing. The true teacher will remember for us, ever calling to us on whatever levels we are receptive, or simply existing as an external expression of our own conscious wish to live lives of freedom and surrender.

Reasons Not to Obey

As beneficial as obedience to a true teacher can be, it cannot and should not occur before its rightful time and circumstance. There are many reasons we choose not to obey, and they are best considered with understanding, respect, patience, without judgement, and with an appreciation for rightful timing.

THE TEACHER'S LEVEL OF MASTERY IS NOT DESERVING OF OUR OBEDIENCE

Obedience should never be engaged in before one is confident in the teacher, especially if following the teacher's advice leads to life-altering choices. We may choose to study with a well-meaning, and perhaps even very good teacher, but one who is not transparent to Objective Will such that they are capable of directing our lives to the degree where we would benefit from obedience to their direction. Claudio Naranjo tells the story of a time during his initial three years of "enlightenment" during which he was able to provide students with suggestions for major life changes, such that their lives evidenced tremendously beneficial change upon following his direction, but how then his precision in providing direction eventually waned to such a degree that he stopped making suggestions altogether. There is value in obedience, but only to the teacher who clearly exemplifies a capacity – and an impeccable track record – of directing students well.

Before considering obedience to a teacher, we should focus our attention on becoming conscious disciples, for only through our own consciousness will we be able to sense the degree of mastery within a teacher accurately.[3]

FURTHER TRUST MUST BE BUILT

Trust involves two distinct processes: the trustworthiness of the teacher and our own capacity and willingness to trust. Both must be in position in order for an effective student–teacher relationship to take place. If we obey the wrong teacher, we may find ourselves in serious trouble.

When we choose to obey because of an adopted, ethical, spiritual mandate that tells us that "good students are obedient", our efforts are likely to be thwarted at some point because our gestures are coming from an ethic imposed from without, rather than from a calling from within. Our efforts are more likely to be fruitful through smaller "experiments" with obedience to the teacher – following a minor suggestion by the teacher wholeheartedly and without reservation, and then observing the results. When we finally decide to place our cards on the table, we should be sure that we are in the right game!

OBEDIENCE IS TOO HARD

Obedience is hard; too hard for many. When somebody we trust asks us to do something that is either far beyond our imagined capacity or which we do not

– and may never – understand, it is difficult. We cannot understand the ways and means of the mystery. We can only be as conscious as we are able to be in any circumstance. Sometimes the risk feels too great; other times we are more daring.

Even when we do trust the teacher, it is difficult to obey when we simply don't *feel* like doing what is asked. I recall a time when my teacher asked for volunteers to serve cocktails at a trade show for a German commercial photography firm at a conference center in Las Vegas for a week. It wasn't even a mystical request; it was practical. One of his students who owned a company that produced trade-show booths had an important contract and needed help. The task was about as unappealing as anything I could think of doing. I would rather have experimented with being a garbage collector or a homeless person on the street. I told him that I did not *want* to go, that if there were other volunteers I would rather not, but that I was willing if necessary.

In the end, one more person was needed, and he asked me to go, so I went. Through countless hours of serving beer with all the heartfulness I could muster (not because I was selfless but because I needed to make it bearable for myself), unanticipated conversations and interactions opened up, and not only was I able to serve a few of those suffering businesspeople in a way that was helpful to them, but through "trying on" the identity of a cocktail waitress for a few days I was able to see how smug my ego had become in its identity as a writer.

WE MAY NOT GET WHAT WE WANT

To choose to obey means that "I" may not get what I want. The question is, which "I" among the many within me is not getting what it wants? Anybody who gets deeply involved in a life of spiritual practice quickly discovers the many opposing forces within themselves that are at play in the soul's thirsty journey toward its source, and never are the forces of opposition and denial so evident as when one begins to work seriously with an authentic teacher.

The teacher's job is to devote him- or herself wholly to the "I" within the disciple who wants God or Truth. Nothing else. The teacher must skillfully work with the multiple aspects of psychology and psyche which support and express that emerging truth, as well as with those that appear to counteract the student's true aim. But the teacher's ultimate loyalty must be to the "I" that wants only God. When the student is not identified with the "I" that is the same as God or that seeks Union, the teacher's requests are likely to clash with what the student *wants* to do, or *feels* like doing.

There are times in my discipleship when I know that my teacher is asking something of me that will support my deepest longing and Truth, but I capitulate to seemingly "lower" desires anyway. At those times I may simply be indulging something that needs or wishes to be psychologically satisfied before I am willing to relinquish it. Who could ultimately judge such matters? I suggest that we simply be conscious and honest in relationship to them. In response to a student who was struggling with the clash between worldly desires and their desire for God, Arnaud Desjardins advised: "Leave *nirvana* for now, and cross the ocean of life."

Disobedience

In his early twenties, Krishna Das, now a popular musician on the Western *bhajan* circuit, traveled to India in search of God. A contemporary of the Western mystic Ram Dass (Richard Alpert), Krishna Das became deeply devoted to Ram Dass' teacher, Neem Karoli Baba, the Indian saint who is widely revered for his extraordinary realization, miracles, and compassion. Like so many fervent but inexperienced seekers before and since, Krishna Das devoted himself wholly to his teacher and his practice, leaving behind sex and relationships in a belief that they were obstacles to God, rather than acknowledging that it was his own fears that caused his renunciation.

Neem Karoli Baba, perhaps suspecting what was really going on in his still-youthful disciple, after three years of this informal "renunciation" sent Krishna Das to the United States to sort out his foreign visa and earn enough money so that he did not have to continue to live off of others. As is a common occurrence in such circumstances, no sooner had Krishna Das arrived in the land of power, distraction and sexuality, than his hormone-charged body predictably began to crave sex, power, and a wide range of experiences. He began touring with Ram Dass, and soon found himself in lust with a beautiful woman who came to live with him. A few months into this affair, he received a fax from India written by a close student of Neem Karoli Baba suggesting that he return to India.

As Krishna Das was but one of thousands of devotees of his master, he knew that such a personalized invitation was anything but casual. Still, by this point he was having *fun*, and although he swore he loved his master more than life itself, and as far as his conscious awareness was concerned he wanted God more than anything (including really great sex), he managed to convince himself that there were many important and justifiable reasons why he should wait just a little bit longer before returning to his life as a celibate monk in

India. He wrote his teacher and logically explained that he had not earned quite *enough* money to live in India for as long as he would like to; that whereas he had applied for his visa, it had not yet come; and that he hadn't fulfilled *all* of the requests his master had made of him when he had sent him to the West. As any true master who respects his disciple's free will would, Neem Karoli Baba lovingly acquiesced to his student's wishes. Three months before Krishna Das was to return to India, his master died. Krishna Das never saw or spoke with his living master again.

There will be poignant moments even in the most conscious discipleship in which the voice of the teacher seems to be in direct conflict with a strong inner voice or sensing, and these are extremely difficult junctures in the process of studenthood. Some people are able to make great gestures of obedience in relationship to the teacher – whether it involves the investment of money, or doing austere practices, or taking on daring tasks – but there are times for each of us when we get pushed up against the line, whether that line be our vanity, our material desires, or some idea or object or person we are attached to and unwilling to let go of, even though it is impeding our spiritual progress.

There was a time in my own process with my teacher in which I was about to make a conscious choice of disobedience because I was unconvinced of what he was asking me to do, although my experience of his recommendations until that time had been that of flawless accuracy on his part. I was discussing my decision with him, asking both him and myself, "Why, if I know that the choice of disobedience is a mistake, would I choose to do it anyway?"

"Because you don't *know* it is a mistake," he responded. "Just go ahead and do it. Test me. Test yourself. Test your practice. You didn't come here to do your spiritual life perfectly. The reason you came here was to make conscious experiments *and* mistakes, and then to learn from them."

Sometimes our greatest lessons of obedience are learned through disobedience. Mistakes are only mistakes when we do not grow from them. It is the very process of engaging and then wrestling with the principle and practice of obedience – not the flawless fulfillment of it – that deepens our understanding of what it means to obey the true Self that exists within each of us.

If our experiments with obedience are successful, we will have occasional experiences in which we notice ourselves becoming free of ourselves. We will note that our experiments are worthwhile and effective. Then the teacher will ask us to do something else we don't want to do, and we will again question whether or not obedience is worthwhile at all. But if the teacher is trustworthy, over time we will gain a reference for its value, and make further choices accordingly.

Blind Following vs Conscious Obedience

Because frequent abuses and disappointments occur between spiritual teachers and their students in the name of obedience, the process of conscious discipleship requires learning the distinction between surrender and submission, between conscious obedience in relationship to spiritual authority and blind following. Blind following is the expression of childish and unconscious discipleship; conscious obedience represents the fruits of mature studenthood. Unfortunately, the latter usually comes through one's repetitive mistakes with the former.

I was wrestling with the idea of obedience during the period when the infamous cult scandal of Heaven's Gate arose, in which cult leader Marshall Applewhite convinced 38 followers that a spaceship, hiding behind comet Hale-Bopp, would deliver them to the next phase of their lives after committing suicide by consuming lethal doses of phenobarbital and vodka. One night I was sitting in the ashram office pouring over articles about the event in various magazines and newspapers when my teacher came in and sat down. "According to the teachings of obedience you regard so highly", I challenged him, "if you asked us to commit suicide because a spaceship was going to take us to heaven, we should do it."

"That is the most preposterous and irresponsible thing you have ever said!" my teacher retorted, he who had expounded such sublime teachings on obedience now enraged. "If anyone who calls themselves my student would actually do anything that stupid, they should closely reconsider what they are doing here." He got up, walked across the office, through the door, slammed it and left.

There is a crucial distinction that needs to be made between obedience to something that *emotionally* feels outlandish – as in the case of the woman who was asked to be a world-class blues singer having never even performed in the elementary school chorus – and acts of aggression and insanity that involve violence, damage to one's body or health or to that of another, disregard of children and the like. We ourselves are ultimately accountable for all of our acts of obedience and disobedience, and we must constantly ask ourselves if we think we can live with (or die with, at an extreme) any given choice. If the answer is "no", it is far better to pass up a given opportunity to be obedient, confident that if our intention remains pure and strong, another chance will eventually be given us.

Layla, a long-term disciple of the renowned Rajneesh, recalls her profound ignorance and naïveté when first engaging with her master: how she would regularly and indiscriminately offer her time, money and emotional well-being at the whim of the commands of her teacher's senior disciples. Years after his death, she is once more considering involvement with a spiritual teacher, yet is understandably wary that she will again find herself in a compromised position. She is uncertain whether or not her subsequent years of maturity can withstand the temptation to capitulate to power in a childish way rather than from a conscious and informed perspective. She values the need for direct and personalized feedback from a spiritual teacher, but she still lacks confidence in her own capacity to engage with a teacher in a manner that will promote more growth than disillusionment.

Layla's predicament is valid; yet, paradoxically, it is her awareness of the dangers and temptations involved, combined with her years of unconscious obedience, that put her in a position finally to be able to engage in a process of conscious surrender if that is what she chooses to do. Her greatest asset on the path at this point is her knowledge of her own weaknesses.

SUBMISSION VS SURRENDER

When people warn against the danger of surrendering to a spiritual authority, they are actually referring to *submission*. Submission, even when enacted from sincere intentions, is what happens when psychologically insecure and needy human beings project and then cling to the notion of the spiritual teacher as savior or good parent, fully expectant that something outside of themselves can and will take responsibility for their liberation or the relief of their suffering. As in the Heaven's Gate example, my teacher's frustration at my interpretation of obedience was due to my inability to make a distinction between blind submission and conscious surrender. Surrender, or conscious obedience, can simply not arise when we are stuck in childish projections and behavior, unwilling to think for ourselves.

True surrender discovered through conscious obedience is a position of power, never of weakness. It involves an informed recognition and admission, ordinarily gained only through years of spiritual work, that as powerful, independent, and highly functional as we may be, we are still living under the unremitting dictate of egoic domination. This recognition, in the words of Gurdjieff, is that "human beings are machines" – that our functioning is overwhelmingly mechanical and that our true freedom lies only in the admission of that difficult reality, followed by a process of self-observation which allows essence to overcome our mechanicality and eventually sustain a position at the forefront of our consciousness.

This is where the function of the spiritual teacher enters the picture. The teacher is someone who sits outside of our own mechanical functioning and makes suggestions for what may seem to be irrational and impractical practices and activities, but which may nonetheless stimulate and elicit true essence and authentic spontaneity.

Fleet Maull – currently the director of Prison Dharma Network and the National Prison Hospice Association – was at one time the personal attendant of the great Tibetan master Chogyam Trungpa Rinpoche. He stayed by Trungpa Rinpoche's side for days and weeks at a time, and received direct personal teaching from him, as well as his master's intimate regard. He also secretly ran drugs to and from South America. While his life of promising discipleship flourished, his "other" life landed him in an infamous federal prison hospital for 14 years, where he worked as a teacher, taught meditation, and cared for dying prisoners. A few years into his imprisonment, he received a notice of his master's illness, and then his death. Instead of being by his beloved master's side as he died, Maull had to live it out in prison.

The shock of this event propelled him into a life of dedicated practice and conscious discipleship. In spite of having been literally held in the arms of his beloved teacher, physically caressed and encouraged to accept the love that was more true of him than his darkness, it was only upon incarceration that his true discipleship was initiated, and a life of mature practice began. Away from the protective scrutiny of the physical master, he finally understood in a real way that the external master represented his own conscience, or innate wisdom, and was ever inviting him to realize his own basic goodness or "Buddha nature". After his teacher's death, he knew he would have to find this nature on his own ... or not, and that the choice was his alone. He chose "yes", and in retrospect expresses tremendous gratitude for how the predicament he got himself into became the greatest gift of his discipleship. During his 14-year incarceration he introduced hundreds to a path of contemplative spirituality, and worked to reduce the suffering of many dying prisoners.

"Yet what could somebody do in order to really understand what you came to realize, short of the extremes you went to?!" was the obvious question asked of him.

"That is the million-dollar question" was Maull's only reply.

Ultimately, we are learning to obey a source of inner authority; thus, the question becomes: At what point have we mastered our egoic mechanism such that we start taking orders from within instead of from without? There is no answer to this question, although from interviewing Western practitioners from all traditions over many years, my general impression is that most people choose to listen to the inner authority far too soon. The ego is trying to get us at every turn. Whereas it may be true that we have gained a quality of inner mastery or reliability to a specific degree at a certain level, if we want to go further we will have to surmount a still-more subtle level of ego's barriers, and we do ourselves a tremendous disservice to assume too quickly that we are sufficiently prepared for the new level. The inner guru remains the ultimate authority, but the outer teacher is the one who awakens, trains, and refines the inner.

Furthermore, as one's practice and commitment to that which may be called Life, the Teacher, the Lineage, increases, new levels and domains of obedience emerge. For example, in Sufi Sheik Llewellyn Vaughan-Lee's spiritual school, there are no *written* rules or practices. Obedience is not discussed. Yet when I pursued this consideration, he suggested that in one's relationship to the teacher and to God, there is a vast and intricate objective "ethical code" which one must obey:

> *The ethics on this path are incredibly high. You're not even allowed, for example, to have a chair if you don't use it – that's considered stealing. If you keep an overdue library book, that is considered stealing. Maybe somebody else would need it more. You're not allowed to eat more food than you need because even the worms could use it. But it isn't imposed. Nobody tells you that you have to do it. It's not written down. But it becomes the way you want to live because then you entangle yourself less in the density of this world, and then you are free. Then you have more time to be with your Beloved. Things of the world don't hold you so tightly.*

Paradoxically, whereas we ordinarily think of obedience as giving up control, it is the vehicle to true spontaneity. When we operate only under the dictates of our own will, we have relative freedom: we can do what we want, when we want to, but the range of what that "freedom" includes is still subject to the confines of conditioned beliefs about who we are. When we practice conscious obedience in relationship to an authentic spiritual teacher – particularly against our own personal preferences – we exercise the "muscle" of essence and freedom which ultimately leads to objective spontaneity and obedience to inner authority.

The fact is that obedience to a teacher is a deeply personal issue, not a matter of conformity to a moral or ethical code. When we arrive at the moment of death, we won't get points for having been "good girls" and "good boys"; for having obeyed Mommy-Daddy-Teacher. As conscious disciples, we benefit from gaining a deep understanding of the principles of obedience and then experimenting with them in accordance with our own aspirations and perceived needs, making conscious choices about who and what best serve our soul's true longing.

We will need to be able to live and die with the choices we make.

Father Bruno Barnhart

Becoming God

Father Bruno Barnhart is a Camaldolese monk living in Big Sur, California. He is the author of *Second Simplicity: The Inner Shape of Christianity*, and *The Good Wine: Reading John from the Center*. His work has focused upon the Christian wisdom tradition and its rebirth in our time.

Q: I'm interested in learning about spiritual authority and discipleship from a Christian perspective.

BB: In Christianity, ideally, the mediation of the teacher is temporary. Ultimately, the only thing the teacher can do is acquaint you with who you are. The fullness is given to you in your initiation at your baptism. The teacher plays a secondary role. In the early centuries of monasticism, at the time of the Desert Fathers, a monk had what was called a spiritual father – the close, one-on-one relationship of disciple and master. The spiritual father was in touch with every aspect of the disciple's life. But in the West, monasticism became institutionalized. The abbott exists today as a symbol of Christ, but the relationship has become largely externalized and somewhat impersonal.

Q: Have you ever had a close relationship with a spiritual teacher?

BB: When I was a young monk I was looking for a spiritual father – a senior monk who could really adopt me, guide me, and lead me along the path. But I didn't find one. There was one monk whom I looked upon as a spiritual father, yet the intimate communion and deep, interior spiritual guidance wasn't there. It is rare to find that. Most of that has disappeared, at least in the Western Church. Around the time of the Reformation there were tremendous abuses of power in the Church. Now the individual living in the West will no longer accept a permanent and absolute authority of another human being over him.

Q: Yet if you had found your spiritual father, wouldn't his function precisely be to help you to discover your own authority?

BB: It would, and then he'd say, "Go. You don't need me anymore. I'll just be in the way." Even Jesus did that. He had his disciples around him for three years, and they all felt that they couldn't live without him. Then he disappeared. He gave them the Holy Spirit, as we say in Christianity, which means that what was in Jesus was discovered in them.

Q: It sounds like the principle of transmission.

BB: Yes, it's the transmission principle, but Christianity translates it to mean your immediate relationship to God or Christ.

Q: Why, if spiritual authority is outdated in Christianity, is there such a strong model of Jesus and his disciples?

BB: Let's look at Jesus. Jesus is divine and human at the same time. The point of this, which is very often missed by Christians, is that we are meant to be what Jesus is. The fathers of the Church would say that God became a human being in Jesus, so that human beings might become God. That's pretty strong, but it is at the core of Christian theology. Do you see the non-dual aspect of it? It's not non-dual consciousness like the Eastern traditions, where everything is seen as one, but more of a channeled non-duality. It becomes like a river, an organic thing. The non-duality is contained within a *body*.

Q: If I'm not mistaken, that sounds very much like the traditional teachings of the guru principle. The student and master are not separate, and the point of the relationship is to realize that you are that – that you are Jesus, in terms of our discussion.

BB: Then Jesus goes away so that the disciple can awaken as Jesus. Now that's not the common Christian teaching, but it's the heart of the Christian truth. In John's Gospel, Jesus can be seen as having a non-dual relationship with God when he says, "I am." He assumes that Divine identity, and then gives that same identity to us so that those words are also true of us. When we look at it that way, it's very similar to the Buddhist and Hindu traditions. The essence of the initiation of baptism is to drown in God and be reborn as that which Jesus *is*, and if you are what Jesus is, you have a non-dual relationship with God. All the teacher can do is help you to descend into that non-dual relationship with God and Christ.

Q: But many are baptized and very few seem to abide in that non-dual relationship with God.

BB: That's true. But I think there is a non-dual relationship which consists of living and acting in God no matter where one's consciousness is at. That is what faith is about. In faith, Jewish and Christian people relate to God as embodied beings, with limited consciousness. Yet this life of faith begins to be a non-dual participation in God. Christianity then takes a further step by making Jesus human and Divine at the same moment, so that one's faith puts them *in* Jesus in a unitive way, even when one is not conscious of it. I think there are a lot of simple people of great faith who live that way. They never have a great enlightenment experience. Yet their life of faith, paradoxically, is a life of non-duality.

Q: If that's the case, why are there still teachers? Weren't you the Prior at your monastery for 18 years?

BB: The teacher—student relationship is still very important. The role of the teacher is to help a novice through obstacles. A teacher guides them and shows them the pitfalls and helps them to discern their own inner movements. When the monastic life is a solitary life, there is a real danger [that you] start to see solitude as absolute. If ego identifies with that absolute, you can be in real trouble.

Q: How so?

BB: Think of living by yourself in a hermit's cell, listening *only* to God, attempting to live a purely interior life without any human interaction or feedback. There is something about it that really appeals to both the individualist and to the introvert, and it can lead someone into a spiritual cul-de-sac. Spiritual experiences, in that kind of lifestyle, may easily lead to ego inflation.

Q: Is that why you need the Prior?

BB: Yes. You need an authority to pull students back down to earth. In the old days, the Desert Fathers said, "If you see a young man climbing up to heaven by himself, grab him by the leg and pull him down." Christian tradition emphasizes the spiritual *descent*, but it's very hard for the male ego to make a descent. It needs to collide with something. The rule of St Benedict is built entirely upon obedience to the authority figure as a means to deal with the ego.

Q: That leads me to the question of obedience in your tradition. What do you think the limitation of obedience is, and what do you think its value is?

BB: At its worst, obedience can be a perfect suppressing of the emergence of the person. Certain people pick an external thing to obey and conform to as a substitute for a real response of the heart. Those are generally people who are submissive. They never dialogue about something they are asked to do, instead remaining as a child because they haven't allowed the conflict to become conscious.

Q: What is that conflict?

BB: There is a tension between my ego – my own ideas and preferences – on the one hand, and the external voice of authority (and ultimately of reality, or the will of God) – on the other. Ideally there should be a dialogue going on between those two poles within us, and if I suppress my ego to the extent that I don't permit that, I won't grow. Somehow ego has to be able to engage with the contrary reality, like Jacob wrestling with his mysterious opponent, rather than immediately surrendering and going limp.

Q: Is there another side?

BB: Of course. I think the value of obedience is that it can relate you directly to God through the mediation of somebody else. It also enables you to transcend your own will because the only thing that can reach into you and *really* get you is another human being. It is the only thing that will really find your ego and kill it. You can outwit almost anything else, since anything else can become a servant and tool of ego, but obedience to another human being can get in there and find it. A willing and conscious obedience can expose your ego perfectly to the transforming power of the Spirit, opening you to a will that is intelligent and flexible enough to find you. Then you can become a perfectly pliable instrument in the hands of the Spirit.

Q: What are the important lessons you have learned over your decades in the monastic tradition?

BB: Over the years, the "peak experience" of transmission or enlightenment disappears into the ordinary. I have become aware of a solid but unspectacular kind of spiritual growth in which the person becomes more and more able to do what he or she has to do. Divinization becomes manifest, paradoxically, as the person becomes genuinely human. Everything luminous and remarkable is disappearing, simply, into *what is.* Just as the honeymoon phase of a splendid love gives way to a day-to-day existence, the original charismatic experience disappears into the ordinariness of life. The Spirit incarnates itself in our bodily existence, becoming simply human. You can see a manifestation of the divine compassion, the divine "humanity" here. Spirit pours down into humanity, which devours it. Spirit does exactly what it must do: it permeates the ground like rain, disappears into the body of humanity.

CHAPTER 12

Imperfections in the Teacher

The purity of the guru is secondary to the purity of the student.

ANDREAS BRAUN

Teachers will be imperfect. What you need to be able to count on is them doing their job.

ARTHUR DEIKMAN

I know what it is to consider the possibility that my teacher is imperfect, even highly flawed. I have considered it many times. In fact, when students are afraid to entertain doubts about their teacher, I am slightly suspicious about their conviction. The capacity for intelligent skepticism – to doubt deeply and to follow that doubt to its end without spiraling into cynicism and negativity – can be a great asset on the path and is a skill that requires tremendous courage. Paradoxically, deep doubt can lead to a sense of inner confidence in a way that few things can, as that which survives doubt and ruthless questioning has the capacity to become a conviction that arises from within, rather than an adopted belief system imposed from without. When students are unwilling to look at imperfections, insisting upon an idealized notion of perfection in the teacher, the slightest expression of imperfection can be experienced as an internal avalanche so immense as to create a chasm, if not a complete break, in the relationship between them.

There came a point in my discipleship when I had doubts and frustrations about many things. I was bored with routine and practice, deeply discouraged by the dawning realization of how long integrated transformation takes, and wondering what I was doing with my precious life. I was vigorously contemplating questions such as: "Do I really want to live on an ashram?", "Am I sure that I want to practice in the ways my teacher has prescribed?", "How would I feel if, by chance, I were to do this practice for the next 20 years, only to discover there was some flaw in my teacher that I had overlooked?", "Am I certain that my choice to work with my teacher so intensively is current, and not an outdated commitment based upon a previous conviction?" My teacher had taught me about the depth of our mechanical conditioning, about ego's tendency to project and conform, and I wanted to make sure my whole relationship to him and the community was just not more of the same. I trusted that the path I was on was a *good* one, but was I certain it was the *right* one for me?

So I went to talk to my teacher about it.

"Why don't you just take a break from all this for a time?" he suggested.

I was taken aback by his totally unexpected suggestion, and immediately assumed he was testing me. "Why are you saying that? Is this some sort of strange guru test?" I asked defensively.

"No. It isn't. Why don't you follow your doubts through to their end? Go away for a while. Greece is lovely this time of year. You could go to the beach. Or move to some city – London, New York. I don't know what you would like to do, but why don't you do whatever you want, for as long as you want, and see what happens. You can come back any time."

"You're giving me a back door," I pressed further, still suspicious of his motivations. "I'm not going to fall for that guru trick. The better option is to stay here and break through this resistance."

"It's not about better or worse. It's about finding your own personal destiny within – or outside of – the tradition."

"But what if I lose everything?" I argued. "My conviction. My years of practice. My trust in the tradition."

"That's the worst-case scenario. Although it would feel terrible for a time, you'd get over it. If there is something inherently false in me or the tradition or your practice, much better to find out now while you're still young than after another 20 years of this."

His words were a song to my heart still hungry for experience, though I had not dared to imagine that a beach in Greece could be part of the trajectory of my spiritual unfolding! I had given the tradition six years of my life, and I wanted to find out for myself if there was anything I was missing. I am adamantly averse to the "blind-sheep" phenomenon so commonly found among gurus and in spiritual groups, giving teachers and their communities a bad reputation, and leaving those who are considering approaching such groups understandably wary. I wanted to be certain I hadn't unconsciously fallen into a blind-sheep mentality, and to be sure I was with a teacher who fully supported my own experimentation and freedom.

Within a week, I had gone from six years of being a semi-renunciate living on a desert ashram in a room the size of a cell with almost no belongings save a few boxes of clothes and a laptop, slated to spend the rest of my life there if need be, to living on a hilltop in the pristine hills of northern California, the proud owner of a used car, a room with a view, and far from the scrutiny of the external spiritual leader. Upon my own request, I had been cast out into the sea of worldly life, with no idea what awaited me.

Granted, the first couple of weeks were very odd – learning to use a debit card, navigating San Francisco traffic jams, grocery shopping and cooking for one person instead of 40, being alone. Whereas during my renunciate years I had been on book tours throughout the States, and research trips and conferences in Asia and Central America, being back in familiar California ready to challenge the context of my spiritual practice was a greater culture shock than I had experienced in years of traveling to and from foreign lands. I was in paradigm shock. But I knew what it was to be a traveler, and now once again I found myself with an internal one-way ticket, but where would this one lead to?

I was determined to discover and fulfill every latent and repressed desire I had experienced during my years as a card-carrying spiritual practitioner. I took my teacher's suggestion seriously, and I decided to challenge every spiritual ideal, practice, walk, talk, and internalized moral conviction I had taken on during my years of searching. I was ready to party: wine, men, salsa, flirting with power and fame. I had done it all before, but now it was time to try it once again while carefully observing the results of my experiments from the perspective gained from years of dedicated and disciplined practice. "To experience consciously within limits" was my mantra, provided me by Arnaud Desjardins – words his master, Swami Prajnanpad, had once used to guide him.

But what were the limits? Each time I feared I had gone too far, I would consult with my teacher about my activities, only to be met with a version of, "Don't ask me. You went out to discover that for yourself." He was right, and I was grateful for the freedom.

So I took another trip around the world. I was nostalgic for the life of a backpacking traveler. As I romped from exotic temples to coral beaches, I often thought of the journey as Le Tour de Emptiness – and not the spiritual kind of emptiness, either. It was empty of purpose, conviction, fulfillment ... yet that discovery itself become its value.

At one point during this journey, I found myself on Paradise Island – an exquisite half-acre land mass of unblemished perfection placed perfectly in the center of the China Sea. I had spent the morning with new friends and two Rastafarian boatmen snorkeling in celestial coral reefs and prancing around the beaches of various local islands, and was now awaiting my lunch of freshly caught fire-baked rare fish. Sipping a fine Filipino beer, smoking my first cigarette in years, I was highly conscious of the fact that by conventional standards I should be on top of the world, having achieved the height of worldly pleasure and splendor.

Treasuring my fleeting nicotine high, I was contemplating the fact that no scenario could be more idyllic than my present one, when suddenly the song *Suzanne*, my favorite piece by my musical hero, the poet-songwriter Leonard Cohen, came sounding in my ears. I thought I was having an auditory hallucination, and smiled to myself at the power of the mind. But then I noticed that the others with me were swaying to the music, and realized it was real – that even here in my precious, manifest fantasy, Leonard Cohen had made an impact. I was astounded by the brilliance of universal intelligence, to have orchestrated such a personalized packet of experience for me, and I began to laugh hysterically – to the bewilderment of the others around me, who were of course oblivious to my inner experiments.

Swooning in the sensations of sensual contentment, the question of the hour was evident: Is external paradise what I want? Does it bring happiness? Is it the fulfillment I have been seeking since the age of five, if not since forever? As exquisite as I felt in my tailor-made paradise, and as unashamed as I was of my deep gratification and appreciation for the opportunity to experience such pristine beauty, the answer was clear: No. Outer paradise does not create inner nirvana.

At another point in Le Tour de Emptiness, I was in Varanasi, India. I had gone there specifically to engage in a solitary two-week meditation at the ancient cremation grounds along the banks of the Ganges River – where sacred fires have been burning bodies every day for 10,000 years, promising believers the most holy and sanctified passing from this life to the next. I had planned to sit wrapped in a shawl as a *sadhu*; to contemplate death as hundreds of bodies were burned before me, inhaling the putrid smoke of burning flesh and turning toward, rather than away from, my inevitable future. Yet within hours of beginning this retreat, I had been discovered by the local hustlers, who attempted to swindle money out of me for a pretend hospice, and I had further attracted their wrath by trying to warn other foreigners against falling for their scam. This rendered any chance of uninterrupted meditation virtually impossible. Besides that, I experienced the burning of the bodies as very natural, so much a part and parcel of life that it did not unravel me nearly as much as the plague of crickets that had hit the city – millions of them – followed by pre-monsoon rains, which had arrived unexpectedly early and left the already-sizzling city, with its temperatures of around 120 degrees, smelling pungently of reconstituted urine.

Meanwhile, I had been given a challenge by two young Israeli friends I had made along the way, who were also wrestling with the guru question. Intelligent and intense, these two had suggested to me that if my relationship with my teacher was real, and that if I wished my present experiment to be complete, I should be able to throw my teacher out of my system completely without leaving a trace, and then see what came back.

I thought their challenge fair, so I made internal preparations and went down to the edge of the Ganges, where I lodged myself behind a staircase in an attempt to find some relative solitude amidst the Varanasi madness. I was ready to stay there all day, and all night if necessary, in order to engage in the task of throwing the guru out of my system.

I gathered all my courage and took the plunge ... or tried to. It didn't work. I tried again, mustering more force, and then again, attempting even deeper surrender. I was trying to throw my teacher out, but as I did I felt I was throwing *myself* out, and it simply didn't work. It was like attempting to remove your own hands, or trying to take the subtle heart from the physical one. It cannot be done because there is a fusion and interconnectedness so intricate that one does not function separately from the other. I intuited that the process of union and fusion between student and teacher had already begun; that there truly was no separation. My teacher was in me, as me. Not his personality nor my own, but as a fusion, or connectedness, of consciousness itself. A sigh of long-awaited relaxation and a sense of profound contentment arose within me. I had gone as far as I was able to go, had stretched my capacity further than I had ever done before, and had discovered something new.

Whether we participate directly in a relationship with a Hindu guru, a Zen roshi, or a Native American shaman, the teacher we follow is not the human person, but the representative of a body of teaching. Depending on the tradition, through practice or transmission or grace or alchemical physics those teachings become a part of us. The transformation they engender penetrates right into our cells, our consciousness, our very own minds and bodies – and the thoughts and movements they produce as a result. The conglomeration of conditioning we once called "ourselves" becomes refined, changed, merged and infused with the body of teachings we often mislabel as "the teacher".

I will say once again that we must take full responsibility for our relationship with the spiritual teacher. If we are going to go for perfection – whatever we imagine that to be – we should focus on cultivating our own perfection while doing our best to ensure that the one who is guiding us is reliable, sincere, and capable. The teacher is human and will inevitably have accompanying human imperfections. We simply need to decide how we will come to terms with this fact, and what is ultimately right for ourselves. When we get to the gates of death, there won't be anyone there giving out gold stars for disciples who were good little girls and boys in relationship to their teacher.

What Is Perfection?

In considering how to navigate the issue of imperfections in the spiritual teacher, we must first consider what our unconscious images of perfection are. This is a very difficult intellectual and psychological challenge. Western biblical images of God promise a benign authority who spares His children if they refrain from sin. The concept of perfection the Bible portrays has not been reflected in people's lives in the manner promised, leaving many, consciously or unconsciously, to believe themselves to be shameful sinners, or betrayed by a lie of God.

On the level of democracy and government, people have been met by similar failed promises and betrayals (which particularly affect the psyche when the so-called authorities lie, steal, and kill innocent people). Betrayals occur on the level of family as well, as the child psyche projects the role of God/Goddess onto the mother and father to a degree that can never be fulfilled. When the idea of the "perfect master" is then introduced in the West, how else could people respond other than with skepticism and mistrust – particularly when it becomes clear that the teacher has a personality that most likely includes an array of neurotic behaviors and conditioning? The fact is that Western teachers have been raised in the same spiritually devastating cultural matrix as the rest of us have. Some have emerged more affected, some less. The value of authentic teachers is that regardless of their conditioning they remain capable of transmitting potent teachings and energies.

To accept "perfection" in the realm of spiritual mastery, we must first consciously deconstruct our images of psychological perfection. Our capacity to perceive perfection in the teacher should be broad enough to include infinite possibility, while realistic enough to respect and include the laws of human incarnation, conditioning, and psychology.

What Is Your Bottom Line?

The question of whether the teacher is perfect is not really the issue. It is safe to assume that most Western teachers will not comply with our mental concept of perfection and therefore will eventually "betray" us, or at least betray our projections and expectations of them. We *will* become disillusioned at some point, at some level. It may be more useful to consider that the teacher *transmits* perfection, rather than that he or she is perfection itself. The question, then, is how much do imperfections in the teacher interfere with this transmission? Does their clarity outweigh their obstructions to a significant enough degree that we as students can trust them to make our investment of energy and learning worthwhile?

To ask whether the teacher's imperfections are too significant to make it profitable for *us* to study with him or her is distinct from making an objective evaluation of his or her teaching capacity in general. For this reason we should be careful not to evaluate a teacher's value for someone else too quickly, nor to become righteous about our own choices. It is really not a matter of right or wrong regarding which of the teacher's imperfections are worthy of amnesty in the Spiritual Supreme Court and which are not, but what serves a given student's needs. It is again a circumstance for which the rulebook just does not suffice, because the issue is a deeply personal one.

Ultimately, the question comes down to: What is our bottom line? What can we handle and what can we not? Drugs? Sex? Prudishness? Puerileness? Dirty jokes? Poverty? Inflation? Vanity? Pride? Righteous indignation? Demanding rigor? We can rest assured that somewhere there will be a "bottom line". There will be *something*.

For example, let's say a married Zen teacher has an affair with another woman. On one hand, this does not necessarily mean that we cannot trust him in his function of spiritual master, as it is likely that our personal relationship to him and the transmission he offers have nothing to do with either sex or his personal life. On the other hand, if we have been betrayed in our own past and are using the relationship with the teacher in an attempt to unravel core beliefs around betrayal – perhaps through an unconscious erotic transference onto the teacher – then the teacher's weakness or apparent lack of integrity in this arena may be an important consideration.

Another example: Some teachers discourage the practice of relationships, especially marriage and childraising, suggesting that these constructs inhibit the optimal possibilities for awakening, at least within the traditions they are conveying. If we find ourselves drawn to such a teacher and we aspire to having a family, we must ask ourselves such deeply personal questions as: Do I trust the teacher's assertion that an intimate romantic relationship and/or children would interfere with my path to God or Truth? Is my connection with this particular teacher so strong that I'm willing to sacrifice my wish for a family? If I do make this sacrifice, am I likely to resent the teacher in the long run? Am I willing to attempt to negotiate with the teacher about this issue so I can proceed in my spiritual life in a way that includes my desire for a family?

In what domains do we personally require the teacher to teach in accordance with our own subjective and psychological needs and preferences in order for our studenthood to be fulfilling and worthwhile? In what areas can we accept either apparent or actual imperfections, and in which do we have limits? How much capacity do we have to tolerate our own ambiguity when it is unclear whether the teacher's behaviors are, in fact, expressions of imperfection or simply in conflict with values that are a product of our own cultural and psychological conditioning? What do we *need* and what do we *want*? Are we willing, as Mick Jagger suggests, to sacrifice some of our wants in order to get what we need? The conscious disciple asks these questions of him- or herself until he or she gets satisfactory answers, then assumes responsibility for the outcome that follows.

Furthermore, when we do hit our bottom line, how do we choose to engage with our teacher with respect to this blockage in the relationship? Do we attempt to repress it? Do we immediately leave? Do we consider attempting to talk about and perhaps even negotiate "terms" of some kind with our teacher?

I do not believe it is wrong to argue with one's teacher, and believe it preferable to either angry and victimized reactivity, or remaining stuck in a childish need to be a "good disciple" in order to receive the love we imagine the teacher will bestow upon us if we do everything right. Gilles Farcet, assistant teacher in the lineage of Arnaud Desjardins, suggests having a "frank, open, and clear discussion" with the teacher regarding the issue in question.

I have repeatedly spoken with long-term "senior" practitioners who are frustrated because they feel that "dissent" in the form of questioning the teacher is not allowed within the community. It is true that there are teachers who are intolerant of being challenged – some are great saints who are simply unwilling to appease disciples" psychological needs, and others are individuals with unconscious psychological "holes" that they are unwilling (unconsciously, of course) to allow to be uncovered. Still, in many other instances it is the disciples' fear of taking the leap into the well of emotion that comes when they challenge the fabric of their psychological relationship with their teacher – that weave of clarity and projection, godliness and humanness – that constitutes their unwillingness to risk confrontation with the teacher. They would rather assume that the teacher cannot handle being challenged than admit to their fear-driven projections of confrontation and rejection which continue to dominate them so many years into their discipleship.

Imperfections in the Student

There is a story of a man who went looking for the perfect teacher. He finally found him and asked to be his disciple. The perfect teacher responded, "Has it never occurred to you that the perfect teacher requires the perfect disciple?" Even after our questions about the teacher's perfection have largely abated, they will continue to arise from time to time. But in order to sustain a position of empowered, conscious discipleship, at some point our attention must shift from the teacher's imperfections to our own. For, truly, the teacher's imperfections, as long as they do not inhibit our own growth, are his or her own responsibility, and problem, to work out. Conversely, no matter how perfect the teacher and how much he or she can point us in the direction of our own liberation, we are and must always be fully responsible for our own imperfections.

After many years of apprenticeship to and apparent trust in my teacher, I passed through a period in which I questioned him and the community around him with intensive scrutiny and unabridged criticism. He and I talked extensively through letters and in conversation, and I argued that I believed every disciple must exercise similar scrutiny to avoid the dangers of blind following. In response, Lee told me to question and challenge him and the community as much as I wanted, to the degree I desired, and for as long as I wished ... and then, when I was finally ready to, to trust unreservedly and unconditionally in order to receive the full possibilities of discipleship.

Fullness sees fullness; emptiness sees emptiness. The eyes of mistrust see one facet of the diamond; the eyes of faith see another. But it is the eyes of discrimination, pointed inward, that are the most indispensable of all.

"It is only in taking into account who you are as a disciple", suggests Arnaud Desjardins, "that you should consider what type of guru can you legitimately hope to meet, and what are you then entitled to expect." Our focus should be on our own growth, our maturity, our responsibility, our increasing capacity to mine riches from mountains. When this is our focus, we will naturally attract spiritual authorities of equal integrity who are willing to grow continually and take responsibility for their own actions. Armed with the willingness to accept our own imperfections, we know how to accept imperfection in others without blaming them or feeling victimized by them. Should we then find we are in the presence of a teacher who is unprepared to fill our spiritual needs, we can consider what it is within ourselves that attracted us to him or her. We can let these teachers go, if necessary, and forgive them for the imperfections of their humanness without becoming disillusioned or needing to reject all spiritual authorities because we feel so let down by the failure of our own projection of perfection.

Neither perfection in the student nor in the teacher is a requirement for successful *sadhana*. What is required is sincerity and discrimination and, ironically, a tolerance for *imperfection*. At the end of the day, expressions of human integrity – including reliability, tenacity, mutual devotion, forgiveness, and faith – far outweigh any projection of imagined perfection.

Llewellyn Vaughan-Lee
The Bond with the Beloved

Llewellyn Vaughan-Lee is a Sufi Sheik in the Naqshbandi lineage, and the successor to the Sufi master Irina Tweedie. He is the founder of the Golden Sufi Center in Inverness, California, and is the author of over a dozen books including *The Bond with the Beloved, The Circle of Love*, and *The Face Before I Was Born.*

Q: The topic I am addressing in this book is a deep consideration of the issue of spiritual authority and discipleship.

LVL: You will be totally misunderstood.

Q: I want help to elucidate this topic from a variety of perspectives in order to increase the likelihood of conveying some understanding on the matter.

LVL: I'm sure you do! So are you proposing a six-volume book? You see, in the West it's become very complicated because spiritual authority is understood on the wrong levels. The difficulty for me in talking about this is that it has never been a problem for me personally. I met Mrs Tweedie when I was 19 years old. When you encounter a real spiritual authority, something in you just bows down. I was always a rebel in school and never accepted any authority and got into a lot of trouble because of that, so it was a bit strange suddenly to find myself in the presence of somebody to whom I would unconditionally do anything she said. But something in me just bowed down and accepted her authority.

Q: Yet people are afraid to agree to such a relationship because they fear they will be taken advantage of in some way.

LVL: A real master is totally free and wants to give you freedom, and therefore has no interest in imposing his or her will on you. He or she doesn't even have any will because their will is the Will of God. What is not understood is that a real teacher will never threaten the free will of a human being because they know that it is a gift from God. A real teacher will never force somebody to do something against their will because they respect the freedom of the human being. Before the master tests a human being, he or she has to give permission to be tested. He or she has to say "Yes." Because certain things can't be done to a human being, spiritually, without the human being saying, "Yes, do with me as thou wilt."

Q: What can't be done without permission?

LVL: The human being has to be turned inside out, has to be burnt to ashes, and a master can't do that to a human being unless they say "yes." They don't have the right to. Because everybody is free. The disciple, at each place along the way, is given a choice: Do you want to continue, do you *not* want to continue? The teacher is there to open your heart, to tear you apart and feed you to the lions of love. But not everybody wants that. They would prefer to argue about authority dynamics. It's so petty and so irrelevant. There are some souls that come into this world already surrendered to God. There is a desire to be with God that overrules any human desire. But those people are rare. Most people say they want but they don't want. This is the whole struggle of the spiritual path – do they want to surrender, or do they not want to surrender? Do they want the world? Do they want a love affair? Do they want all the illusions that come up? The teacher has to respect their free will in regards to each of these issues.

Q: The free will you speak about seems very different than a teacher's freedom. Is it really free or just some mechanical function?

LVL: You have the choice to say yes to God or to say yes to your ego. And it's a very definite choice. I have seen people choose – not necessarily knowing that they have chosen – but I've seen it. They rapidly drift away from the path, and suddenly they are back in the world. Maybe they get something they always thought they wanted like a new career, or a new lover in their life, and they don't know that they have said no, but they have said no. They were given a choice.

Q: Even if they don't know they were given a choice?

LVL: They know somewhere within. It depends how strong the longing is in the human being, and how much pushes them from within. It is said that even until the last initiation, the teacher does not know what choice the disciple will make. The disciple can say yes, or the disciple can say no. It *has* to be like that.

Q: What is the function of the teacher?

LVL: People make the mistake of thinking that spiritual power is about telling somebody what to do. Spiritual power is about being able to take a human soul and turn it back to God, to be given the authority to work with the soul of a human being, to work in the secret places of the heart that belong only to God. That is *real authority*. And that requires tremendous humanity. In the West, individuality is so important and we project that into this relationship with the teacher and make a mess of it. We stir it up and get confused, and fight imaginary demons, but the teacher wants nothing from the disciple, because the teacher is free. How can the teacher want anything from a disciple? If they do, they're not a teacher because they're not free. But the disciple projects into this empty space of the teacher all of their psychological dramas. They find something that the teacher said that they disagree with, and then they fight about it and go off and say, "The teacher said this and this and this." Maybe the teacher did and maybe the teacher didn't. It really doesn't matter. The disciple is given the opportunity to play out all of their dramas, all of their psychological problems, and some people get stuck in the psychology of it all. And I've seen that happen. They walk away angry and resentful. And that's fine too, because human beings are free. Those who don't walk away – who begin to see that there is something else underneath – start to find what is there. They get a little bit closer to themselves, to their own true nature. They walk another few steps on the path and the teacher just watches.

Q: How do you handle people's psychological projections onto you?

LVL: I did discover people like to play power games against me, but I also discovered that "It takes two to tango." If I don't involve myself in it, then there is no game and the person is left chasing his or her own shadow. I have other things to do with my time. You see, the relationship of the teacher to the disciple is just love. The love is present there at the beginning and the love is present there at the end. As a teacher, you see the disciple's potential to realize.

You have no interest in playing authority games. Occasionally you have to be a bit rude – to wake something up in them. Sometimes they take it right and sometimes they don't, but that's up to them. If they don't want to remain a student they are welcome to go. Sometimes they come back after a few months or a few years. Sometimes they don't, and that's fine too.

Q: Tell me about your teacher.

LVL: I went from upper middle-class, English boarding school, to sitting at the feet of a woman intoxicated with God. And I stayed there. It was my only reality. My wife and I lived and stayed in the same house with Mrs Tweedie for 10 years, and she was always under orders from her teacher. So we lived in a house with somebody who was under orders. And there was never a question. We couldn't have lived there if we didn't jump when we were told to jump. What I'm trying to say is that with *real authority*, you can't question it.

Q: How should a student work with their struggles?

LVL: It's different for each of us and a mystery as well. The moment you try to crystallize it, it's like a dream, like a butterfly. The moment you try to hold it, it's gone. Spiritual life is alive! One day it's like this, the next day it's like that. The Sufis say it has more to do with inner attitude. There is no rigidity. This is why it is so difficult for people in the West. They want to be told what to do. They want to remain like children, so they project the father or the mother onto the teacher. Then there is an inevitable authority conflict and all sorts of exciting dynamics. But spiritual life is *not* about that. It is about catching this golden thread of your own destiny, and looking for the signs of God everywhere. Those hidden signs in yourself, in the outer world, listening to your dreams, your intuitions, what books come your way, what your teacher says and what your teacher doesn't say. The moment you try to crystallize a spiritual path in the rules of this world you've lost it. Because the whole purpose of the spiritual path is you attune to something which isn't quite in this world, which is faster than the vibrations of this world, which isn't caught in crystallized patterns.

Q: Given the ambiguity of it all, how should a student proceed?

LVL: You will attract the experiences you need. You will learn what you need to learn. If you need to learn to be deceived by a charlatan, a charlatan will deceive you. You will learn something and you will go on. And the next time, if your *karma* allows, you will find a real teacher. It is so simple. It is your attitude that matters. The light of the higher self will guide you where you need to go. If your attitude is correct then you will see what you need to see. You will get the experiences you need to get. And that's the way it is. It is the attitude of the disciple that matters.

Q: Can you do it without a teacher?

LVL: You can't do it on your own. You need a certain energy – what Sufis call the *grace of the guru* – to reach reality. It is given into the heart, given to the higher organs of consciousness. That's what the teacher does. The teacher makes sure that you are living in a way that doesn't interfere with this inner process so that you can develop, get in touch with, and awaken to your higher consciousness. That's all. Those who want to find the way to God will find the way to God, because God wants them to find the way. He will guide them and He will show them the way. Even if it's not apparent. Even if it's not visible at the beginning. He will give them hints. He will give them signs. He will talk to their hearts. That is how it happens and that's how it always has happened since the beginning of time. And you can't convince anybody else about it, because you either have experienced it and you know it's real, or not. It is like trying to explain the effect of being drunk to somebody who has never tasted wine. You can't. You can write books about it, but being drunk is something else. When you have sat at the feet of a true spiritual teacher – it doesn't even have to be *your* teacher – you know. Something inside you knows. And you can't explain how or what. The mind can argue with it and the personality can defend itself against it, but it's *real* and you know that it's real.

Q: What do you do until that clarity arises?

LVL: You know, once you have really meditated it is so fulfilling. That's why all these power dynamics seem so odd to me. Why would anybody want to engage [in] messy power dynamics when they could go into meditation and be with their Beloved? Why?

Section Five

For the Glory of Love

Separation exists purely and wholly for the glory of Love.

The authentic teacher will only and always empower the disciple, urging him or her toward the expression of fullest possibility. The primary job of the true teacher is to conquer the student's current enslavement to egoic domination, releasing him or her into an ever-widening identification with consciousness itself, and the teacher's suggestions and interventions are singularly designed to serve this end. The source of true power is always within, and every authentic teacher knows this. Beyond this, however, lies the possibility for a magnificent celebration of Love between student and teacher. Those who have tasted the nectar of this Love implicitly understand it as a dynamic reciprocity, embedded in union but manifested through apparent separation; its essence impersonal, while its expression profoundly personal. Love of the One is experienced by the Two, and extends itself to all. Both student and teacher are slaves to the same source, and thus experience their essential equality while cherishing apparent separation in order to bask together in a celebration of the glory of Love.

CHAPTER 13

The Source of True Power

*You receive exactly what you give ... you take all, you accept all without
any sense of obligation. Your attitude toward life is the attitude of one
who has the right to make demands and to take – who has no need to pay
or earn. You behave that all things are your due – simply because it is you.
None of this strikes your attention, yet this is precisely what keeps one
world separate from another.*

JEANNE DE SALZMANN

It was a sizzling, irritating afternoon sometime in those first months with Yogi
Ramsuratkumar – the days before he was discovered by the whole world, and
we still sat with him in a small group. My mind was obsessing over my own
spiritual inadequacies, my eyes fixated on a spot on the ceiling. I was begrudg-
ingly contemplating the fact that, as wondrous as this saint who sat before me
appeared to be – his realization so undisputed that the great *Shankaracharyas*,
the keepers of the Hindu faith, had traveled from all corners of the subcontinent to honor him on his birthday – the reality remained that he was He and I
was me, and there wasn't a hell of a lot in common between us. He had surrendered his mind, vanity, pride, selfishness, greed, and attachment in order to
serve humanity, while I became infuriated when the guy in the local cow-shack
coffee shop charged me seven cents for a cup of coffee that he only charged
the Indians five-and-a-half cents for. Yogi Ramsuratkumar sat wrapped in blankets enduring the 120-degree heat, pouring out compassion to all he encountered, while I could not travel to the market without internally, and sometimes
externally, cursing rickshaw drivers, beggars, vendors, leering men, and
whichever sun god in the Hindu pantheon thought up the Indian summer. He
was preoccupied with the healing of all beings in the cosmos – seen and
unseen, animate and inanimate – while I was obsessed with myself.

Suddenly my focus was jolted back to Yogi Ramsuratkumar, pulled by the
force of objective command. As I turned toward him, I saw a look on his face
that blazed straight through my chest, burning all my mental garbage to ash in
an instant. I quickly looked behind me to see what extraordinary expression
of manifest reality could possibly have catalyzed this most naked expression of

beauty I had ever seen. There was no one behind me. I looked again. No one. Nothing ... "Holy shit," I gasped internally. "He is looking at *me*."

He was looking at me. He was *bleeding* love at me. Not a sappy, sentimental love. Not the all-encompassing, impersonal love of a god to all of his children. What I saw was the deeply personal, intimate, direct expression of a heart broken open upon seeing itself reflected in another. It was a love that included every "sin" I had ever committed – a love that was fully aware of each wicked, demented, and vindictive thought I had ever directed toward another or myself; of all my imagined and actual inadequacies; of all my crimes of ignorance and unawareness; even of the ways I would continue to hurt people in the future out of my own blindness and fear. Love without reason. Love without conditions.

I had traveled 20 countries and five continents. I had had lovers of every exotic creed, met mystics of all traditions, found God in secret pockets of nature few people even believe exist ... but I had never witnessed anything remotely near this, much less directed toward me. It was my Self, seen for the first time in the reflection of the Other.

Although I tacitly understood that it was still the beginning of the beginning, I knew Love could never rightfully be denied again, no matter if it took the rest of my life and beyond to come to rest in that knowledge. That evening, eyes still puffy, hands still shaky, I took out my twice rain-soaked, cheap Indian notebook and scribbled an insufficient tribute to the moment I knew would fade, but the reality of which I would be responsible to for the rest of my life.

> *I was moved to tears. It was due to the feeling, deep, deep within, that my soul is now being taken care of: a deepest knowing that I have been found. Even now I cry. Never alone again. Never alone again. A past of imagined craziness, believed inadequacies ... erased in an instant. It is all gone. Now comes years and years of hard work and a new kind of suffering, but if I do not cease to know, to believe I am being held, it will be different.*

Five summers later I am sitting in the funky, 15-foot trailer that is as old as I am and that has become my bedroom and work studio. It is stationed in the sandy parking lot of my teacher's ashram in Arizona. I am wearing a damp yellow bikini that I hose down by the garage each time it dries out. Table fan on, I pass hour after hour with my fingers on the keyboard while the pores of my skin sweat out the Arizona desert heat as the pores of my still-distrusting mind sweat out the old, false beliefs that I am inept, inadequate, lacking in knowledge, incapable of manifesting the high capacity my teacher insists I am capable of.

It is my fourth book. This time Lee has asked me to write about "the error of premature claims to enlightenment". I am once again certain that *this time* he has surely gone off his rocker, and I tell him as much. *This time* he has utterly overestimated my abilities. Given the fact that since the very day I met him he has systematically destroyed every false idea I had about what enlightenment is, what spiritual life is about, even what it means to be fully *human*, how the hell am I supposed to now write about enlightenment, much less about those who claim it prematurely? I tell him that this time he is being totally unrealistic, and, as each time before, he tells me I don't have to do it. And this time, once again, I choose conscious trust in his seemingly limitless faith in me over my conditioned, ego-engraved convictions of personal inadequacy.

As I begin to ascend the internal Everest that this particular book represents to me in my writing career, the daemons of denial wage warfare with the Self upon the battlefield that is my body. My only grace is my stubbornness, as my obstinate but still-moving fingers gesture to universal intelligence a refusal to capitulate to perceived limitation, trusting my teacher to estimate my capacity more accurately than I can. Frustration is my daily companion as, at many points in the writing, I find myself not only at a loss for words, but at a loss for some piece of knowledge necessary for the book, at which point I demand of whatever universal force that commanded my teacher to ask me to write this book that *it* supply the required information. Although I cannot prove it, I tacitly comprehend the fact that the book has somehow already been written in an unseen world, and it is my job to midwife it into concrete reality.

I would love to say that at these moments I choose to appeal to Saraswati – Goddess of Wisdom – to bestow knowledge upon me, and she then descends in a beatific cloud, caresses my fingers and reveals all knowledge through them. But it is not like that. At these moments, all there is to do is endure tremendous tension in the body, use all internal weapons to keep the daemons even inches at bay, keep the fingers on the keyboard, and literally *insist* that whatever gods or gurus or whoever the hell runs the show should write what is needed in order to serve the reader. I curse the gods. I tell them I don't even know if I believe in them, but that they must work regardless. And then knowledge comes. It does not shower itself in glittering rainbows of grace; it comes up in hacking coughs and gasps. But it comes.

I finally perceive the source of this knowledge, and with this realization comes a sober, unsentimental, humbling awe for the guru-function and how it operates in and through my life and body. I understand that the seed of the divine, or Truth, lies dormant within us, awakened to greater or lesser degrees. The guru or true teacher is someone in whom that seed is more awakened than it is in myself. In the meeting of guru and disciple, the more awakened force sparks the lesser awakened, much as a flaming candle ignites the wick of an unlit candle upon contact. Whenever that moment occurs, whether the process is conscious or unconscious, transmission has taken place. The teacher has catalyzed the dormant energy of Truth within the disciple. At that moment the process is both complete and is only beginning. For whereas the transmission is alive, it has yet to emerge and be integrated. A lifetime, or even lifetimes, of false conditioning obscure its transparency and consistent expression. The whole process of spiritual *sadhana*, or practice of purification, awaits the student who is committed to allowing the transmission of Truth to express itself through the vehicle of his or her own body.

My teacher has not asked me to write books to serve humanity, though that is a most beneficial side-effect. Taking orders from his Boss – whether we call that authority Universal Intelligence, Transmission, Truth, or Love – he has requested this clearly difficult and painstaking task of me to serve the unfolding of my optimal capacity in incarnation. In my rare moments of true prayer, I have asked both Yogi Ramsuratkumar and Lee to give me *Everything* as quickly as possible. I have told them that I will endure whatever pains and sufferings are required in order to serve according to the highest possibility available to me in this lifetime. I have let them know that I might scream and fight and resist and probably act in ways that appear as though I am retracting my vows, but that they should ignore all of it, and persist in the shared task we have agreed upon.

And they have persisted, according to my request, giving me work at the highest level my body-mind can handle, insisting that the seed of transmission express itself. I have gradually come to recognize that once these seeds of transmission have been expressed through the written word and, particularly after I have shared them with the world at large, I become responsible to that knowledge. This comes as a great, and largely unwelcome, surprise to the ego, which still wishes to enact spiritually adolescent and self-gratifying behaviors. Whereas I do not fulfill this new obligation much of the time, it does not lessen the demand. The tension between my former self, with its limiting habits and tendencies, and my true capacity is as uncomfortable as it is creative, and will ever nag me until I fulfill my highest possibility. A thorny blessing which I would never wish to be otherwise.

The benefit of the manifest teacher is that he or she can orchestrate a highly individualized transformational "packet" according to the needs and abilities of each student, a packet that diminishes the power of obstacles and augments the student's strengths. Whether the teacher supports the student in becoming a famous rock star or a loving parent, a true teacher would never take away the student's own power, capacity, or objective autonomy, but does precisely the opposite. The authentic master serves as a fountain that directs power into our lives. The fountain flows endlessly, in excess and abundance; yet we must make ourselves increasingly receptive to that outpouring. Otherwise we will continue to squander the resources of transmission available to us while complaining that grace and transmission are not present in our lives. In the words of George Bernard Shaw, we will become "a feverish, selfish little clod of ailments and grievances complaining that the world will not devote itself to making [us] ... happy". A false teacher will energetically feed off of the student's energy; the true teacher will dig the well within the student's psyche until it is overflowing to the point that its abundance saturates everything in its vicinity. It can be no other way.

We Are All Slaves to Something

We are all slaves to something. Understanding this point is essential before it is possible to comprehend and appreciate the objective value of the spiritual teacher as manifest in the world, and the precious opportunity of conscious interrelationship that exists between teacher and student.

Whether we believe that the infant is born as a "blank slate" and conditioned at birth (or during the perinatal period), or whether we resonate with the wider perspective of *karma* – which implies coming into the world with pre-conditioned tendencies accumulated through an unspecified quantity of lifetimes in which the individuated soul journeys before its eventual return to its oneness with God – the fact remains that the human or egoic mind (as opposed to the essence or soul) is shaped and sculpted by an indeterminate number of factors and influences. What we understand to be "ourselves" is comprised of a set of tendencies that have engraved themselves so deeply upon the psyche as to create and re-create repetitive sets of experiences that we come to know as our "personality". Whereas some people have personalities that are more pleasant to live with than others, as wonderful or awful as any particular personality might be, it remains largely mechanical and predictable.

When we understand this, we come to appreciate that, no matter how much relative freedom we have, and how good our lives have become, until we have the capacity to function free from even the most subtle attachment – positive or negative – to our conditioning, we remain slaves. Sometimes we must fulfill our worldly desires before we are willing to acknowledge the emptiness that remains – the "wound that only God (Truth) can heal", in the words of Lee Lozowick. A classic historical example is the life of Siddharta Gautama, also known as the Buddha. Destined to rule the kingdom into which he was born and to have all riches, women, pleasures, and even knowledge at his beck and call, he saw with unwavering clarity the inevitable facts of suffering, old age, sickness, and death, which prompted him to relinquish all forms of outer wealth in favor of the "kingdom of Heaven" within. The life of songwriter Leonard Cohen is a contemporary illustration of this principle. With riches and women at his fingertips, he chose to spend many years as the personal attendant, cook, and housekeeper of Japanese Zen master Sazaki Roshi.

When we finally comprehend that we are indeed slaves to our own limitations, we naturally look for help from someone who is not enslaved to the same degree as we are. The teacher who has discovered even relative freedom has necessarily undergone tremendous inner purification – "trial by fire" – and possesses knowledge of how to endure such heat and use it to fuel the mysterious process of alchemical transformation.

A recent news clip told about a train that caught fire as it was entering a tunnel in the Alps. While everyone else was panicking, one man who clearly saw the predicament told the others, "Our only chance to survive is to go toward the fire and then go around it." Even though the passengers didn't have to go directly through the fire to be saved, only 12 were willing even to approach it. Those who followed the man's advice and went in the direction of the fire got out alive, whereas the remaining 150 died. The egoic mind's insistence on saving itself without external help is equivalent to those who feared to walk toward the fire. The true teacher is not only the one who calls us to move toward the fire, but the one who will stay by our side in order to assure our safe passage.

We are all slaves to something – generally a combination of our personal ego and the cultural and collective egos, which express themselves through conditioned mechanical behavior. If we want to be slaves to Truth, we must become apprentices to Truth. In the context of conscious discipleship, this comes through apprenticeship to the teacher. The seed of true power is within. The teacher waters that seed through transmission, and through his or her skillful means prunes the growing plant to perfection in order to feed the masses. The true teacher will only and always direct us to an essential knowledge of, and contact with, our own personal power.

Master as Disciple

I was recently asked by a Jewish cantor whether I thought it was harder to be a master or a disciple. I told him it is harder to be a true disciple than a false master; but it is harder to be a true master than a true disciple, for the true master is simultaneously both master *and* disciple. True masters continue to have the full responsibility of discipleship in relation to their own master, as well as all the responsibilities of masterhood in relation to their disciples. The true master *is* a true disciple. One who claims to be a master but is not also a disciple *in some form* leaves his or her mastery open to question.

The source of the master's true power is his discipleship, not his mastery. This is an interesting proposition, for the master's function, appearance, and even his outward attention will largely be expressed through his role as master. Still, the teacher's locus of internal attention is on his discipleship, and all actions he performs are an expression of that discipleship.

Spontaneous awakenings do occur, and there are occasions in which an authentic master has not had a living teacher. In such cases "discipleship" is to a deity, a body of teachings, or ultimate Truth itself. Arnaud Desjardins addresses this consideration in the question, "To whom do you *pranam* [bow]?"

The purpose of "bowing" to the other – even if the "other" is the Teachings, the lineage, the tradition, the ancestors, or the Ineffable – is both for protection and to keep ourselves humble. The lineage and the living or once-living master who comes to live within and as one's conscience offer the disciple profound *karmic* protection and mediates the forces of denial that may arise even in the midst of profound awakening.

To be humbled in relationship to the teacher and lineage is a far cry from powerless submission. It demonstrates respect for an intelligence far greater than that of the ordinary untrained mind. To "bow" to another represents a humble willingness *not* to know or understand everything while refusing to capitulate to cynicism regarding the preciousness of human incarnation.

Ultimate Equality

At the level of *essence*, everyone is equal. Period. It is the law of non-duality. There is no need to argue this point, nor to react against it. To do so would be to refute the sages and mystics of every tradition in every time, as well as the truth we all know within us if we dare to admit it. It just *is*, and every true teacher knows this. If they don't, they are not true teachers. At the most essential level of existence, the teacher is no different from the student.

There was a moment just weeks before my mother's death when I knelt by the side of the couch where she lay, surrendering to the inevitable. We were both devastated by the imminent loss of one another as we sat together waiting, loving, grieving. In a moment of shared acceptance of a reality that neither of us could deny, I told her, and we both understood, that whereas at that moment it was she who was lying on the couch and I who knelt beside her, no sooner would I turn my head, or blink my eye than it would be me there, my yet-to-be conceived daughter kneeling by *my* side. And then it would be *her* daughter ... So utterly the same. Beyond equal, to the point of One. And still, it was two. She fulfilled what she was able to, given her *karma*, will, incarnation, circumstances; and I would fulfill what I could, given mine.

Within non-duality is duality; within equality is hierarchy. If we return to Ken Wilber's concept of *holarchy*, we can describe it as concentric circles upon circles of ever-greater inclusion in a process of relative evolution on all levels, while, at the same time, everything is already complete. To make a distinction between different levels has nothing to do with morality, good and bad, higher and lower. It is only the multiple levels of psychological wounding that convince us that the existence of relative levels of power and knowledge is dangerous to us.

THE GURU IS NONE OTHER THAN THE CONSCIOUS SELF

The Upanishads teach that "the guru [or true teacher] is none other than the conscious Self." This simple statement reveals a truth that, if understood, undermines all false notions and misunderstandings regarding the true teacher and his or her objective function in the world. The false guru is the unconscious self; the sincere but weak teacher is the self striving toward unitive consciousness; and the true teacher is the conscious Self. The true guru or teacher is not *my* separative self, *my* personality, *my* conditioning, but *the Self*, housed in the body and mind of the teacher's own humanity. The teacher is not limited to a separative identification, and thus abides in connection with the same Self that is Consciousness Itself. We love the teacher because we love our own Self – not in a narcissistic and self-aggrandizing manner, but because we love Truth or God as expressed through the teacher. We respect the teacher for having made that bravest of leaps – to die to their own individuality for the selfless task of connection with, and service to, everything. We bow to them as a gesture of remembrance of our own intention to make that same leap of surrender.

In many forms of psychological work, we project onto the therapist those qualities of our psyches that we have disavowed because our conditioning and wounding have limited our range of mental and emotional experience and expansion. As therapy progresses, healing occurs through reclaiming the disowned aspects of ourselves. The guru principle works in a parallel manner, albeit on a different level: we project onto the teacher our highest Self, eventually (ideally) coming to embrace this full possibility for ourselves. In the student–teacher relationship, the teacher ideally *is*, in essence, that which we project onto him or her, as well as being an ordinary human being. In fact, we may only come to perceive such a vast possibility consciously for ourselves by seeing it *lived* through another.

When we finally come to appreciate the guru or teacher – not the personality but the expressed essence – as none other than our own Self manifest in another, all subjective power-differentials collapse. Relative distinctions become relegated to the domain of form. The teacher remains a construct that is ultimately impersonal while at the same time expressing itself through the personal as a most intimate connection between the authentic teacher and the conscious disciple. Respect becomes an organic response to the relative circumstance of less-learned in relationship to more-learned.

Power ignites power, force feeds force, divine reflects divine. To discount this possibility because of an intellectual contradiction, an outdated psychological fear, or crimes of ignorance committed by others or by ourselves is to deny ourselves the option of engaging with a vehicle that will carry us to the fountainhead of our own true source of power. Perhaps we will not choose to walk the road of the student–teacher relationship, but the conscious disciple of Truth benefits from having all paths of integrity available to them.

Ram Dass

The Predicament of Ram Dass

Ram Dass, also know as Richard Alpert, is the renowned Harvard professor-turned spiritual icon. In the late sixties he traveled to India and met Neem Karoli Baba – the famous Indian saint – who gave Ram Dass his blessing to write *Be Here Now* – a book that was unprecedented in bringing knowledge of Eastern spirituality and the guru to the Western world. Ram Dass has endeared himself to the public by being candid about his own spiritual unfolding – the relentless antics of ego incessantly trying to be somebody. He is uncompromisingly passionate in his longing for the function of the guru to be understood in the Western world.

Q: You are a great advocate of the guru—disciple relationship. Were you receptive to the idea from the beginning?

RD: When I first visited India in the sixties, my attitudes were still very Western. I met Neem Karoli Baba, and saw people touching his feet, but I decided I wasn't going to get sucked in to bowing down like that. After all, I was a Harvard professor. But he worked on me – the whole cultural scene of India worked on me – and I came back committed to the relationship with my guru. But here in the West, there was no opportunity to talk about it.

Q: Even though people wanted to hear you speak, they didn't want to hear about your guru?

RD: They wanted to hear about him as a spiritual figure, but they didn't want to understand anything about guru yoga. The West is so antagonistic toward gurus. I am careful when I talk about my relationship to my guru because of the way it will be interpreted by this culture. People will always listen through their own cultural ideas, and will therefore always misunderstand the guru. Every time they hear the word *guru*, they freak out, thinking it will be another

Jim Jones. And so they put up a wall. It doesn't bother me as much as it affects the way I communicate with others. This is perhaps the most difficult problem I have: how to share my spirit. My *sadhana* is guru yoga, and there is no room for it in this culture.

Q: But there is room for *you* in this culture. If what you are representing is your guru, even if others don't quite understand it, won't people still get the guru through you?

RD: People need to look within and discover what they want from the guru: Do they want the guru as a good daddy? Do they want to have decisions made for them? Do they want a guru for *sadhana*? Do they want a spiritual scene? If people in this culture want a guru, they are forced to deal with their own truth.

Q: But they see *you* as a guru, even though I've never heard you refer to yourself that way.

RD: People don't understand the guru, and if they don't understand the guru, they can't understand what my function is in relationship to Neem Karoli Baba. I am not what he is. He is the most important being in my universe. I feel so lucky to have him. But he's dead now, so I can't offer him to people in a tangible way, only subtly, through my books and stories. So now people look to me to be that lineage. They say to me, "You're my guru. I know you're a real one." But I'm not a real one. I can't give people that. It just doesn't work. A guru is somebody who is a doorway to the infinite.

Q: Are people insistent upon putting you in that role in spite of what you tell them?

RD: Yes. I'll give you an example. I was at a conference last week, and afterwards there was a party. I was sitting stationary in my wheelchair, and various people came up to visit with me. A woman came in who was very argumentative, and since I wear these dark glasses to protect my eyes, people don't know exactly what I'm up to. I decided to be silent instead of engaging her trip. A man who was in the room watching me came up afterwards and said, "How do you stand the vibration you get when you meditate that way?" He thought I was meditating, when I was really trying to avoid the woman. But he projected meditation onto me, so that's what he got.

Q: Did he only get his projection, or did he get something else?

RD: Well, he *was* getting something. But what? What is *it* compared to the saints?

Q: But since he wasn't *doing it* onto a saint, and instead doing it onto *you*, could he still receive the benefit of the transmission – even if you are not functioning at the same level as your guru?

RD: People will get my teacher, Neem Karoli Baba, through me, even though it is colored by my psychology and my hang-ups. I can tell you that these people are driving me – that's for sure. Driving me not to drink, but to spirit.

Q: What do you mean?

RD: They are wanting something I can't give them, or that I can only partially give. But their wanting drives me to look inside for what the truth is.

Q: If people are unable or unwilling to understand the guru principle through you – the infamous Ram Dass who is perhaps accepted more widely than any other Western spiritual leader – how are they going to get it?

RD: I'm such a phony! What are they getting? People think of the guru as a role. The guru is not a role. The guru is an internal message. It's heart-to-heart resuscitation. The role is a power position in this society. For me to take on the role of wise man, or the guru, is very corrupting. Yet, I don't mind being wise and spiritual, and therefore I want to help others to become wisdom and become spirit. In this culture, people see me for the roles I play and have played: I was at Harvard, I was featured in *People* magazine. It is very important to people that I am famous. But it's horrible. Of all possible motivations, being near to somebody famous is not the reason to have a guru.

Q: If people's primary interest in you is their desire to associate with your fame, how do you deal with the temptation of it?

RD: I deal with a lot of false motivations within myself. Fame is one of them. People come to me because I'm famous. I remember a time when I was giving a talk and women were running up to me and pulling buttons off my jacket as souvenirs.

Q: You are painting a pretty devastating picture here.

RD: It's too devastating!

Q: Does it make you suspicious?

RD: It sure does, and it should. It means there is something to look at.

Q: You've gotten yourself into an interesting situation: You have the capacity to reach the masses with your guru's teaching, and at the same time you are offered every possibility to fulfill ego's dream.

RD: This is the *sadhana* I have come to embrace. I have to be truthful with myself, because things like my power needs, my sexual needs, my psychological needs to feel wanted or needed, are all potential traps. When somebody says to me, "I want you as my guru," I laugh because of the massive discrepancy between my guru's realization and my own. He sees over the mountain; I only see him. But I tell myself, "He set me up to do this. He must assume I can handle it."

Q: So you're in a situation in which you can run any number of power trips and get distracted from your *sadhana*, and nobody will stop you but yourself because you're Ram Dass and everybody wants something from you. For most of us, the universe just won't mirror our egos and give us what we want, but in your case, particularly because your teacher is not alive, you have to catch yourself. What an admirable and precarious position you find yourself in.

RD: That's how it is. Yes. You understand it. Oh lucky, lucky me [laughing]. Fortunately, my guru is with me inside all the time, and having him with me keeps me straight.

Q: Perhaps people really can get something from you they aren't willing to get from one of the hard-core, traditional gurus.

RD: Here's the picture. There are many gurus who come from guru-loving cultures like Tibet and India, and within their own cultures they function impeccably, but they start falling like flies once they come to the West because they can't deal with this culture – the sexual promiscuity, the materialism. People get disillusioned by these gurus, and then come to a psychologist like me saying, "I can't get what I'm looking for from these cultures like Tibet, but I can get it from you because you are sensitive to my situation." In Western culture, we have four recognized modes of spiritual guidance: rabbi, priest, therapist, or teacher. Most people want me to play one of those traditional roles. In order to give them what I want to give them, I find myself playing into one of these roles. So I therapize to them, but only to get into them, to get my foothold.

Q: When people come to you for what you really have to offer, what do they get?

RD: I love the Beloved so much, and that's what makes me the guru in moments. But the guru is never a role. The roles attract people to me, but when they get close, what they get in their heart is my love for my Guru, which is my love for God, my love for spirit. We have to transcend the roles that we meet in, and then we're heart-to-heart. We meet and their spiritual heart is mirrored by my own. They can get close to me through the roles, but when we get close enough they see reflected in me their own spiritual heart – that's the function of the guru.

Q: What would you like people to understand about the guru?

RD: In your book, portray that the guru is real. Let people know there is something there. But let them know that the guru-disciple relationship is ultimately an inner mood. It is not one of roles. It's not social. It's not a relationship. It's an inner sharing. You have an *atman* (Self) and I have an *atman* and it's the same *atman*. The guru represents that *atman* to your heart. When my guru died, some people were sobbing. But I knew that he and I were related internally, and death didn't have anything to do with that level.

Q: Has your relationship with your guru changed since he died?

RD: The only thing that has changed is that before he died, I was always thinking, "He's in India. I've got to get to India." Now I know he's right here.

CHAPTER 14

For the Glory of Love

Don't ever listen to the so-called swamis who tell you that you have to become cold and dead in order to make spiritual progress. They can say such things only because they have forgotten what it means to have a heart.[1]

THE AGHORI VIMALANANDA

Yoga is falling in love, not a choice of a carrier.[2]

IRINA TWEEDIE

It was an "average" day during those initial months of anguished purification in India, if anything around a God-mad saint could be considered to be average. The scene was in full play: Yogi Ramsuratkumar, Master of masters, on his simple, wooden platform, the same rags and blankets he had worn during five decades of living as a mad saint on the streets of Tiruvannamalai now covered by layer upon layer of jasmine and rose garlands. His devoted attendants sat nearby, their eyes gazing lovingly at their master, alert to the subtle shifts in his every mood or need, their insides melting as they endured the searing burn of divine heat invisibly transforming their subtle internal organs. Disciples and visitors sat in rows several feet away, approaching the Yogi to make their requests for enough money for a daughter's dowry, or for a miracle cure for a loved one's cancer, or to express praise and adoration for the gifts already given through the glory of God as manifest in the form of the personal Beloved.

And there I sat, playing my part as disciple, supplicating God to allow me to taste a morsel of the sublime divinity that sat before me. My inner moods shifted continuously. At one moment I assumed an arrogant stance of condescension toward the visitors who came before the most transcendent, compassionate, and gift-bestowing expression of humanity they would likely ever set eyes on, asking for favors as mundane as for their child to pass their university entrance exams. At the next I would be plunged into feelings of essential unworthiness as I pleaded to this One who appeared to be outside of myself to give me some unknown substance I believed that I lacked. Then would arise gratitude and praise for the glory of God transmitted so evidently, yet mysteriously, by this form before me.

In a moment, and clearly to no credit of my own, my vision took a 180-degree turn. Suddenly, the Great Game, the cosmic love affair, the grand explosion of duality, "the play of consciousness" as Swami Muktananda referred to it, was palpable. There was no division, no separation, no "other". Only supreme, unwavering equality. Each of us was simply playing out our specified role in the divine script at this moment of manifest existence. Yogi Ramsuratkumar played the part of the great Yogi – feted, worshipped, adored. But it meant nothing, even and especially to him. The cast featured his noble attendants as the select of all disciples, renouncing personal desires and finding fulfillment in service of the Great One. The rest of us played the crowd – supporting actors, extras, wannabes – perceiving ourselves either as gracious recipients of others' sacrifices, or as under-recognized pious disciples of God – seekers of the Truth who imagined ourselves to be separate from the Great One.

The forms were as diverse as the actors in the play, the differences simply a lawful expression of the infinite manifestations of duality – the differentiated aspects of the Divine Mother with heart, lungs, eyes, kidneys inseparably intertwined to form the whole of Her body. This vision of supreme equality manifest arose with such heartwarming delight that it caused me nearly to double over in laughter. At the same time it brought about an unprecedented calm, trust and acceptance in this one accustomed to seeing separation, contradiction, disparity.

The question is always the same: If all abides in Oneness, why apparent separation and difference? Why forms? Why "higher" and "lower"? If God is One, Indivisible, Everywhere, in All Things, Whole, Unified, why all this mess? Philosophers and mystics in every tradition take their guesses. One appealing answer is that separation exists purely and wholly for the glory of Love. People who argue about the limitations of a tradition in which the student doesn't eventually "graduate" and surpass the teacher surely have never sampled the flavor of love for the teacher.

Love makes us grow like few things do. From time immemorial, people have been motivated to do things for romantic love that they would not do for any other reason: to grow, to transform, to sacrifice selfishness, pride, and even their own limited identification in order to join with another in a greater whole. Divine love catalyzes these same processes on another level. The projection of our higher self as expressed through the living form of the teacher symbolizes our own highest possibility, and the externalized locus of this attention can pull us toward our Self, push us from beneath, arouse our conscience, or simply bring us running toward it through the longing its own beauty kindles in us.

The *Ras Lila* depicts the great love games surrounding Lord Krishna, who played his flute so beautifully that when the *gopis*, or cowherd girls, heard it, it "made the love-god, Ananga, grow stronger within them".

> *Some Gopis had been milking, but in their great eagerness they left their milking and rushed to Him. Others had just put milk over the fire to boil, but they left it. Still others left without removing the wheat-porridge which they were cooking over the fire. And all of them went to Him ... Some Gopis were serving their husband his meal, and they left that. Some were giving milk to their babies, and they left that ... Still others were eating their own meal, and they left that.* [3]

The Form of the Master

My very first vision of my teacher was seeing him in the role of disciple, receiving benediction and direction from his teacher. In truth, it was the fact of his discipleship that initially drew me to him. After years of chasing false gurus, hearing that a Western spiritual master was coming with 20 disciples to visit his master got my attention. I was intrigued by the possibility of a teacher who might possess enough integrity and humility to reveal himself in the so-called "submissive" role of disciple in the presence of his own students. At the time, I did not know that his discipleship was one of the most potent forms of teaching he used with his own students. He was not a teacher who asked students to submit to him while he took off in private jets to Hawaii, but one who lived in visible surrender to his teacher while serving others in a parallel manner.

Forever imprinted in my mind is an image of Lee dressed in a baby-blue traditional Indian *kurta*, hands folded in a gesture of *pranam* to his master as the Yogi walked out of the *darshan* hall one day. It was the look in his eyes that got to me, even though at the time I did not understand the implications of what I was seeing. It was a look of utter and abject adoration, a surrender arising from completeness, a whole-bodied submission to the awesome expression of One in the form of the personal Beloved. Lee's eyes and yearning heart followed his master's every step as the Yogi walked past him and out the door. I recognized clearly in that moment that no matter who this man was to become to me, and in whatever crazy-wise manner he might express himself in his function as guru, I had already seen that he was first a Lover. His connection to the teachings and to his teacher was that of a disciple, and my longing heart and doubting mind was thus reassured.

In a public talk addressing the students of Yogi Ramsuratkumar, Lee told them:

> *If we are afraid to love the human master, we are denying ourselves one of the sweetest and most tender aspects of relationship. When we bring the Beloved into our bodies, hearts, and minds, there is a literal rain of nectar in the body itself which is neither metaphorical nor mystical. The body itself becomes an ocean of nectar and sweetness that is the result of the Beloved's blessing in our hearts. When we bring the Beloved into our hearts, bodies, and minds, we become pervaded, permeated, and soaked in the ocean of the Beloved's blessings. This is a quality of devotion that many of us miss out on because we are afraid to love the human master.*

Reflecting upon his own decades of discipleship, Arnaud Desjardins, teacher to thousands, suggests:

> *... Don't insist too much on the impersonal side of the guru. Don't be afraid to take the human side of the guru to heart. Because he is your guru; he is the form for you to be led beyond form ... For us the beyond form, the Infinite, is found in the human guru, in human shape. So we have to see and feel, "He is my guru, the mouthpiece of Reality." And when we are convinced, then don't hesitate to take completely into your heart the physical form of the guru. Don't make the mistake of saying, "This is the divine aspect of the guru, this is the human aspect of the guru" ... Don't hesitate to take the human being of the guru into your heart.*[4]

When You Meet the Buddha on the Road, Invite Him In!

"I thought if you meet the Buddha on the road you're supposed to kill him" is a comment often directed to me as a challenge in the various talks I give on the value of conscious discipleship. It's usually accompanied by a look both poignant and slightly smug which suggests that this insightful observation will close the conversation. I have found that rarely do such people have any actual experience with the high-sounding dharma they expound.

It is true that we must eventually "kill the master" in the sense of allowing the sense of "otherness" to be destroyed. But, at the same time, we *cannot* kill the guru because the guru as an expression of the guru-principle is eternal. This is a tacit reality, a lived principle attested to countless times by individuals even in traditions that do not use words such as "guru" or "master". We can kill Jesus, but not the Christ; we can slay the body of the master, but not God. The personal guru is a teacher contained within a human body accompanied by a particular personality, but the Guru is Consciousness itself.

To "kill the Buddha" means to kill the projection of separation between ourselves and the Buddha, not to kill the human being who embodies Buddha-nature. Far better to kill the projection and then invite the one who has realized and embodied their Buddha-nature to come live in our house. Better to honor and serve the one who has served scores of beings through his or her realization; to learn from them how to live *after* one has realized Buddhahood; to dwell in the company of awakened realization.

If I met the Buddha on the road I would certainly not kill him! I would cook up a tremendous feast and invite everybody I care about – and even those I despise – and let us all be fed until our minds and hearts and bellies were overflowing to the point that we could do nothing but share the glory of our own richness with others.

Non-duality vs Enlightened Duality

It happens, no doubt, that, when the good and faithful servant enters into the joy of his Lord, he becomes intoxicated with the immeasurable abundance of the Divine house. [5]

HENRY SUSO

Non-duality is the path of oneness. It is the realization of the essential non-separation of all things. The context of the non-dual teachings is the essential emptiness and illusory nature of all phenomena. This is the key to achieving the furthest reaches of self-understanding available within the human experience. Yet, in spite of the realization of essential oneness and the "illusory" nature of all phenomena, there remains the outer world. "Form is emptiness," the Buddhist scriptures teach, "but emptiness is also form." There remains a world of physical and emotional suffering, of mass environmental destruction, of war, of profound loneliness, isolation, and widespread dissatisfaction and depression ranging from the personal to the global. Georg Feuerstein suggests that it is not the forms of life that are illusory, but rather that our *relationship* to those forms is based upon an illusory, or false, perception.

"Enlightened duality", a term coined by Lee Lozowick, describes the principle and practice of an abidance in non-dual realization which is then expressed through all facets of dual experience, infusing and transmuting that duality within the context of Oneness. In enlightened duality, apparent separation is acknowledged. Even suffering that is based upon misperception is still recognized as suffering. The teacher and student exist independently at the same time as they are one. In lived enlightened duality, nothing is denied. Everything exists, yet is seen through a recognition of its essential non-dual nature.

Non-dual realization is, in itself, unchallengeable. However, when the teachings and insights of non-duality interface with a wounded Western psyche, mistaken perceptions arise. Human beings commonly seek enlightenment from a conscious or unconscious urge to have their personal suffering alleviated, which exists alongside a true longing for reunion with Truth or God. All too often, however, the Westernized ego, informed by a psyche that is programmed for independence, disconnected from the body, and wounded by betrayals co-opts the insights of emptiness, non-meaning, and illusion and uses them to build a solid spiritual-intellectual fortress that paradoxically separates the insightful one from him or her own very real humanity and the individuals closest to him or her. What is expressed as non-dual realization is often the *memory* of a non-dual insight.

The greatest masters in the world, in spite of their realization of emptiness and void and illusion and nonseparation, are masters of love. This is what they teach, and this is what they express through their humanity. Arnaud Desjardins tells of his first encounters with such masters over four decades ago when he was a young seeker of truth:

> Long ago I had the chance to meet some well-known Tibetan gurus. Still at that time I was dreaming of mysterious esoteric teachings, occult powers. But I found these masters to be so simple, with such humility, even if their only teaching was compassion, compassion, compassion. According to my feeling, this is one of the greatest teachings: to insist upon compassion.

The 16th Karmapa was dining with students in a lovely restaurant high above the city of Hong Kong when he suddenly got up from the table and went outside. After some time, a concerned student went out to see where the master had disappeared to and found him weeping uncontrollably. Shocked by the scene of the enlightened master sobbing like an inconsolable child, the student appealed to him to share the source of his anguish. The Karmapa explained that he had been sitting there at the elegant restaurant, enjoying the refined company of mature students of the dharma, when suddenly his attention had been drawn to the city below. He began to consider all the millions of people who were suffering endless expressions of human misery and affliction. He then reflected upon how few of them would ever have the fortune to come into contact with the great teachings, which represented the only real possibility for them to be relieved of their suffering. This awareness was devastating, and it was for them that he wept.

Great disciples of all traditions are lovers. Their tremendous efforts of will, sacrifice, discipline, and selfless service are enacted not for the purpose of self-fulfillment or personal satisfaction, but as expressions of love. Mother Teresa repeatedly taught her nuns that they were not social workers, but Lovers: "Your vocation is not to work for lepers," she told them. "Your vocation is to belong to Jesus." In *The Woman Awake*, Regina Sara Ryan writes:

> *Mother Teresa held her source and her payoff as no secret. Her work was not to help the poor, although that is what she was always doing; her work was to serve Her Beloved Jesus, who had first loved her. Her work was her faith – in knowing that the sick, the poor, the deformed, the destitute were the faces and forms of her Beloved, and that her God was not separate from humanity.* [6]

Practitioners of all traditions may express their realization and understanding through an abidance in emptiness or through an appreciation of form. Regardless of the degree and consistency of their realization, and irrespective of the language which they use to describe their intention, true disciples of all traditions have willingly submitted themselves to serve as slaves of Love. Through their sacrifice, Love begins to dominate and consume them, pouring forth from a fountain whose Source is everywhere, and thus cannot be depleted. Such lovers often choose, or are chosen, to engage in the form of the student–teacher bond in order to apprentice to the multifaceted forms of love – personal and impersonal, form and formless – which are revealed within the context of that relationship.

What Can I Give?

You have given me everything.
What shall I offer to you, O Master?
I offer salutations, with folded hands.

The teacher, the tradition, and the specific practices of the tradition serve simultaneously as a means to an end and as an expression of that end. There was a period in my discipleship when, frustrated to the brim by the recognition of my egoic motivations to practice (to get love, to gain approval, to arrive somewhere), I decided, after years of unwavering obedience, to not practice the disciplines recommended by my teacher and my tradition. I wanted to see what would happen. To my surprise, what happened was nothing. I felt totally loved, connected to my tradition, and free of guilt, which prompted me to consider why one would practice at all. I shared my reflections with a trusted senior practitioner, who suggested that I not draw any quick conclusions, but simply wait and watch.

One day several weeks later, walking in the hills by my California home, I found myself in a mood of extraordinary contentedness and gratitude to my teacher, life, God. Overwhelmed with appreciation for my precious birth and the intersection of my life with the great teachings and an authentic teacher, I became filled with a desire to give something back in exchange for the extraordinary gifts I had received. The response to this desire was immediately obvious: Practice. Practice was revealed to be both the means to an end and an expression of that end. For although my life remained full and plentiful even upon relinquishing my practice for a couple of months, it was clear that the present bounty of my experience was the fruit of years of internal resolve accompanied by external discipline. Even more important, I understood that a lifestyle of consistent practice was the most natural and respectful means of acknowledging the gifts that are given to us the moment we encounter the teacher and the spiritual path. To respect the body through conscious eating and exercise, to study the great mystics, to spend time daily in silence, to pursue ever deeper knowledge of our own existence: the means, the end, and the expression of that end are one and the same.

The question of the student–teacher relationship takes a radical shift when we turn from a consideration of *What can I get from the master?* to *What can I give to the master?* We are so accustomed to thinking of the teacher as an "other" who is going to give us something we don't already have, rather than as a symbol of that which we have already been given through the transmission that occurs immediately upon our association with a tradition. We think of the teacher as someone who *owes* us something, rather than an advocate of the soul, a "cosmic cheerleader" who urges us to express the fullness of our own inherent divinity. We think of the teacher as someone who must serve us, rather than as someone we can assist in serving the liberation and surrender of all humanity.

Years ago when I was ranting to a senior practitioner about the decrepit condition of my spiritual practice and my teacher's refusal to express his love for me in the way I thought he should, she asked me to consider the possibility that I was never going to get anything more from my teacher than that which I had already been given. "What if what he has already given you", she challenged, "is the full extent of what he is ever going to give you? What if what you have now is all you are ever going to get? Could you live with that?" My mind had to do a backbend to wrap itself around this new perspective, and when I finally managed to, I saw that she was absolutely correct.

What if we already have everything? What if our lives – including our difficulties, strengths, sorrows, confusion – are already so saturated with grace that there is really "nowhere to go and nothing to do"? What if we have already been fully found, and that everything is *really OK*, even if we sometimes fail to realize it? What if the very fact of finding the path, of walking the road of an endless unfolding into eternity is all there is, and we are already doing it, and will continue to do it, and that we are already there even as we walk?

If we have already been given everything, the only task that remains is to acknowledge our gratitude for that gift, and then express it through our own giving with as much consistency as possible. This profound shift in the underlying attitude of our discipleship – from one of trying to "get" to one of seeking to give – marks a mature phase of conscious discipleship in which the apparently distinct roles of teacher and student merge in the shared task of service to God or Truth through service to humanity.

Love in Separation

When there is only oneness, there is no one to love. No Lover and no Beloved. There is Love, but not the *play* of love. One particular expression of discipleship involves consciously choosing to express the perceived distinction between guru and disciple in order to live the play of enlightened worship and enlightened love. The gopis were no different from Krishna, but chose, or were chosen for, the role of enlightened lover for the sheer joy of worship and adoration. They chose to forgo an immersion in impersonal Oneness for the experience of love in separation – to live their yearning through the very cells of their body. The Sufis refer to this as "the path of longing". Their passion for the God within is consciously projected onto the externalized Beloved, and this passion increases through a process of purification, prayer, practice, and praise until the heat of it becomes a fire that turns all obstacles to ash and they surrender to the fire. Some describe an experience so delicious it is painful, so exquisite it is agonizing, so joy-full that it grieves, so hot that it sears the heart in ecstasy. The longing itself becomes the fulfillment, and the possibility of actual union is avoided at all costs, as it would eliminate the sought-after longing.

Layla and Majnun is a great Persian love epic of an unconsummated longing between lovers. In it, Majnun says:

> *Oh Lord! Let her berate me, castigate me, punish me – I do not care. I am ready to sacrifice my life for the sake of her beauty. Do You not see how I burn for her? And although I know that I shall never be free of this pain, it does not matter. For that is how it has to be. And so, dear God, for Your own sake and for the sake of love, let my love grow stronger with each passing hour. Love is all I have, all I am, and all I ever want to be!* [7]

Irina Tweedie, upon completing years of a purification process under the guidance of her Sufi master that few people would ever wish to know existed, much less endure, wrote in her journal:

> *From now on I will have to live with the Glory and the Terror of it [Love] ... It is merciless, inescapable, sometimes nearer, sometimes receding into the distance, but never far away, always just around the corner on the edge of perception; a throbbing, dynamic, intensely virile, intoxicating "Presence" so utterly joyous, boundless and free* [8] *... It is said that the river takes no rest, the wind knows no fatigue, and the sun can only shine and shine forever. The child plays for the joy of playing. It does not think of the benefit; all its joy is in playing. Yoga is falling in love, not a choice of a carrier ... I know that there is nothing left to do for the devotee who has surrendered himself. For from then on He takes over and the will of the devotee becomes the will of the Beloved ...* [9]

To live such longing often involves a long process of apprenticeship to Love. Egoic desire and pure love are often intermingled within the psyche; human love and divine love each playing off of the other. Yet even mundane or selfish or conditional love, when attended by the conscious intention to know ultimate Love and Truth, becomes the training ground for divine Love.

I learned this lesson one day when Yogi Ramsuratkumar called me to him, handed me a small stack of papers, and asked me to read them aloud, one by one, to his disciples. First was a poem Lee had written to him. It was a poem expressing the poet's intention to praise, to serve, to love without reserve, without expectation of fulfillment, for the sake of love itself. The next was a poem I had written to him – a poem also of intention, and hunger, and desire, but of my own wants and needs and demands of God. Then he had me read two more of Lee's; then one of my own. Then Lee's, then my own. Most of the hundreds of disciples who sat and listened thought that I was being honored, acknowledged, recognized, and compared favorably to my teacher. Very few understood the chasm between the demanding nature of my own love and the selfless offering of my teacher's love as it was revealed in Yogi Ramsuratkumar's play. My love was for myself, Lee's was for God, a reflection of a vow to serve all of humanity. With gratitude, and touched by the compassionate wisdom through which the message was delivered, I understood the lesson.

My teacher chooses the path of love in separation, and I as his student thereby become an apprentice to this most difficult form of practice that is as agonizing as it is fulfilling. We cannot know, or even begin to guess, when our ordinary love will become divinized. Our surest possibility is to offer authentic and dedicated love to the extent which we are able. If we water the tree through intention, practice, longing, clarity and integrity, one day – whether today, tomorrow, or in thousands upon thousands of years – the fruits will come.

The higher expression of this practice takes the inexplicable form of a chosen separation that is literally whole, complete, and One, at the same time as it is two. From its roots in the ineffable and ultimate Oneness, it wills itself into separation in order to burn in the creative fire of the dynamic tension of Two.

In *Death of a Dishonest Man: Poems and Prayers to Yogi Ramsuratkumar*, Lee appeals to his master:

> *If to realize You*
> *is to lose Your Form,*
> *then spare Your son this agony*
> *and give him Your Feet.*
> *Let Your son, this bad Poet,*
> *stay separate from You*
> *so he can long for You*
> *and beg for Your glance.* [10]

In *The Hunger of Love*, Princess Sita writes to her Guru and Lover, Lord Rama:

> *The vow I made today, Beloved, has put me in chains,*
> *kissing Thee has cost me my life.*
> *Yet, I do not grieve, for these chains I wear are made of the finest silver.*
> *They bind not only my hands and feet,*
> *They also wrap around the chambers of my heart ...*
> *Please hear Eternal Husband,*
> *I do not wish to be released from these chains*
> *These chains do not clink or clatter,*
> *They do not rip into the skin or cut into the muscle,*
> *No, they tinkle with the sound of my vow to Thee.*
> *I do not long for freedom, for these chains enslave me*
> *In Your Prison of Love.*
> *I hope to die in these chains,*
> *I long to leave my body with these chains*
> *still wrapped around my full but broken heart.*[11]

Who but a madman or madwoman would make such a choice? And why would they make it? Only because they were mad for love, and it is this very madness that is the fire that has drawn the greatest lovers of all times and traditions to it. It is the fire of Rumi and Shams-i Tabriz, of Romeo and Juliet, of Radha and Krishna, of Camille and Rodin, of Heloise and Abelard.

We are all capable of a love as great as this; to think otherwise is a disservice not only to ourselves but to Ultimate Reality, which loves and longs to be loved by each of us equally. All of us are made of the same God. Jesus and Buddha were made of the same stuff as we are, only they made another choice. The choice they made is available to each of us in every moment, but the responsibility of making it is so terrifying that we shield ourselves from it as if it were the plague, while, at the same time, we live forever unable to extinguish our longing for it.

It is now almost seven years to the day that I first met my teacher, an event that followed seven years of chasing the charlatans within me who manifested themselves in the form of false or disappointing teachers. These years have produced a stripping-away of everything I once thought spiritual, replaced by a vision of ordinariness that is so veiled it appears altogether mundane, yet is so refined it can be found in few places on this earth.

I sit in a small office in the French countryside at my teacher's summer ashram. Lee sits six feet away, a portrait of Yogi Ramsuratkumar behind him, studying an esoteric Gurdjieffian text and responding to his children and then his students as they wander in, asking for everything from a game of cards to an explanation of sexual alchemy. Sometimes he looks up and smiles at me. At other times he does not even seem to register than I am here. I have finally begun to understand that neither response has anything to do with the process of transmission that marks the core of our relationship. The guru is not the person, and the task of conscious discipleship is mine alone.

I have watched the years go by in this most unique love affair that bears similar qualities to other forms of love, yet is distinct from all. During these years I have undergone an infinite variety of experiences in relationship to my teacher. I have attached to him in an enormous variety of neurotic and divine ways. I have been a dependent child attempting to gain the affection of a projected and unavailable father, and I have experienced qualities of divine love too intimate to desecrate with words. I have challenged his motives, actions, behaviors. I have been angry with him to the point of being outright abusive. I have been an exemplary disciple and an embarrassing appendage. I have tested him in every way that my imagination could fashion, and if I come up with another way I will probably test him again. I have trusted and mistrusted; worshipped and cursed; surrendered and betrayed. Under his careful eye, I have raised myself into conscious discipleship. All of this, and I am just beginning ...

I am fully cognizant that the labyrinth of the conscious disciple is one of the most challenging paths that one can follow to God, but equally aware that it is one of the most gratifying. It is the opportunity to be in relationship with one "whose circumference is nowhere but whose center is everywhere", as Saint Thomas Aquinas said.

It takes great courage, or sheer desperation of the soul insistent upon union, to walk into a living labyrinth and take up residence there, indefinitely if need be. I suspect that those who do it have no other choice. Even if they cannot remember their true identity, they also cannot forget. It is less a matter of what we believe than a willingness to turn without barriers toward what is already True. In the far, far distant future we will all know reunion with our source, but some will know this sooner, and some much later. Conscious discipleship means that we step into the maze with full consciousness and complete self-responsibility, offering ourselves *now*.

I once believed that I would gain something from spiritual life; that enlightenment would be mine if I played my cards well. My teacher taught me that spiritual life is about giving instead of getting. I thought there was something in it for me, but in spite of myself I have learned that it is only about Love, and that Love is about God, and that relationship to God is about ceaseless praise of the One in the form of service to the many. The last great request that the Indian saint Mother Krishnabai made of God was to be allowed to take the suffering of the whole world into her own body. She became ill immediately as she experienced the *karma* of the world eating up her body until she died nine months later. Yogi Ramsuratkumar lived as a bleeding open heart, rarely sleeping, sacrificing himself each moment in an endless stream of pure giving.

Love is bondage and liberation, both at the same time. The true master is fully surrendered to Love in the form of his master and his disciples. The disciple likewise surrenders to Love in the form of his or her master and to the world which he or she is ultimately called to serve. It is the sublime manifestation of the play of God through the expression of humanity. It is all and only for the glory of Love.

Om. May we, Guru and disciple, be protected together.
May we enjoy the fruits of our actions together.
May we achieve strength together.
May our knowledge be full of light.
May we never have enmity for one another.

GURU GITA [IN] SRI SKANDA PURANA

Bibliography and Recommended Reading

Anthony, Dick, Bruce Ecker and Ken Wilber. *Spiritual Choices: The Problems of Recognizing Authentic Paths to Inner Transformation* (NY: Paragon House, 1987)

Aryashura. *Fifty Stanzas on the Spiritual Teacher* (2nd edn; Dharamsala, India: Library of Tibetan Works and Archives, 1991)

Aurobindo, Ghose. *Integral Yoga* (Twin Lakes, WI: Lotus Press, 1998)

Avabhasa, Da. *Divine Distraction: A Guide to the Guru-Devotee Relationship* (Clearlake, CA: The Dawn Horse Press, 1991)

Bache, Chris, *Dark Night, Early Dawn* (Albany, NY: State University of New York Press, 2000)

Barnhart, Bruno. *Second Simplicity: the Inner Shape of Christianity* (Mahwah, NJ: Paulist Press, 1999)

Barrett, William E. *The Lady of the Lotus: the Untold Love Story of the Buddha and His Wife* (Los Angeles, CA: Jeremy P. Tarcher, 1989)

Berzin, Alexander. *Relating to a Spiritual Teacher* (Ithaca, NY: Snow Lion Publications, 2000)

Bly, Robert. *The Sibling Society* (New York: Addison-Wesley Publishing Company, 1996)

Bogart, Greg. *The Nine Stages of Spiritual Apprenticeship* (Berkeley, CA: Dawn Mountain Press, 1997)

Chadwick, David. *Crooked Cucumber: the Life and Zen Teaching of Shunryu Suzuki* (New York: Broadway Books, 1999)

Charlton, Hilda. *Saints Alive* (Woodstock, NY: Golden Quest, 1989)

Chodron, Pema. *When Things Fall Apart* (Boston, MA: Shambhala, 1997)

Cohen, Andrew. *In Defense of the Guru Principle* (Lenox, MA: Impersonal Enlightenment Fellowship, 1999)

Crane, George. *Bones of the Master* (New York: Bantam, 2000)

Crook, John, and James Low. *The Yogins of Ladakh: A Pilgrimage Among the Hermits of the Buddhist Himalayas* (Delhi, India: Motilal Banarsiddass Publishers, 1997)

De Boulay, Shirley. *Beyond the Darkness: a Biography of Bede Griffiths* (New York, Doubleday, 1998)

De Mello, Anthony. *Awareness: a De Mello Conference in His Own Words* (Image Books, 1990)

Deida, David. *Wild Nights* (Austin, TX: Plexus, 2000)

Desjardins, Arnaud. *Jump into Life* (Prescott, AZ: Hohm Press, 1994)

—. *L'Ami Spirituel* (Paris, France: Les Editions de La Table Ronde, 1996)

Dorje, Rig'dzin. *Dangerous Friend* (Boston, MA: Shambhala, 2001)

Dowman, Keith. *Sky Dancer: the Secret Life and Songs of the Lady Yeshe Tsogyel* (Ithaca, NY: Snow Lion Publications, 1996)

—. *Buddhist Masters of Enchantment* (Rochester, VT: Inner Traditions, 1998)

Evans-Wentz. *Tibet's Great Yogi Milarepa* (2nd edn; London: Oxford University Press, 1969)

Farcet, Gilles. *Radical Awakening: Cutting Through the Conditioned Mind: Dialogues with Stephen Jourdain* (Carlsbad, CA: Inner Directions, 2001)

Fedorschak, V J. *The Shadow on the Path: Clearing Psychological Blocks to Spiritual Development* (Prescott, AZ: Hohm Press, 1999)

Feuerstein, Georg. *Holy Madness: The Shock Tactics and Radical Teachings of Crazy-Wise Adepts, Holy Fools, and Rascal Gurus* (New York: Penguin, 1992)

—. *Tantra* (Boston, MA: Shambhala, 1998)

—. *The Yoga Tradition* (Prescott, AZ: Hohm Press, 1998)

Frager, Robert. *Heart, Self & Soul* (Wheaton, IL: Quest Books, 1997)

Gold, E J. *The Human Biological Machine as a Transformational Apparatus* (Nevada City, CA: Gateways, 1985)

Harvey, Andrew. *The Direct Path* (New York, Broadway Books, 2001)

Keen, Sam. *Hymns to an Unknown God* (New York: Bantam, 1995)

Kinsley, David. *Tantric Visions of the Divine Feminine* (Berkeley, CA: The University of California Press, 1997)

Kramer, Joel, and Diana Alstad. *The Guru Papers* (Berkeley, CA: Frog Ltd., 1993)

Krishnamurti, J. *The First & Last Freedom* (New York: Harper & Row, 1975)

Krishnamurti, U G. *The Mystique of Enlightenment* (3rd edn; Bangalore, India: Sahasramana Prakashana Press, 2001)

Leonard, George, and Michael Murphy. *The Life We are Given* (Jeremy P. Tarcher/Putnam, 1995)

Lewis, Rick. *The Perfection of Nothing* (Prescott, AZ: Hohm Press, 2000)

Lozowick, Lee. *The Only Grace is Loving God* (Prescott, AZ: Hohm Press, 1982)

—. *The Alchemy of Transformation* (Prescott, AZ: Hohm Press, 1996)

McBrien, Richard. *Lives of the Saints* (San Francisco, CA: HarperSan Francisco, 2001)

Martin, Sita. *The Hunger of Love: Versions of the Ramayana* (Kanyakumari, India: Yogi Ramsuratkumar Manthralayam Trust, 1995)

Martin, Valerie. *Salvation: Scenes from the Life of St. Francis* (New York: Alfred A. Knopf, 2001)

Merell-Wolff, Franklin. *Experience and Philosophy: A Personal Record of Transformation and a Discussion of Transcendental Consciousness* (Albany, NY: State University of New York Press, 1994)

Merton, Thomas. *Contemplation in a World of Action* (Notre Dame: University of Notre Dame Press, 1998)

Nalanda Translation Committee. *The Life of Marpa the Translator* (Boston, MA: Shambhala, 1995)

Nizami. *Layla and Majnun* (London: Blake Publishing, 1970)

Nyanaponika, Thera, and Hellmuth Hecker. *Great Disciples of the Buddha: Their Lives, their Works, Their Legacy* (Boston, MA: Wisdom Publications, 1997)

Patterson, William Patrick. *Eating the "I"* (Fairfax, CA: Arete Communications, 1992)

—. *Struggle of the Magicians: Exploring the Teacher–Student Relationship* (Fairfax, CA: Arete Communications, 1996)

Rabten, Geshe. *The Life of a Tibetan Monk* (Le Mont-Pelerin, Switzerland: Edition Rabten, 2000)

Ram Dass. *Be Here Now* (New York: Crown Publications, 1971)

—. *Still Here* (New York: Riverhead Books, 2001)

Ray, Reginald. *Indestructible Truth* (Boston, MA: Shambhala, 2000)

—. *Secret of the Vajra World* (Boston, MA: Shambhala, 2001)

Redington, James. *Vallabhacarya on the Love Games of Krsna* (2nd edn; New Delhi, India: Motilal 1989)

Ryan, Regina Sara. *The Woman Awake: Feminine Wisdom for Spiritual Life* (Prescott, AZ: Hohm Press, 1999)

Sekkizhaar [condensed English version by G. Vanmikanathan] (Madras, India: Sri Ramakrishna Math, 1985)

Shaw, Miranda. *Passionate Enlightenment* (Princeton, NJ: Princeton University Press, 1994)

Smith, Ingram. *Truth is a Pathless Land: a Journey with Krishnamurti* (Wheaton, IL: The Theosophical Publishing House, 1989)

Steiner, Rudolf. *Rosicrucian Wisdom* (London: Rudolf Steiner Press, 2000)

Svoboda, Robert. *Aghora* (Albuquerque, NM: Brotherhood of Life Inc., 1986)

—. *Aghora II: Kundalini* (Albuquerque, NM: Brotherhood of Life Inc., 1993)

—. *Aghora III: The Law of Karma* (Albuquerque, NM: Brotherhood of Life Inc., 1997)

Swami Prahavananda and Christopher Isherwood (trans.). *The Song of God: Bhagavad-Gita* (New York: Penguin Books, 1972)

Tart, Charles. *Mind Science: Meditation Training for Practical People* (Novato, CA: Wisdom Edition, 2000)

Thakar, Vimala. *On an Eternal Voyage* (Ahmedabad, India: Vimal Prakashan Trust, 1989)

Trungpa, Chogyam. *Cutting Through Spiritual Materialism* (Boston, MA: Shambhala, 1973)

—. *Shambhala: Sacred Path of the Warrior* (Boston, MA: Shambhala, 1988)

—. *Crazy Wisdom* (Boston, MA: Shambhala, 2001)

Tweedie, Irina. *Chasm of Fire* (Inverness, CA: The Golden Sufi Center, 1986)

—. *Daughter of Fire* (Inverness, CA: The Golden Sufi Center, 1986)

Ullman, Robert, and Judyth Reichenberg-Ullman. *Mystics, Masters, Saints and Sages* (Berkeley, CA: Conari Press, 2001)

Upton, Charles (trans.). *Doorkeeper of the Heart: Versions of Rabi'a* (Putney, VT: Threshold Books, 1988)

Uspenskii, P D. *In Search of the Miraculous* (New York: Harvest, 2001)

Vaughan-Lee, Llewellyn. *The Bond with the Beloved: The Mystical Relationship of the Lover and the Beloved* (Inverness, CA: The Golden Sufi Center, 1993)

—. *The Face Before I Was Born: a Spiritual Autobiography* (Inverness, CA: The Golden Sufi Center, 1997)

Vivekananda (Swami). *Râja-Yoga* (revd edn; New York: Ramakrishna-Vivekananda Center, 1955)

Welwood, John. *Toward a Psychology of Awakening* (Boston, MA: Shambhala, 2000)

Wilber, Ken. *One Taste* (Boston, MA: Shambhala, 1999)

—. *Integral Psychology* (Boston, MA: Shambhala, 2000)

Willis, Janice D. *Enlightened Beings: Life Stories from the Ganden Oral Tradition* (Boston, MA: Wisdom Publications, 1995)

Wilson, Colin. *Rogue Messiahs: Tales of Self-Proclaimed Saviors* (Charlottesville, VA: Hampton Roads Publishing Company, 2000)

Young, M. *As it Is* (Prescott, AZ: Hohm Press, 2000)

About the Author

Mariana was educated at the University of Michigan in Ann Arbor, the California Institute of Integral Studies in San Francisco, and the Union Institute and University in Cincinnati. Her degrees are in Cultural Anthropology, Counseling Psychology, and Contemporary Spirituality. However, she attributes the majority of her education and inspiration to years of research and practice in the world's great mystical traditions, and to studying and living in villages and spiritual communities in India, Central and South America, and Europe.

She lectures internationally, and is a popular guest on radio and television due to her passionate, no-nonsense style and her emphasis on the need for authenticity, sanity, and spiritual discernment in a troubled world. Mariana resides in the San Francisco Bay area, as well as in Prescott, Arizona. She is a freelance writer for various magazines, teaches at the California Institute of Integral Studies, and has a private practice in counseling.

Mariana offers a range of seminars and trainings based on her previous books. Topics include: Spiritual Choices; The Promises and Pitfalls of Spiritual Life; Writing Your Way to God; Halfway Up the Mountain; and Touch, Intimacy & Embodiment. She can be reached through her website at www.realspirituality.com

Further Resources

Spiritual Authority:
Surrender, Submission, or Conscious Discipleship?
Leading Experts Speak to the Challenge!

With:
Claudio Naranjo
John Welwood
Lee Lozowick
Robert Svoboda
Angeles Arrien
Andrew Harvey
Mariana Caplan
Jai Uttal

Eight leading figures in the field of contemporary spirituality, along with hundreds of students, gathered in San Francisco at the California Institute of Integral Studies in the Spring of 2002 to discuss the challenge of spiritual authority in Western Culture.

Topics discussed included: Trials and Tribulations of a Modern Mystic; The Psychology of the Student–teacher Relationship; Crazy Wisdom, Rock n" Roll and Slavery to the Divine, the Guru as Heavyweight; Promises and Pitfalls in the Student–teacher Relationship; The Direct Path; Conscious Discipleship; and Hindu *kirtan* and dialogue with Jai Uttal.

8-Cassette Series: $70.00

Available through: Conference Recording Service
www.conferencerecording.com   Telephone in USA: (510)527-3600

References

SECTION I: THE DILEMMA

Chapter 1: You Get What You Ask For (But You Need to Know What You Want)

1 John Welwood, *Toward a Psychology of Awakening* (Boston, MA: Shambhala, 2000): 273–6
2 Ken Wilber, *One Taste* (Boston, MA: Shambhala, 1999): 28–30
3 From personal interview conducted with Vimala Thakar in Dalhousie, India, in July, 2000
4 Mariana Caplan, *Halfway Up the Mountain: the Error of Premature Claims to Enlightenment* (Prescott, AZ: Hohm Press, 1999): Chapter 11: "The Inner Guru and Other Spiritual Truisms"
5 Welwood: 275–6
6 Ken Wilber, *Integral Psychology* (Boston, MA: Shambhala, 2000): 28–32
7 *Karma* is a term readily thrown about but rarely understood in spiritual circles. As used here, it suggests that according to a law of cause and effect, there are circumstances and attachments we create in the journey of the soul in this lifetime or another that must eventually come into balance. Excellent study on this subject can be found in, Robert Svoboda, *Aghora III: the Law of Karma* (Albuquerque, NM: Brotherhood of Life, 1997)
8 Public talk at Open Secret bookstore, San Rafael, CA, July, 2001
9 Private interview, March 22, 2000
10 Swami Muktananda, *Where Are You Going?* (South Fallsburg, NY: SYDA Foundation, 1981): 138

Chapter 2: "Guru" Is a Four-letter Word: The Nature of Spiritual Scandals

1 Ken Wilber, "Transpersonal Hotspots: Reflections on the New Editions of Up From Eden, The Atman Project, and Eye to Eye", *Journal of Humanistic Psychology* vol. 37, No. 4 (Fall 1997): 97
2 Roger Walsh, "The Search for Synthesis: Transpersonal Psychology and the Meeting of East and West, Psychology and Religion, Personal and Transpersonal", *Journal of Humanistic Psychology* vol. 32, No. 1 (Winter 1992): 31
3 Swami Muktananda, *Where Are You Going?* (South Fallsburg, NY: SYDA Foundation, 1981): 144
4 A full account of Naranjo's story can be found in *Halfway Up the Mountain* (Prescott, AZ: Hohm Press, 1999), Chapter 21: "The Sadhana of Disillusionment"
5 Ken Wilber, *One Taste* (Boston, MA: Shambhala, 1999): 43
6 Mariana Caplan, *When Sons and Daughters Choose Alternative Lifestyles* (Prescott, AZ: Hohm Press, 1996)
7 Wilber (1999): 238
8 John Welwood, "On Spiritual Authority", in *Spiritual Choices*: 299–300

Chapter 3: The Need for a Teacher

1 William Patrick Patterson, *Struggle of the Magicians: Exploring the Teacher—Student Relationship* (Fairfax, CA: Arete Communications, 1996): 269
2 Rudolf Steiner, *Rosicrucian Wisdom* (London: Rudolf Steiner Press, 2000): 6–7
3 Georg Feuerstein, *Holy Madness: The Shock Tactics and Radical Teachings of Crazy-Wise Adepts, Holy Fools, and Rascal Gurus* (New York: Penguin, 1992): 90
4 Greg Bogart, *The Nine Stages of Spiritual Apprenticeship* (Berkeley, CA: Dawn Mountain Press, 1997): 36

SECTION 2: A WORKING MODEL OF RELATIONSHIP: THREE NECESSARY QUALITIES FOR TEACHER AND STUDENT

1 Swami Muktananda, *Where Are You Going?* (South Fallsburg, NY: SYDA Foundation, 1981): 153

Chapter 4: Basic Psychological Sanity

1 Private interview, Boulder, CO, 1998
2 Private interview, Berkeley, CA, 1999
3 Ibid.

Chapter 5: Conscious Relationship to Power Dynamics

1 William Patrick Patterson, *Struggle of the Magicians: Exploring the Teacher—Student Relationship* (Fairfax, CA: Arete Communications, 1996): 264–6
2 See Lee Lozowick, *Conscious Parenting* (Prescott, AZ: Hohm Press, 1997)
3 Further discussion on this topic can be found in *Halfway Up the Mountain*, Chapter 14: "The Consequences of Assuming a Teaching Function Before One is Prepared"

Chapter 6: Mutual Trust and Surrender

1 Swami Muktananda, *Where Are You Going?* (South Fallsburg, NY: SYDA Foundation, 1981): 151
2 An exemplary depiction of the intelligence use of psychoactive substances can be found in Chris Bache, *Dark Night, Early Dawn* (Albany, NY: SUNY Press, 2000)
3 Pema Chodron, *When Things Fall Apart: Heartfelt Advice for Difficult Times* (Boston, MA: Shambhala, 2000): 135
4 Arnaud Desjardins in Lee Lozowick, *Death of a Dishonest Man: Poems and Prayers to Yogi Ramsuratkumar* (Prescott, AZ: Hohm Press, 1998): 43
5 Lozowick: 45
6 Private discourse. February, 1993; Tiruvannamalai, South India

SECTION 3: FINDING YOUR TEACHER: THE FINE ART
OF DISCRIMINATION

Chapter 7: Meeting the Teacher: Defining Criteria for Teacher and Student

1 A full set of criteria for considering the master is found in *Halfway Up the Mountain*, Chapter 19: "True Teacher – or False?"
2 Georg Feuerstein, *Holy Madness: The Shock Tactics and Radical Teachings of Crazy-Wise Adepts, Holy Fools, and Rascal Gurus* (New York: Penguin, 1992): 143
3 Frances Vaughan, "A Question of Balance: Health and Pathology in New Religious Movements" in *Spiritual Choices*: 275
4 Arnaud Desjardins, "Am I a Disciple?" in Lee Lozowick, *Death of a Dishonest Man* (Prescott, AZ: Hohm Press, 1998): 51

SECTION 4: HOT ISSUES

Chapter 9: Spiritual Monogamy vs "Sleeping Around"

1 William Patrick Patterson, *Struggle of the Magicians: Exploring the Teacher–Student Relationship* (Fairfax, CA: Arete Communications, 1996): 255

Chapter 10: Guru Games and Crazy Wisdom

1 Irina Tweedie, *Daughter of Fire* (Inverness, CA: Golden Sufi Center, 1986): 350
2 See Evans-Wentz, *Tibet's Great Yogi Milarepa* (2nd edn; London: Oxford University Press, 1969)

Chapter 11: Obedience

1 Swami Prahavananda and Christopher Isherwood (trans.). *The Song of God: Bhagavad-Gita* (New York: Penguin Books, 1972): 37
2 For further resources, see E. J. Gold, *The Tibetan Book of the Dead* (Nevada City, CA: Gateways, 1999); Sogyal Rinpoche, *The Tibetan Book of Living and Dying* (San Francisco, CA: HarperSan Francisco, 1993)
3 A further discussion on criteria for genuine spiritual teachers can be found in my earlier book, *Halfway Up the Mountain* (Prescott, AZ: Hohm Press, 1999) in Chapter 19

SECTION 5: FOR THE GLORY OF LOVE

Chapter 14: For the Glory of Love

1 The Aghori Vimalananda, in Robert Svoboda, *Aghora III: The Law of Karma* (Albuquerque, NM: Brotherhood of Life, 1997): 106
2 Irina Tweedie, *Daughter of Fire* (Nevada City, CA: Blue Dolphin Publishing): 819–20
3 James Redington, *Vallabhacarya on the Love Games of Krsna* (2nd edn; New Delhi, India: Motilal 1989): 56–7 (Stanzas 5 and 6)
4 Arnaud Desjardins, in *Tawagoto* vol. 14, No. 2 (Spring 2001)

5 Henry Suso, *Little Book of Eternal Wisdom* and *Little Book of Truth* (trans. J. M. Clark; London: Faber and Faber, 1953): 185

6 Regina Sara Ryan, *The Woman Awake: Feminine Wisdom for Spiritual Life* (Prescott, AZ: Hohm Press, 1999)

7 Nizami, *Layla and Majnun* (London: Blake Publishing, 1970): 36

8 Irina Tweedie, *Daughter of Fire* (Nevada City, CA: Blue Dolphin Publishing): 813

9 Tweedie: 819–20

10 Lee Lozowick, *Death of a Dishonest Man: Poems and Prayers to Yogi Ramsuratkumar* (Prescott, AZ: Hohm Press, 1998): 815

11 Sita Martin, *The Hunger of Love: Versions of the Ramayana* (Kanyakumari, India: Yogi Ramsuratkumar Manthralayam Trust, 1995): 14–15

Index